An Appointment with Somerset Maugham

For Shirley Williams —
we may be each other's last
reminders of when newspapering
was still fun — with respect & affection,
Dick Costa
2-3-07
College Station, TX

An Appointment with
Somerset Maugham

AND OTHER LITERARY

ENCOUNTERS

RICHARD HAUER COSTA

Texas A&M University Press   *College Station*

Library of Congress Cataloging-in-Publication Data

Costa, Richard Hauer.
    An appointment with Somerset Maugham : and other literary encounters
/ Richard Hauer Costa. — 1st ed.
        p.   cm.
    Spine title: An appointment with Somerset Maugham.
    Includes bibliographical references and index.
    ISBN 0-89096-618-4 (alk. paper). — ISBN 0-89096-619-2 (pbk. :
alk. paper)
    1. English literature—20th century—History and criticism.
    2. American literature—20th century—History and criticism.
    I. Title. II. Title: Appointment with Somerset Maugham.
PR473.C67   1994
820.9'0091—dc20   94-12375
                                                             CIP

For Jo, who spared me;
for Hop, who fueled me;
and to the memory of Maurice Beebe,
who saved me

Contents

Illustrations

Preface

> The following of such thematic designs through one's life
> should be, I think, the true purpose of autobiography.
> —Vladimir Nabokov, *Speak, Memory*

If I read him rightly, Nabokov believes that we find the keys that open the door of our lives by locating the "designs"—the patterns—from which they have been made. Only by following them unblinkingly over the years can we chronicle the past faithfully. If we have been moths, we shouldn't look for tracings of butterflies. In this memoir, I have looked back not only for the patterns but for what I take to be the pattern makers. In crucial ways that these pages seek to illumine, I have indeed lived for books and writers. To the lyrics of "September Song"—"the days dwindle down to a precious few"—I would add one word—"books." I remember a class Reader from high school bearing the title, *Literature and Life*. I know there is a distinction, but I have never been able to make it.

Aboard a World War II troop train coursing down the spine of the United Kingdom from Glasgow to Southhampton, I forgot when we stopped in London that I was heading for infantry combat in Germany. I thought of H. G. Wells and the newspaper photo I had just seen of him shaking his fist at the *Luftwaffe* bombers overhead. How near was Hanover Terrace and the house Wells had purchased from Alfred Noyes—the one he refused to leave in the midst of the blitz—and why couldn't I go there to meet the first of my literary heroes?

Six months later, on rest leave in Nice, I looked out to the Mediterranean near Monte Carlo at a finger of land jutting into the sea—St. Jean–Cap Ferrat, where the second, Somerset Maugham, had a villa to which I assumed he had returned after the war. Why couldn't I go there?

Honeymooning as a summer student at Mexico City College in 1950, I tried to follow on weekends the bibulous trail of Malcolm Lowry without even knowing that the setting—Quauhnahuac—of the then recently published *Under the Volcano,* my all-time favorite novel, was the Indian name for Cuernavaca, the city my bride and I twice visited as guests of our Mexican landlady.

One book leads to another, one writer to another. For a time, I found myself reversing the process. As a journalist-turned-teacher, I returned in my forties to some of my first books. In the classroom, one comes to know books, if no more intimately, at least more fully, than as private advocate. To borrow from Melville's shock-of-recognition tribute to Hawthorne, by "confessing" old gods anew, I grew to confess others until I "braced" a community of letters—James and Wells, Joyce and Lowry, Conrad Aiken and T. S. Eliot, Dostoevski and Joseph Heller, Edmund Wilson and John Dos Passos. *Appointment with Somerset Maugham & Other Literary Encounters* interweaves memoir and scholarship. Early debts to Wells and Maugham and Lowry have long since evolved into late dividends in such books as *Ulysses, Ushant, Notes from Underground, Something Happened, The Ambassadors, Lucky Jim.*

This book is not a collection of previously published or presented essays, although seven have appeared in journals and two contributed to international symposiums on Wells and Joyce. Like a plot or character trait whose outcome is the more galvanic for being tracked down at its source, each of the fifteen formal essays becomes a benchmark in an odyssey from innocence to experience which memory—remote and recent—seeks to bring to fuller circle. Twelve newly written informal memoirs complement the more scholarly.

Part one—"The Troubling Case of Somerset Maugham"—traces the fate of one abiding god in critical killing fields where prurient disdain lurks in the guise of literary reassessment.

Part two—"The Dismantling of Favor"—is about quarreling. The issues between James and Wells, Eliot and Aiken, Dos Passos and Wilson, Turgenev and Flaubert may seem literary and political, but collectively they point to something more important—the difficulty of friendship between titans and, with Joyce and Alessandro Francini, the toll of fame on friendship.

Part three—"The Serious Business of Comedy, Innocence, and Homage to the Hemingways"—attempts to analyze laughter and to demonstrate how hard-earned yet necessary it is in books as a buffer to the sheer difficulty of living outside them.

Part four—"The Consul and Other Notations from Underground"—is about three antiheroes of fiction who to me are unforgettable and heroic. The three seem to me to be defined, finally, by Dostoevski's notion that we are all marked by the things we cannot tell even to ourselves.

Finally, and above all, *Appointment with Somerset Maugham* is an attempt by one who loved literature early and tried to teach it late to help preserve books and the reading public from destruction. We who meet literature classes, as Frank Kermode recently wrote, can deconstruct or neohistoricize among ourselves but we should be honor-bound to make people know books well enough to understand what it is to love them.

—Richard Hauer Costa

Acknowledgments

For permission to reprint seven essays which appeared earlier, sometimes in slightly different form, I should like to thank these publications: *Nimrod; CEA Critic; H. G. Wells: Reality and Beyond* (Critical essays, Champaign, Illinois, Public Library and Information Center and the Library of the University of Illinois; *New York History; Journal of Modern Literature; Cimarron Review;* and *Texas Studies in Literature and Language.*

Special mention goes to Noel Parsons, editor-in-chief of the Texas A&M University Press, and to my book's patient first reader, James Thomas, professor, Department of English, Wright State University, Dayton, Ohio, for their encouragement over the long haul. I am fortunate to have had Mary Lenn Dixon, managing editor, to oversee this book into print, and I have benefited from the intelligent and conscientious copyediting of Sally Antrobus. Her keen eye has spared me a number of embarrassments. The embarrassments that remain are all my own doing.

Finally, I should like to thank novelist, short-story writer, and Yeats biographer Frank Tuohy of Somerset, England, for making available to me his wide knowledge of many of the figures I discuss in this book. His friendship has been inspiring.

PART ONE

The Troubling Case of
Somerset Maugham

Prologue
Abiding Gods

Many of my heroes have been writers. I grew up spending many otherwise lonely hours reading their books. Much later, teaching literature and writing about it, I have been trying to repay that early indebtedness. It took me years with caring mentors before I was able to feel worshipful about an author long dead. *Appointment with Somerset Maugham,* to reverse a famous title, is about *gods who succeeded*—at least with me. The first of them, H. G. Wells and W. Somerset Maugham, were in their sixties when I encountered their stories in my teens. I never thought of them as old. Indeed, they were younger than I, a recently turned septuagenarian, as I write this.

The journey to Wells and Maugham required early rites of passage which I have only now begun to recognize. Without my maternal grandfather and my mother, neither of whom ever had time to indulge themselves with great books, I could never have booked passage. The first set of books I ever looked into, excluding *Compton's Encyclopedia* and the *National Geographic,* was my grandfather's *Little Journeys into the Lives of Famous Men* by Elbert Hubbard. The first volume was inscribed by the author himself in honor of an occasion long before I was born, when my grandfather, a Grand Exalted Ruler of the Elks of Lebanon, Pennsylvania, introduced the famous author-lecturer-wit—and Elk. I devoured these books; they spawned a love of biography. But all I remember is an essay on a certain Alfred R. Wallace, a contemporary of Charles Darwin's whom Hubbard pictured as coming independently to the same conclusion about origin of species as his famous peer while sharing none of the credit. That was my first intimation that the wages of discovery could become the wages of neglect. It was a lesson whose application to some of my literary heroes would be compelling.

If I had often skimmed the Hubbard sketches, I read page for page the two thick books I spotted at seventeen in the basement of Strawbridge & Clothier's, Philadelphia, during a characteristic Saturday shopping spree with my working mother. I remember reading my way through quarantines in my mid-teens and finding short-story collections especially congenial. You could take a story, leave it completed, and take up a new one at your own convenience. That Saturday in summer in the bargain crypt of the store where Mom's charge tag was good I made my first acquaintance with a writer firmly established in what much later I would hear termed the canon. Huge placards touted the availability as a boxed set of the *Joseph* trilogy by Thomas Mann, "the world's greatest writer." But I had given up on his *Magic Mountain,* one of the first big books I ever attempted, on the fobbed-up excuse that it was a translation. Shelved far below the peaks of Mann were the two story collections that would change my life.

The first, *Tellers of Tales,* contained one hundred stories from the United States, England, France, Russia, and Germany. The stories had been selected— and there was an introduction—by W. Somerset Maugham, a writer I already knew because he was the author of *Of Human Bondage,* a novel longer even than *The Magic Mountain* but one I could barely put down. The other was *The Famous Short Stories of H. G. Wells.* It even included *The Time Machine,* which I still read frequently, and a work I would hear Arthur C. Clarke in 1986 extol, with *Gulliver's Travels,* as the only work of science fiction that also merits being called literature.

My birthday was coming up, so my mother added two expensive books— twenty-five hundred pages—to her charge account as a shopper and to my credit account as a reader. To use terms sports writers applied to a pair of sparkling running backs for strong Army teams during the war years, Maugham and Wells were "Mr. Inside" and "Mr. Outside" throughout my adolescence and well beyond. To convey inner worlds ranging from Euro-pean cosmopolites to narrower societies in the Orient and South Seas, I turned to Maugham's stories. Whenever the world was too much with me— for a socially inept, pimply teenager, that was much of the time—I fled to Wells's fantasies, those "atrocious miracles," as Borges has it.

In Wells, from Time Traveller to sojourner in the Country of the Blind, a sense of anything-is-possible took over from the banality of the empirical. In

Maugham, as with the dramatic monologues I would encounter later in Browning, the speaker's urbane exposure of human fallibility became irresistible. Enchanted by stories like "Mr. Know-All" and "The Alien Corn," I did not then see that, given a slight flick of the persona's dial, the wise and mellow narrator could turn into a prig.

It is undoubtedly a confession of the inverted values that have often characterized my life to say that my most memorable day was neither the day of my marriage nor the day our son was born. The best day of my life was the morning after Labor Day, 1959, in a place where the holiday is not celebrated. Shortly before eleven on Tuesday, September 8, on the balcony of his villa called La Mauresque, overlooking the Mediterranean at St. Jean–Cap Ferrat in the south of France, I met Somerset Maugham.

How pretentious these words sound. But for anyone who believes the world of books surpasses any other, they make sense. I have encountered imaginative works of greater power than Maugham's. No single *oeuvre* has provided as much pleasure. I can think of no more satisfying reader's experience than to have shared a morning with the writer who holds this position and to have been able to tell him so.

Part one, "The Troubling Case of Somerset Maugham," consists of three essays that mark three distinct stages in my involvement with the storyteller who has been the companion of a lifetime. In the first, in The Driffield position, I find myself recalling our—my wife's and my—adventure that September morning at Villa Mauresque. If I have conveyed it rightly, it unfolded less like an interview than a tale Maugham might himself have enjoyed telling. The essay was originally published in *Nimrod* as "A Pleasure, Mr. Maugham" seventeen years after the fact. The middle essay puts Maugham's diffidence about his chances with posterity to a test. It looks at "Sanatorium," the final of his Ashenden stories, and aligns it with Tolstoy's "The Death of Ivan Ilych" in an attempt to extrapolate Maugham's often faulted distinction between talent and genius into a statement about two kinds of truth—that of art and that of life. It first appeared in the *CEA Critic* in 1981. The final one, "WSM: The Wages of Notoriety," confronts the recent—and rare—flurry of critical interest in Maugham and the abyss into which this prurience over his homosexuality has plunged Maugham studies. The essay originates here.

I.

Somerset Maugham and the Driffield Position

Years before becoming the unchallenged grand old man of British letters, W. Somerset Maugham, writing of Thomas Hardy, called veneration one of the continuing ordeals of authors who are cursed with long lives. When Maugham himself reached eighty-nine, he passed the age at which Hardy died and crept to within five years of George Bernard Shaw's record among the giants: ninety-four. At the time of Maugham's death in 1965, one month before his ninety-second birthday, I recall feeling a peculiar regret. There would be no more of those seemingly annual birthday quotes, invariably waspish, in which the Very Old Party would repeat that he was only too glad to step down as an author; that creativity was the prerogative of youth; and that he enjoyed nothing so much in his old age as filling out a foursome for bridge.

I thought of Maugham again recently while watching a rerun of the three-part BBC/*Masterpiece Theater* dramatization of his own favorite among his books, *Cakes and Ale*. That novel, in part at least, tells how survivability often confers genius on a writer whose works might otherwise have settled comfortably in the limbo of the highly competent. Edward (Ted) Driffield, Maugham's fictional "last Victorian," was like that—his name, in a reversal of A. E. Housman's "To an Athlete Dying Young," outliving his performance. Nearing death, Driffield wanders away from still another affair in his honor and limps to the same pub where he had met and successfully propositioned (for marriage) the loving barmaid, Rosie Gann. In such an atmosphere, one free of parasites like his second wife and unctuous suppliants like Alroy Kear, his biographer-to-be, Driffield can die happier.

What crossed my mind after the last reunion between Rosie and Willie Ashenden, her one-time part-time lover, had played out its final irony was this: Did the creator of *Cakes and Ale,* writing in 1929 about the fickleness of literary reputation, ever in his wildest dreams picture himself thirty years later in the Driffield position, obliged to accept from sycophants the mantle of literary senior statesmanship?

Thirty-five years ago I was, if not a sycophant, certainly a suppliant: an upstate New York newspaperman who, in December, 1958, had written a column on the occasion of Somerset Maugham's eighty-fifth birthday; had received a gracious reply from the subject; and who, vacationing with my wife in France that summer, sought to meet the man whose books have given me more pleasure than any other's. I even had with me a second letter, over Maugham's signature and received in Paris, inviting me to phone his villa in the south of France to see if his health would permit an interview.

I was on a month's leave from the *Utica (N.Y.) Observer-Dispatch.* Two weeks were vacation, two on my own time, unpaid. My wife Jo and I were in the final week of a four-week, five-hundred-dollar Experiment in International Living package that was wearing thin along with our spending money. And Jo's morale.

With the package, you paid in advance and took whatever was on the itinerary. For the final phase, a sojourn on the French Riviera, we thought we could at last look forward to decent accommodations, perhaps even a hotel—Nice, Cannes, St. Tropez. But that Saturday night, when everybody back in Utica would be enjoying the Labor Day weekend, our rickety chartered bus arrived, but barely, at a place off the maps and with an un-Gallic name: St. Aygulf.

We Experimenters were hustled off to what had been billed as "comfortable accommodations on the Côte d'Azur." What we saw resembled army barracks. Jo had become carsick as the bus snaked around hairpin turns in the approach through the French Alps to the sea. She began to cry.

Somerset Maugham wrote an ironic story about an elderly verger who, after losing his job because he is found to be illiterate, succeeds in a commercial venture and saves the bankrupt church that had fired him. Looking at Jo and the telltale dark circles that had formed under her eyes, I felt at low ebb, spiritually bankrupt, and I knew of no verger who could save us. I reached into my pocket, as I had done a hundred times, for the letter, now dog-eared, that had been held for us at Experiment headquarters when we arrived in Paris in mid-August:

Thank you for your letter and for sending me the article, etc. I am not disposed at the moment to give any interviews—I am tired and in a rather indifferent state of health. When you arrive in Nice in September, if you telephone my secretary at _____ perhaps something can be arranged, but I make no promises.

Yours sincerely,
W. S. Maugham

I had written to Maugham from Utica a few days before our chartered prop flight left from New York for Paris. I tried to tell the truth. I was an American about to vacation in France who had read everything he had written and would like to meet him. Without explicitly identifying myself as a newspaper person, I enclosed the eighty-fifth birthday column which, presumably, he had already seen: the one in which I expressed regret that there would be no more books from him; that he was the only author I could enjoy while riding in a coach of the New York Central Railroad as it changed engines at Albany en route to Utica.

From the moment I received Maugham's letter I found it impossible to participate with enthusiasm in the program of the Experiment. Five days in Paris had dragged by under the weight of the course in cathedrals; a week's homestay with a young French family in a village eighty kilometers north-east of Paris was, despite formidable difficulties in communication, a well-intentioned implementing of the Experiment's philosophy that the best way for people of various nationalities to learn to live together is to try it on a host-guest basis; the annual meeting of the delegates on the campus of the University of Grenoble, near the Swiss border, was a rampantly congenial week-long series of earphone seminars. Now, at the end of it all, we had earned a week's winding down on the Riviera.

Among the members of our group with whom I shared Maugham's letter, the Americans expressed characteristic optimism over my chances. The Europeans—especially the British—were skeptical.

"Why should Maugham bother with you?" demanded Mike Goldsmith, the Associated Press bureau chief in Geneva, whom I looked up during a stopover in Switzerland. "It's an old Maugham pattern: to lead reporters on and shut the door at the last minute."

"Nothing but the old run-around," said and English dowager. "But don't fret over it. You're fortunate. Saw him on the BBC last year. Gave his inter-viewers a frightful time. Dreadful, insolent old man. Worse than Malcolm

Muggeridge." I could not help but wonder if her hostility toward Maugham was entirely detached. Had he not written that he could not feel relaxed until he'd put the Channel between himself and England?

I tried to comfort Jo that dismal night of our arrival at St. Aygulf. "First thing in the morning we'll get away from this hole. We'll go straight to Nice and maybe hire a car and drive down into Italy." She laughed in that mock comic way of hers. "Look, Dick, we're broke. We've got fifteen dollars. The only way we could manage a car would be to steal it."

I wanted to say that she would feel differently after a fruitful phone call to Somerset Maugham, but I could not.

A second-class train, like the one in Hitchcock's *To Catch a Thief,* with stops at all those worldly resorts along the sea, got us into Nice just a few minutes to noon. We brought along swimsuits, cameras, my portable typewriter. Walking beside the sea, along the Promenade des Anglais (as I had done fourteen years earlier during a World War II rest leave), provided a tonic. We decided on a swim before trying to place a phone call to Maugham.

I left Jo sunning herself on the sandless public beach and walked to the Negresco, Nice's largest hotel. My nerve deserted me—acute anxiety set in—as I placed the call from a lobby phone. The hotel operator told me to stay on the line. After an eternity—it could not have been more than three rings—someone answered in machine-gun French. I stammered something about wanting to speak to *le secrétaire de Monsieur Maugham.* The Frenchman put me off. The only words I could be sure of were *rien* and *demain.* It was clear that Maugham's Villa Mauresque did not take kindly to phone calls on Sundays.

We returned, gloom-laden, to our barracks. Among the Experimenters word of our failure to see Somerset Maugham could not have helped but get around. But no one, not even the Englishwoman, mentioned it.

Next day—Labor Day back home—we returned to the Negresco. I placed the call again. The voice, this time a woman's, was again French but only for a moment. The abrupt Frenchman of the day before, still evasive, took over. I protested, spewed into the phone a phrase I had memorized about possessing *une lettre de Monsieur Maugham.* There was a pause. The next voice was crisp but friendly, an Englishman's:

"I'm Alan Searle, Mr. Maugham's secretary. I'm afraid I can't be too hopeful for you. Mr. Maugham has not been feeling at all well. Can you phone tomorrow at ten? Meanwhile, I'll do my best."

I phoned Villa Mauresque promptly at ten the next morning. This time

Few story-tellers have lived to see so many of their works coverted into successful motion pictures. Here, just after WWII, Maugham was photographed during a recording session for the blind of parts of *Of Human Bondage*. His biographer Ted Morgan reported that Maugham broke down and could not finish. *Photo by Fred Plaut.*

there was no Gallic interlude. Alan Searle asked me to hold the line. I imagined him walking into the master's study, asking Maugham's pleasure: "It's that American. You know, the one who likes to read your books on trains. Do you think you're up to seeing him?"

"Can you be here at eleven?" Searle's voice broke in. "Mr. Maugham is working but will be finished by then. I say, have you a car? . . . Then I would suggest you take a taxi. Go on to the Grand Hotel in Cap Ferrat. Just walk one hundred yards straight up the hill. You'll know the place by the sign on the door. It's the emblem that appears on all his books."

Overjoyed, I hung up and said to Jo, "We've got to hunt up a cab."

"*Cab*—what for? Why can't we take a bus?"

I approached the first cabbie I saw and told him our destination. He quoted a price, clearly exorbitant, but I was in no mood to haggle. Jo was. It was already twenty past ten. I heard my own voice—straining: *"Damn you! We have an appointment with Somerset Maugham and you worry about the fare!"*

"Do you realize we'll have five dollars left if we pay him what he's asking? There are still four more days before the plane leaves. I haven't even bought myself a single bottle of perfume."

"Get in, we're going," I said.

St. Jean–Cap Ferrat points like an accusing finger into the Mediterranean at a position halfway between Nice and Monte Carlo. Our cab proceeded among olive groves, the sea shimmering in the sun on both sides of us. During an earlier ride among the salmon-colored hills overlooking Monaco, I had tried to make a note or two of questions I would ask. I held in my hand a British edition of selected Maugham nonfiction under the title, *The Partial View*. It included *The Summing Up*, the nearest thing Maugham had written to an autobiography. I opened the book to a passage which, for me, had always pointed up a paradox. He had made a point of stressing how carefully according to plan his life had proceeded. That plan had brought a lifetime of renown and riches known to few of his contemporaries. Yet nowhere does Maugham give the impression that it had brought contentment.

I am not a pessimist [he writes a few pages from the end]. Indeed, it would be nonsensical of me to be so, for I have been one of the lucky ones. I have often wondered at my good fortune. I am well aware that many who were more deserving than I have not had the happy fate that has befallen me. . . . With all my limitations, physical and mental, I have been glad to live. I would not live my life over again. There would be no point in that. Nor would I care to pass through the anguish I have suffered. *It is one of the faults of my nature that I have suffered more from the pains, than I have enjoyed the pleasures, of my life* [emphasis mine].

The taxi pulled into the courtyard of the Grand Hotel. It looked to be a resort hotel and unique among such places in France that summer in that we saw no one in the lobby who looked the least like an American. Then I felt alarm. I could see our images in the lobby mirror, our tourist appendages— our cameras—showing.

"Do you want to wait here with our stuff?" The words must have sounded mock apologetic, an old fault of mine.

Jo gave me a sharp look. "Do you think after all the sacrifices I've made that you're going to leave me behind? I'm going up there, too, at least as far as the villa. I'll wait in the garden or on the back stoop, but I won't wait *here*."

Alan Searle's directions were perfect. The Moorish mark against the evil eye—the toothed crest looking for all the world like an upside down television antenna—leered at us from the top of the hill. We entered the gate and followed a path two hundred feet or so among tropical flowers and cactus until we reached the door.

I rang and a Frenchman, perhaps the one I recalled from the telephone calls, opened the door. He retreated, the door ajar, but we were not invited to enter. Searle came promptly, a pleasantly handsome man who looked more like a prospect for tennis than the companion who had served Maugham for more than thirty years.

"Can my wife wait in the garden?"

"Goodness, no," said Searle. "Mr. Maugham would never forgive me for leaving a lady outside."

He took us to a terrace overlooking the sea, sat us down, and began chatting. I was glad, all at once, for Jo's presence. She held up our end of the conversation while I stirred uneasily in anticipation of the master.

Fifteen minutes went by. Finally Searle said, "I'd better give Willie a jog. Perhaps he's forgotten."

He returned alone. I kept my eyes on the door until I glimpsed through the screening a figure heading for the patio. William Somerset Maugham, shading his eyes, shuffled into view. "Would you rather sit inside?" he asked distinctly. "It appears quite cool out there." He rejected his own suggestion and took the sun seat. He was wearing a tweed jacket, sport shirt open at the neck, moccasin shoes.

My instant impression was of a very old man but all the same one of vitality. The stammer—result, it has been said, of unhappy boyhood experiences—was quickly apparent; so, too, a barely controlled shaking of the fingers as we talked. But the voice and eyes were clear; the figure and hairline those of a younger man; the descriptions I had read of a face lined like the skin of a crocodile exaggerated.

We had been reading, I began, of his plans for an ocean voyage in October to the Orient, the scene of many of his stories. Would he respond to an old urge, make a note or two of things that struck his fancy in some remote port of call?

"Oh my, no," he said, his hands making a nervous tracing in the air. "I'm absolutely out of business as a writer, a has-been, and I know it. I shall be happiest on the voyage when I can exploit someone on the ship to play bridge. I'm expecting Charley Goren any day. He's taught me all I know."

I asked if, as had been reported, he was working on his memoirs and whether they would be published during his lifetime. He replied, right out of one of those *London Times* birthday interviews, that no more books would be forthcoming while he was alive. There had been a huge fire, very recently, he said, in which he had burned all his correspondence and any other materials future biographers could get at after his death. (*Was he taking precautions against future Alroy Kears?* I thought this question but did not ask it.) The only writing he did was one hour on mornings when he felt up to it—mostly correspondence. His one habit that continued undiminished was reading. He expressed the fear that his eyesight might go the way of his hearing.

"You know, blindness for me would be like the end of life. I don't know what I should do. What do I read? Everything, particularly the thrillers. One of my favorites is the American, Raymond Chandler, who died not long ago. Several weeks ago I received a letter from the woman who took care of him in his last illness. She asked Chandler if she might read to him. He was at first opposed. Then she began. It was something I had written about him. After she finished, Chandler expressed pleasure over it. Then he closed his eyes for the last time. A most touching thing, don't you think?"

He spoke of death, of contemporaries who had died in bitterness, of "poor H. G. Wells who visited us regularly before the war, a most congenial guest but, finally, an old man who could never live with the fact that his creative talent had left him. As for me, I am only too content to step aside."

Each year, he said, brings the passing of close friends, most recently—it had actually been in 1956, three years before—that of Max Beerbohm, "a dear, delightful man." I asked him about Joyce Cary, whose courageous battle with a progressively crippling illness had ended in death shortly before we'd left the States. The reference appeared to puzzle Maugham. He looked to Searle for clarification.

"You know, Willie, he means the Highlander," Searle prompted.

"Oh yes, Joyce Cary. A dreadful way to die, little by little. But his case is an interesting one for writers. Cary didn't succeed until he was in his fifties, but he was fortunate all the same. He lived to see his work acclaimed. Young writers so often start writing without anything to write. One must live a good bit before putting anything down. One cannot wait for experiences to happen to one. One must go after them."

Maugham's speech had a slight period flavor. It gave his answers a fullness quite the opposite of the brusqueness the English Experimenter had led us to expect. All evidence of the stammer had by now disappeared. He spoke of that summer of 1959 as one of the happiest he had known since the war.

"Nearly everyone's in Europe this summer, especially the Americans. We've had Adlai Stevenson; the columnist Art Buchwald—his wife's even funnier than he, we think she writes the column; Moss Hart, the world's best talker; S. J. Perelman, a most amusing man.

"I believe the reason so many Americans are on the Riviera is Grace Kelly. What a perfectly wonderful girl she must be. She has astounded everyone with the way she has taken to being royalty. It could have been a frightful ordeal for a lesser person not reared in such an atmosphere."

Alan Searle said that while so many Americans were on the Riviera, Mr. Maugham, ironically, would not only like to visit but to settle in the United States. "The taxes and rent are so damnably high here. Mr. Maugham would prefer to live in New York where most of his friends are, but of course the press wouldn't let him alone."

There was a pause. I had the feeling that Searle was on the point of terminating the interview. I reached for *The Summing Up*. I decided to plunge in. Would he mind if I asked him to elaborate on a passage that had always fascinated and puzzled me?

"I don't know how much help I'll be," he said. "I haven't looked at that book in twenty years. But fire away."

I read the passage, the one about his having suffered more from the pains than he has enjoyed the pleasures of his long life. Even before I finished reading, I sensed I had intruded on forbidden territory. Maugham's lips quivered; he appeared to be making an extraordinary effort to find words. The stammer, for the moment, was impenetrable.

My wife Jo, almost silent since Maugham had sat down, interrupted. "Some years ago I cured for tuberculosis. In those days, as you know, it was a long, discouraging process. During my convalescence, I read a short story of yours. It was 'Sanatorium.' Something you wrote in that story I've never forgotten. You said something to the effect that suffering, contrary to the belief of certain romantic novelists and popular clergy, does not ennoble. It only degrades. It makes you bitter and vindictive. I found it easier, reading that, to live with my resentment."

I was surprised by Jo's words but grateful for the diversion they provided. She had never in our ten-year marriage mentioned the passage or spoken about how much it had helped her survive a two-year confinement. The effect on Maugham was immediate—and salutary. Had the reference to tuberculosis awakened in him recollections of his own confinement with the disease during World War I, when he was forty? When he spoke, there was no groping for words:

"That's the way things must be for all of us, whatever our lot, the suffering outlasting the pleasure . . ." He paused; for the first time a smile, different from the one that had seemed pasted to his face at other junctures, crossed his face. Was I only thinking of a key section of *Cakes and Ale* where the aged Edward Driffield appears to have winked at Ashenden in the midst of Alroy Kear's phony solicitude? Did I imagine a twinkle in the eyes of Maugham?

"Now, just ask yourself," he said without the least suggestion of delivering a catechism, *"wouldn't it be a dreadful world if pleasure ruled?"*

Maugham tried to build himself to his feet but settled back again in his chair. "By the way, do you and Mrs. Costa play bridge?"

I had read that Somerset Maugham was a player of near tournament caliber. Jo and I didn't know a finesse from a ruff. How often since that summer have we regretted it. Perhaps—who knows?—Jo and I might have been asked to fill out a foursome that afternoon at Villa Mauresque.

Searle rose discreetly. "Would you and Mrs. Costa like to see the villa?" The interview was at an end.

We left Maugham on the patio while we toured La Mauresque, a miniature Louvre with masterpieces filling every wall. What we saw that day in 1959 were works sold by Maugham at Sotheby's less than three years later for around one-and-three-quarter millions.

Searle's commentary enlivened the tour:

"The one at the head of the stairs is of Rosie from *Cakes and Ale,* our favorite of the novels. Nobody who comes here for the first time ever guesses who painted that one across from Rosie. We make a standing offer of fifty dollars." It was an oil of a male, nude, in the position of a sprinter. We gave up without even a guess. It proved to be an early Toulouse-Lautrec—*Le Polisseur* (the polisher)—uncharacteristic of anything our lay person's grasp of his work could summon up.

We were guided to the highest room in the villa, Maugham's study. We saw the paintings Gauguin had done on the wall of his hut in Tahiti. Maugham had bought the entire wall and built it intact as the ceiling of his garret workroom. Formerly open to the sea on all sides, the room had been closed up by Maugham because the sea distracted him. We were shown the photograph of his mother, beside his bed, whose death when Maugham was eight became a loss from which he never recovered.

The master of the Villa Mauresque was waiting for us when we returned to the patio. I asked him if he would inscribe a note in my book. The request appeared to please him. Taking my pen, he wrote, without prompting, my full name and added "in recollection of a pleasant chat, W. Somerset Maugham." Shambling with us to the gate, he asked Alan if he could not arrange for the chauffeur to drive us back to Nice.

"I'm sorry, Willie. The car's out for provisions."

"It has been an honor," I said, rather too stiffly.

"Please, rather than say an honor, say it has been a pleasure," Maugham called back a moment later.

Alan accompanied us the two hundred feet through the garden to the gate. Just as we were getting ready to say goodbye, a bus lumbered by. Searle sprang into action. He ran after the bus, but it kept right on going. "Rotten luck," he said. "They never stop. Come by so infrequently, too. But it would have saved you the cab fare. I say, it has been a pleasure."

On the train back to St. Aygulf, I asked Jo about her remark to Maugham.

"Oh, don't you remember bringing me *The Complete Stories* while I was in the San?"

"I mean the part about resentments—*your* resentments."

She thought a moment, looking out to the sea. "Oh that," she said. "It was all such a long time ago." Then she looked at me. "But *today*—wasn't today exciting?"

But what of Maugham, surviving to experience the Driffield position, a veneration about which he could only speculate in *Cakes and Ale?* In the final episode of the BBC production, Lord George Kemp, the insolvent coal dealer who is Rosie's favorite of many lovers, begs her to leave Driffield and flee to America with him. Rosie, for the moment only, demurs. "What'll poor Ted do without me?" she asks. "Ted Driffield," snorts Lord George. "Why he's a born survivor!"

For Somerset Maugham, survivor, the 1960s combined draining legal battles with his daughter over his fortune and such horrors of extreme old age that he reportedly told Alan Searle every night into his nineties that he prayed he would be spared seeing the morning.

Against ravishment of mind and body, of what compensation the riches, the continuing veneration?

II.

Maugham's "Partial Self":
The "Unexpected View" on the Way to
Tolstoy's "Death of Ivan Ilych"

Diffidence in a person given to self-imaging is rarely sincere. With an author who deploys it as a buffer in betting on his chances with the ages, it must be seriously questioned. There was always a thou-doth-protest-too-much demurrer about Somerset Maugham's obsession with the distinction between talent and genius.

I do not think that Cervantes had an exceptional gift for writing; few people would deny him genius. Nor would it be easy in English literature to find a poet with a happier gift than Herrick and yet no one would claim that he had more than a delightful talent.[1]

Invariably, rankings serve his own perceived chances. He positively savors a place somewhere in the lower orders;

My sympathies are limited. . . . I can only be myself, and partly by nature, partly by the circumstances of my life, it is a partial self. I am not a social person, I cannot get drunk and feel a great love for my fellow men. . . . And so, never having felt some of the fundamental emotions of normal men, it is impossible that my work should have the intimacy, the broad human touch and animal serenity which the greatest writers alone can give. (*SU*, 528)

So, for Maugham, literary genius is a supreme normality combined with some aberration of chemistry, a fortunate idiosyncrasy, that—he seems grateful to be able to say—arises once or twice in a century. If he cannot join it, he will patronize it to death. Edmund Wilson puts the matter well when he writes that, with Maugham, "We get the impression of a malcontent eye cocked from the brackish waters of the *Cosmopolitan* magazine, and a peevish and insistent grumbling. There is something going on, on the higher ground, that halfway compels his respect, but he does not quite understand what it is, and in any case he can never get up there."[2]

If, as Maugham writes, adopting the same metaphor as Wilson, "talent cannot reach the utmost height, but . . . can show you many an unexpected and delicious view . . . on the way that leads to them," surely Maugham saw his best work proceeding well beyond the foothills.

Why not, then, take an acknowledgedly strong work of "talent"—Maugham's talent—and place it side by side with another that issued from unquestioned "genius," making certain that the two works deal with similar thematic material? Why not, in effect, "test" Maugham's self-reductive assertion that "the frowardness of human nature is such that it falters sometimes when it is bidden to take the broadest of all surveys of human nature?" (*SU,* 528).

Such an investigation may not only contribute to a weighing of Wilson's charge that Maugham's decorous modesty disguises invidious comment about his betters, but may also provide clues as to why all his novels remain steadfastly in print while contemporary scholarship—until the recently declared open season on closet homosexuality in dead authors—just as steadfastly ignores him.

I propose to demonstrate that in "Sanatorium," the final of the Ashenden stories, Maugham places the talent of the master teller of tales in the service of a life-and-death theme that also occupied Leo Tolstoy in "The Death of Ivan Ilych."

Maugham's admiration for "Ivan Ilych" cannot be doubted. It leads off a sixteen-story segment devoted to Russian authors in *Tellers of Tales,* his famous anthology.[3] It is by a wide margin the longest story in the collection. It may, in fact, be the classic expression in world literature of Maugham's often stated notion—the one on which my interview with him turned—that, far from ennobling, suffering makes us vindictive, trivializes.

Maugham, a bridge player of near-professional skill, may even have drawn one of his climactic incidents from a relatively undramatic entry in Ivan Ilych's catalog of horrors. Ilych is playing bridge with a grand slam in sight. Suddenly, once more conscious of the gnawing pain that has taken over his life, he can only regard further interest in the game as absurd. When his partner pushes the tricks toward him that he might have the pleasure of gathering them up, he can only infer general concern over his debility. He goes down by three tricks.

In "Sanatorium," McLeod and Campbell, eighteen-year patients at the tuberculosis hospital where Ashenden is briefly confined, have long devoted themselves to diversions of mutual exasperation. They always play bridge against each other. In the game that is the melodramatic counterpart of the one in the Tolstoy story, McLeod bids a grand slam, Campbell replies by doubling, McLeod redoubles. At the moment of completing the contract, with everyone watching the triumph of his life, McLeod springs to his feet, affirming this signal moment while shaking his fist at Campbell—and drops dead.

This scene is true to certain conventions of story-telling as Maugham practices them, but it undercuts any serious statement on human suffering. It is untrue to life. One accepts McLeod's death because it enables Maugham to resolve the story's two principal subplots. In the first, Major Templeton, an invalided former Grenadier Guard, reads in McLeod's fate the absolute futility of living eighteen years under wraps. "I wonder if it's worth it," he confides to Ashenden. "I wonder if it's not better to have one's fling and take the consequences."

And he does. Templeton, a sybarite, falls in love with and proposes to Ivy Bishop, the youngest and prettiest girl in the sanatorium. She accepts him although both know that the marriage will mean his certain death in a few months. Their decision, in turn, serves Maugham as lever for a heroic, though unconvincing, turn in the attitude of Henry Chester, his Ivan Ilych figure. While it may be true that placing the step-by-step disintegration of Tolstoy's provincial magistrate beside the complaints of Maugham's London accountant is like comparing a massive coronary to gas on the stomach, Chester's plight provides a perfect statement of the donnée of "Ivan Ilych." Maugham is almost as succinct as the Russian:

Henry Chester was born and bred to lead an average life, exposed to the normal vicissitudes of existence, and when an unforeseeable accident befell him he had no means of coping with it. . . . It was no fault of Henry Chester's that he was incapable of the conceptions that might have enabled him to bear his calamity with resignation.[4]

The calamity, of course, is that, with no preparation, Henry Chester faces a sentence of death from tuberculosis. Having no resources in himself, he becomes obsessed by thoughts of his health. He takes it into his head that the doctors regard his case indifferently. To force their attention, he induces the thermometer to register alarming temperatures. During her visits to the sanatorium, he brutalizes his equally commonplace, though loving, wife until she confesses to Ashenden that Henry now hates her because he is to die while she goes on living. "Do we all fear death like that?" she asks.

Tolstoy leaves no doubt that, judging by Ivan Ilych, we do. A dying man who is in no way exceptional, or even likable, Tolstoy's protagonist assumes by the very intimacy of his long day's dying the guise of everyman. Through him we imagine what our own death could be. Maugham, in contrast, introduces us through the briefly hospitalized Ashenden to a gallery of patients. We meet them, not whole but in the selective way this kind of short story necessitates—by brief encounters that are dramatic means to didactic ends. The Maugham voice, issuing from above the sickroom, dominates:

[B]ut for all that the idea of death haunts the subconscious. It is a sardonic song that runs through a sprightly operetta. Now and again the gay, melodious arias, the dance measures, deviate strangely into tragic strains that throb menacingly down the nerves; the petty interests of every day, the small jealousies and trivial concerns are as nothing; pity and terror make the heart on a sudden stand still and the awfulness of death broods as the silence that precedes a tropical storm broods over the tropical jungle. ("S," 515)

The worldly voice has stated its text. It remains to be seen whether, having metaphorized the idea of death, Maugham can earn the actuality of it in the way all fiction must—dramatically.

Although Tolstoy brings to his analysis of disease—in this instance cancer of the stomach—the same clinical precision as in his description of the successive stages endured by the dying man, we are never permitted to view Ivan Ilych's ordeal as students reviewing a case history. Not even the long prologue, in which Ivan has already died, allows our feelings any letup. *Memento mori* will be indelible even before Ivan's story begins. Tolstoy accomplishes this through a temporary persona, a colleague and lifelong friend of the deceased. Peter Ivanovich, viewing the body lying in state, experiences at once the human pull toward death and the recoil from it:

The thought of the sufferings of this man he had known so intimately . . . suddenly struck Peter Ivanovich with horror, despite an unpleasant consciousness of his own and [Ivan Ilych's widow's] . . . dissimulation. He again saw that brow and that nose pressing down on the lip, and felt afraid for himself.

Three days of frightful suffering and then death! Why, that might suddenly, at any time, happen to me, he thought, and for a moment felt terrified. But—he did not himself know how—the customary reflection at once occurred to him that it should not and could not happen to him. ("Ilych," 557)

Tolstoy thus conveys a message that is often echoed in contemporary works like Shirley Jackson's "The Lottery": Death, to the living, is always something that happens to somebody else.

In the pivotal conversation between Ashenden and Henry Chester's wife, Maugham also reveals a truth about the idea of death, but this time as experienced by one of the dying. Such a one cannot bear being alone in facing it. "'He'd be terribly sorry if I had T.B.' [she says]. 'But I know . . . it would be a relief. He could forgive me, he could forgive fate, if he thought I was going to die too'" ("S," 514). This conversation, which occurs halfway through the story, mounts the trivializing-by-suffering theme. It renders indirectly in the words of Mrs. Chester what Tolstoy renders directly by the decline of Ivan Ilych. Considered by itself, it gives us the sort of wisdom about death that Maugham learned at first hand as a medical student at St. Thomas' Hospital in London. But what Maugham tells us about this most abreactive of themes pales beside "Ivan Ilych," where the toll of sickness on personality is experienced in private.

The effects of "indirect evidence" in fiction are a diminishment in reader involvement. When, for three pages immediately after the Ashenden–Mrs. Chester conversation, the Maugham voice absorbs the Ashenden voice, we know the concession that has been made to the "cool" image of the outsider-as-author, the partial self:

People often said he had a low opinion of human nature. It was because he did not always judge his fellows by the usual standards. He accepted with a smile, a tear, or a shrug of the shoulders, much that filled others with dismay. It was true that you could never have expected that good-natured, commonplace little chap to harbour such bitter and unworthy thoughts; but who has ever been able to tell to what depths man may fall or to what heights rise? ("S," 514–15)

So far as the telling can take him, Maugham is able to do so: "an unexpected and delicious view" on the way to the heights. The telling of Henry Chester's redemption—and Major Templeton's—will be the burden of the rest of the story. But the redemptions will filter through the severely limited omniscience of the Ashenden-Maugham persona, the outside-insider who, his own recovery providing "relief" (in both senses of the word) from the state of dying, "continued to read, and with amused tolerance to watch the vagaries of his fellow creatures" ("S," 241).

Maugham gives his story a satisfying, if dramatically unearned, ending. Word of the impending marriage of the officer and the gentle girl sets off a chain reaction of institutional well-being. "All this about Templeton and Ivy

Bishop" provides reconciliation, too, for Henry Chester. "Sanatorium" ends with a reaffirmation of his love for his wife and banishment of his fear of death. "I don't mind dying any more," he says, rising to heights the Maugham voice has vowed are possible even in such as he. "I don't think death's very important, not so important as love" ("S", 527).

As for Ivan Ilych, hardly any less of a "commonplace little chap," no such vicarious situation as delivered Chester can help. In a masterful sentence of concision, Tolstoy goes to the heart of the matter: "Ivan Ilych's life had been most simple and most ordinary and therefore most terrible" ("Ilych," 558). What makes it "terrible" is told almost reportorially. Ivan Ilych is a conscientious minor official whose inner fiber is strung together by a few principles handed down by his parents. He is, in fact, little different from W. H. Auden's Unknown Citizen except that when something goes wrong, we surely do hear. Ivan Ilych suffers a fall from a ladder while hanging curtains and, after a time, the pain begins to grow worse instead of getting better. It begins to live a life of its own. He senses that something dreadful is going on inside him, "something terrible, new, and more important than anything before in his life." A chasm has opened between his world and that of the confident living, and it cannot be closed.

At last, condemned to his bedroom, Ivan Ilych feels unloved, alone. He calls on God for answers, expects none, yet weeps when nothing is forthcoming. Desperate for a sharer of his fate, he carries on endless dialogues with himself. What has he done wrong to deserve such a fate? His need to recall some compensating good for what has befallen him takes him back to the only time where memory is satisfying: childhood. He cannot release his hold on life; somehow the organ that has gone wrong will right itself. His only friend is a servant, Gerasim, who washes and sometimes holds up his feet to relieve the pain. His wife entreats him to submit to Communion; he goes through with it. Then he is seized with terror. He screams. He grows calm. His hands fall on a boy's head, his son's. Ivan Ilych's exorcism of death—a matter of an instant—provides a kind of speculative epiphany, one of the most powerful in world literature (". . . In place of death there was light . . .").

When we finish "The Death of Ivan Ilych," we know at our nerve ends how *un*natural dying from natural causes is likely to be. As Tolstoy's biographer Henri Troyat observes: "We think of ourselves while Ivan Ilych moans in pain in his bed; we pass our lives in review as he draws up the balance sheet for his. At the end of his torment, two things dominate: the terror of what is coming and the emptiness of what has been. No philosophical dissertation can ever equal in depth this simple 'documentary'—unemotional, sharp, cruel, devoid of all artistic effect—of a sickroom."[5]

"I can never forget myself," writes Maugham in one of the many confessionals in *The Summing Up.* "[My nature] will shrink from the splendour of Tolstoy . . . to turn with complacency to Voltaire's *Candide.*" A reading of a superb fiction of galvanic anecdotage and irony, when coupled with a reading of another that never falters as it closes in on the unmentionable, reveals the honesty and justice of Maugham's deepest intimations of himself and his craft.

III.

The Wages of Notoriety
—An Update

"Maugham's homosexuality was well known but excited little comment in the tolerant literary world of London." So wrote Drew Middleton, veteran London correspondent of the *New York Times* in a sidebar to the full-page obituary ("A Major Literary Craftsman of the Century Dies at 91," Dec. 16, 1965). Even if I had known about it—and I hadn't—I am sure I would have been the same awe-stricken suppliant that morning after Labor Day, 1959, at the Villa Mauresque. Nor would I have been likely, having two years after the interview switched from newspapering to teaching, to have introduced the topic in my lectures on *Of Human Bondage*.

Long before Maugham's homosexuality was known to his vast popular audience, a friend and colleague of mine at Utica College made a controlled survey of the ninety-one short stories Maugham published in his long lifetime. Psychology Professor Abe Judson made it a class project to examine, under appropriate headings, Maugham's handling of such themes as love, death, violence, marriage, infidelity. When carefully collated, Abe Judson's survey ("Love and Death in the Short Stories of Somerset Maugham: A Psychological Analysis," *Psychiatric Quarterly* 37 [Spring, 1963]: 250–62) showed a significant association of love and death; preponderance of males as the victims of violence; a tendency of self-aggression in his English heroes but a difficulty in them of violent expression against others, although non-English males do not have such inhibitions; the general failure of marriage; the more frequent unfaithfulness in females compared to males.

Not long after publishing these findings, Abe Judson died. He and I never mentioned any other Maugham tendency, as revealed in the survey, besides his well-known cynicism about *homo sapiens,* generally, and his misogyny, particularly. I believe it probable that Abe, one of the wisest men I have ever known, inferred homosexuality. We often talked about the passage with which I confronted Maugham—the one about his remembering less the fame and wealth than the misfortunes of his life. I wish I had shown Abe another passage in *The Summing Up:*

[N]ever having felt some of the fundamental emotions of normal men, it is impossible that my work should have the intimacy, the broad human touch and the animal serenity which the greatest writers alone can give. *(SU, 528)*

These words appear at the end of a Maugham dilation on the theme I examined in the previous essay, talent versus genius. Now compare them with those he applied to the painter El Greco in his travel book—*Don Fernando*—three years earlier:

Now it cannot be denied that the homosexual has a narrower outlook on the world than the *normal* man. . . . Some at least of the broad and typical emotions he can never experience. . . . I should say that a distinctive trait of the homosexual is a lack of deep seriousness over certain things that *normal* men take seriously [emphasis mine].[1]

It is tempting to apply some such syllogism as this: El Greco and Somerset Maugham are men; Maugham finds El Greco, who he says was homosexual, denied the broad emotions of normal men; Maugham finds himself denied the broad emotions of normal men; therefore, Maugham is a homosexual.

The flaw in this exercise, of course, is that many heterosexuals are also denied "the broad emotions of normal men." Maugham often repeated himself from book to book. *The Summing Up* (1938) is an extended gloss of ideas on truth, beauty and loving-kindness as dramatized in *Cakes and Ale* (1930). Little can be gained, I believe, in playing a game of literary hindsight with Maugham's books. In his recent collection of essays, Joseph Epstein quotes one of his students in a seminar on Henry James as suggesting "there ought to be a statute of limitations on discovery of homosexuality in literature."[2]

British critic A. D. Harvey concludes that "it is the particular nature of Maugham's literary achievement that makes him a useful starting point in any study of the homosexual novelist."[3] However, based on the paucity of evidence he and other sleuths have amassed, the search for clues in Maugham's fiction is unlikely ever to be fruitful as a starting—or any other—point in the currently bullish market in out-of-the-closet shares.

Harvey, in fact, writes as if he had taken on the assignment, only to discover the pantry is bare. Largely on the basis of Philip Carey's ambivalent passion for a woman who physically repels him in *Of Human Bondage,* this critic infers that Maugham has revealed his inverted sexuality. Impatient to convince, Harvey takes out his frustration on Maugham:

> It is a truism that the defects—perhaps one should say *peculiarities*—of a work of literature derive from the *peculiarities* of the author's personality. One may attribute to Maugham's homosexuality his mode of depicting sexual relations with women, perhaps even the general conventionality of his sensibility, but if he had not been a homosexual he would not have been the Somerset Maugham who wrote Of Human Bondage. . . . These facts are surely well established and inextricable; the *mechanisms* are partly visible to inspection. Perhaps in a greater artist they would have been less visible [emphasis mine]. ("Harvey," 78–79)

This, at best, is an unearned conclusion. The "mechanisms" that disclose a psychic disposition to one reader may be dramatically telling to another on different grounds. At worst, Harvey's position is suspect. Since when are an author's "peculiarities" defects? Robert E. Scholes is illuminating on what he calls a writer's "system of notation, which has its focal limits in abstracting from the total system of existence."[4] If I understand Scholes rightly, each significant writer employs "narrative codes" that illumine—even elucidate—his or her "version of reality." All accomplished representations merit consideration on their own terms rather than on any specialized gloss a critic like A. J. Harvey contrives for his own ends.

If, as still another prospector would have it, Philip's affair with Mildred in *Of Human Bondage* is a "fable for [Maugham's] own sexual dilemma"—if Maugham's homosexuality is to be inferred from Mildred's androgyny, her boyish flat-chestedness—why is it that every reader—males, mostly—with whom I have ever discussed the book views Mildred as the archetype of the enigmatically irresistible *femme fatale,* attachment to whom is at once inevitable and costly?

As a study of a youth's search for meaning and truth in a world of cruelty and deceit, *Of Human Bondage* stands apart from the remainder of Maugham's works. It is a masterpiece in any company because of its brutal honesty. No one is spared, least of all its hero, of whom I found myself, in effect, saying early on: "Philip Carey, *c'est moi.*" My son bears his name.

Of all the major English fiction writers whose long lives spanned the reigns of Victoria and four or more subsequent monarchs—Shaw, Wells, and For-

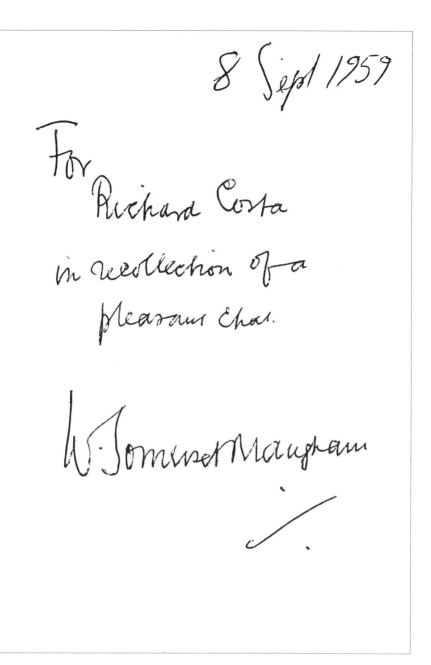

8 Sept 1959

For
Richard Costa
in recollection of a
pleasant chat.

W. Somerset Maugham

Maugham inscribed my copy of *The Summing Up* after the interview he had granted my wife Jo and me the morning of Sept. 8, 1959 at his villa on Cape Ferrat, in the Mediterranean between Nice and Monte Carlo.

ster come to mind—W. Somerset Maugham (1874–1965) has been the least
fortunate in his recent biographers. This is not to suggest that Maugham's
ninety-one years have been mined with any less thoroughness by Ted Morgan (*Maugham: A Biography* [New York: Simon & Schuster, 1980], 711 p.)
than Shaw's ninety-four were excavated by Michael Holroyd. Rather, it is
the collision of changing modes in criticism and biography with the anticipated prurience of Maugham's readers that has always prevented a serious
assessment of his considerable contributions to the arts of fiction and theater.

The most recent full-dress biography since Morgan's a decade before is
Robert Calder's *Willie: The Life of W. Somerset Maugham* (1990, 429 p.),
nearly three hundred pages shorter than the Morgan and with only twenty
pages of notes compared to Morgan's forty. It tells us nothing new. No
matter. Predictably, Calder's only mission is to rewrite Morgan; to convey
gently what Morgan conveyed zestfully: Maugham's homosexuality, which
did not become common knowledge until Morgan proclaimed it—and
named names.

Calder comes to the point in his preface: "Though [Morgan's] treatment
of Maugham's homosexuality is more explicit than anything previously published, it always emphasizes the nasty, procuring side of his homosexual life.
At no time is there a recognition that a homosexual relationship might be
supportive, sensitive, compassionate, and loving."[5]

Granted, Morgan is of the Kitty Kelly school of biography; he often
quotes gossip as though it were fact. Still, Morgan's book never dragged.
Calder's first three hundred pages feature long guest lists, often without
embellishment, as if he were more concerned getting the names right than
forging their connections to Maugham. Morgan came as close to the always
elusive Maugham as anyone ever will—Victoria Glendinning called him the
Great Untouchable—and drew on material about the private Maugham that
was made available for the first time, and against orders, by his executor.
Above all, Morgan did what any chronicler of this particular author must do.
He told his story well.

"My own interpretation of Maugham is obviously very different from Ted
Morgan's," Calder continues. "I am convinced that the long-standing and
inaccurate perception of him as a malicious, bitter, and spiteful misanthrope
must be replaced by a portrait which recognizes his sensitivity, wit, loyalty,
and numerous kindnesses to many people" (*Willie*, xvii).

After the first three hundred pages—eight chapters carrying his subject
into his seventies and the end of the World War II—Calder devotes his final

two chapters, eighty pages, to a passionate demonstration that loving-kindness—a rare (for Maugham) quality which he exalted in *The Summing Up* over such other intangibles as truth, beauty, goodness, and love—was frequently enacted during his ninety-two years.

Calder is a Canadian professor who has devoted his life as a scholar to Maugham. His *W. Somerset Maugham and the Quest for Freedom* (1972) was distinguished by its definitive account of the multilingual Maugham's often risky work as a liaison agent in WW I counterespionage in Russia and elsewhere. Given his rationale, he has produced compassionate hagiography but an unsatisfactory biography.

If Morgan stacked the deck to sensationalize Maugham's closet homosexuality, Calder goes to the other extreme. He is less persuasive than Morgan in the matter of Maugham's almost pathological need for the secret life. Maugham never lived to see the decriminalization of homosexuality in England. It was only twenty-five years ago—in 1967, two years after Maugham's death—that the Sexual Offences Act made homosexuality between consenting adults legal.

Although often urged to do so, Maugham never spoke up in favor of homosexuals for fear he would blow his cover. That is Calder's view. Harvey is more emphatic and brutal: Maugham never, as the current phrase has it, *went public* for fear he would lose readers. "Maugham took himself seriously as a novelist, despite token displays of self-depreciation, and was proud of his enormous commercial success; he had no desire to jeopardize his reputation by quixotic gestures in defiance of sexual prejudice." No one would have dared write a barbed tribute as Clive James does for Auden:

> He wound up as a poor fag at bay,
> Beleaguered in the end as at the start
> By dons appalled that he could talk all day
> And not draw breath although pissed as a fart,
> But deep down he had grown great, in a way
> Seen seldom in the history of his art—
> Whose earthly limits Auden helped define
> By realizing he was not divine.[6]

Rather, long penalized for being a popular writer, Maugham is now being penalized for having been a homosexual in secret.

Both biographies are fair about the checkered relationship between Maugham and his first companion, the American Gerald Haxton, who was parasitic but always loyal, and Haxton's successor, the late Alan Searle, whom

Maugham cultivated as a youth and who performed the often agonizing role of a very old party's Man Friday during Maugham's tortured final two decades. Calder is especially generous to Searle, whom Maugham's friends villified, and to Syrie Barnardo Wellcome Maugham, the famous interior decorator, whom Maugham married and spent half his life discrediting. Nor does Calder blink the most dishonorable act of Maugham's life: his unsuccessful attempt, nearing death, to disinherit their daughter Liza (Lady Hope), by adopting Searle as his son.

Calder, who is a better critic than Morgan, is too busy countering Morgan for the long overdue reassessment of the literary figure, the master storyteller whose universality for the intelligent and literate though not academic reader made him the best read and richest author of his day. But Maugham fell afoul of the prevailing mode in both prose and poetry during his most productive years. The elevation of text over temper—complexity over humanity, the artful over the life-affirming—produced in Maugham a false diffidence and humility that are his least attractive traits as a commentator. Edmund Wilson, who "translated" some of the most difficult texts of modernism, pilloried Maugham for books that were not *written*. But he admitted to me in conversation that he had not read any of Maugham's best works.

Wilson has been outnumbered. Evelyn Waugh called Maugham "the only . . . studio-master under whom one can study with profit." Orwell declared Maugham the writer who influenced him most "for his power of telling a story straightforwardly and without frills." His fan club included Dreiser and Virginia Woolf, Burgess, Perelman, Chandler, Isherwood, Garcia Marquez, and nearly all of Britain's leading critics before WW II.

Robert Calder writes: "When confronted with honesty and warmth, Maugham could let his own guard drop and respond with a warmth often masked when he confronted a more threatening world." He quotes a little-known friend as saying that "to many . . . people like myself with whom he came in contact he was goodness itself" (*Willie*, 226). For me and my wife, no truer words could be spoken. The opening memoir in this volume recalls the kindness with which he and Alan Searle treated us that day, the most memorable of my life: three decades ago and more and not a shade of its bright memory lost.

PART TWO

The Dismantling of Favor

Prologue

In Deepest Regions

In the opening scene of *King Lear*, the King of France expresses shock at Lear's about-face in dismissing his youngest daughter Cordelia, who has been his favorite: "This is most strange," he remarks to Lear, "that she, that even now was your best object, the argument of your praise, balm of your age, most best, most dearest, should in this trice of time, commit a thing so monstrous." He pleads for redress out of his perplexity that in a moment Cordelia's infraction should be so severe as "*to dismantle so many folds of favour*" (stress added); that somehow "reason without miracle" has poisoned Cordelia in her father's eyes.

Thus, a thin-skinned paterfamilias, in a manner unfit for a king, takes honest reticence as inferior to high-sounding lower forms of flattery. A tragedy of relationships is set in motion.

It is a commonplace to say that we have little to do with who our fathers, mothers, sons, daughters, siblings and kinspersons are, but we can choose our friends. In the vulnerable regions of the authorial, however, friendships among peers often assume interactions that are familial, connections that are umbilical. In the fluctuations of literary fortune favor is inconstant, friendships dismantled.

In this century we know that Ernest Hemingway sooner or later turned on everyone who had helped him. In the recent past, only the providential death of Lillian Hellman halted a defamation suit against Mary McCarthy. Surely he was thinking of literary friendships three hundred years ago and more when François de la Rochefoucauld perceived that friends do not take the bad news of their friends with unalloyed sorrow.

And yet, in terms of history—and particularly literary history and the history of ideas—the flow and ebb, the breach and occasional repair of friendships between major writers can be instructive. One learns amidst the quarreling how issues can at once join and divide competing sensibilities. In that deepest region of the psyche—the one to which, as we shall see later, Dostoevski's Underground Man assigned matters we cannot even acknowledge to ourselves—we can locate issues of politics, personal and professional, aesthetic and cultural.

In their conflict over taste and sensibility, Henry James and H. G. Wells appeared to the Edwardians to be battling for squatters' rights. James sought to protect his precious territory, the Novel, from the brash invasion of the younger and more popular Wells. The latter's expressed determination "to have all of life" embraced by fiction ran up against James's charges that writers like Wells and Arnold Bennett "saturated" fiction. His argument would be taken up and given new dimension a decade later—in 1924—by Virginia Woolf in a famous essay, "Mr. Bennett and Mrs. Brown."[1]

For a time, the master bestowed his favors lavishly on the pupil. The pupil received them with the deference of the aspiring pretender. As the relationship deepened, as Wells's burgeoning fame buttressed his cockney impudence, an implication of disapproval crept into James's letters.

James deplored long narratives in the first person because they precipitated the novel into "looseness." Two of Wells's best novels, *Tono-Bungay* and *The New Machiavelli,* are written in the first person and have long monologues. James objected to having characters talk at the reader. At first he excused Wells on the basis of the younger man's matchless vitality. A James biographer, Michael Swan, in his puzzlement over why James should have become so excited over a writer so unlike himself, asks: "Was [James] simply recognizing genius in whatever form it should appear—or was this recognition inspired by some obscure demand of his private psychology? Did he admire Wells as the aesthete secretly admires the athlete? Wells' commonsense pragmatism attracts him in the same way that he was unwillingly drawn towards the mind of his brother William."[2]

James always referred, without disparagement, to Wells's "cheek" and could write to Mrs. Humphry Ward: "I really think him [Wells] more interesting by his faults than he will ever manage to be in any other way . . . a most vivid and violent object lesson!"[3]

The lessons are still being learned and applied today. Their quarrel may have been *the* landmark engagement in the still-seething struggle between literature and journalism. Wells's trumpetings to expand the provinces of fiction, as sounded in 1911, have their parallel in those blown in 1989 by the high priest of vanity-of-vanities fictive journalism. Give us the big picture, blares Tom Wolfe. His *Bonfire of the Vanities,* at least by its length, did just that. The reviews of Wolfe's first novel echo the half-praises accorded Wells by James. Both writers are viewed by the mandarins as more interesting for their flaws than their virtues.

For anyone writing as I was in the early sixties, it was easy to accept the prevailing view that serious literary interest in H. G. Wells had long since ebbed. How otherwise explain how I, a retread from newspaper reporting and columning, obtained a Twayne contract in 1962 to add Wells's name to its burgeoning list of critical studies of English authors? Formalism, generally, and the New Criticism, specifically, appeared to have buried him. Mark Schorer had had what seemed to be the last word. Demolishing *Tono-Bungay* by forming a hangman's noose of words a desperate H. G. Wells had tossed back as a defensive lob against James ("I had rather be called a journalist than an artist"[4]), Schorer damned Wells by his exclusive syllogism: no accepted technique, no achieved content. It did not matter that if read with an open mind *Tono-Bungay* (1908) is as compelling today (at least for my students) as it was when Arnold Bennett reviewed it as an "epic," and D. H. Lawrence was so impressed that he despaired to Jessie Chambers of ever being able to match it.[5]

How many hundreds of times during the fevered composition of my first book did I bemoan Henry James's ever having been born? I wrote the original version in the shadow of an assumed discreditation, and I could not jump over it. It was only after publication of an earnest but less than adequate book that I came to see that the matter between coevals could be more than either/or. After decades of neglect, a combination of science fiction's acceptance and the writings of a small but influential coterie of critics—David Lodge, Colin Wilson, and Bernard Bergonzi in England; Anthony West, Mark Hillegas, and W. Warren Wagar in the United States—has led to a reassessment of the earlier works of Wells, especially the scientific romances and short stories, and found that at their core they imaginatively project a deep pessimism.

Most of all, however, an accident of geography whereby I met Edmund Wilson gave me confidence that, eventually, I could come to terms with James. I needed to be told at an early stage and carefully enough not to destroy me altogether that I had not earned the right to disparage. To Wilson's solicitude I owe the passion both to refresh my loyalty to Wells and to recognize that James's commitment to the art of the novel advanced the genre. James in his final phase was the first modernist.

When Twayne asked me almost twenty years later to revise the flawed 1967 study of Wells, I found myself given that rarity in any context: a second chance. My strategy would be to link rather than divide. For all the psychological prospecting of James and the didactic thrust of Wells, neither ever stopped being novelist-in-charge. Each managed his fiction—"stood next to God," as John Fowles Victorianly puts it in his tongue-in-cheek parody of the "new novel" called *The French Lieutenant's Woman*. Wells saw life as involving dramatic interaction between sensibility and the flow of the times. James *ordered* impressions—*regulated* his viewpoint—out of the necessity to encounter experience without the ability to take dramatic part in it. In the same year that Henry James died—1916—Wells published what in its time was his most popular novel, *Mr. Britling Sees It Through*. To evoke the feelings of a representative Englishman in the agony of the Great War, Wells installs a central intelligence of comparable galvanism to that which operates in *The Ambassadors*, James's favorite novel. *Britling* is Wells's Condition-of-England novel in wartime. *The Ambassadors* is James's Condition-of-Strether's-soul novel. The private Britling is as much Wells's concern as the public one as events move to a tragic conclusion with the death of his son in the trenches. How Lambert Strether comes, at last, to live his unlived life is the burden of James's inside look. Both James and Wells achieve a balanced tension between what goes on "outside"—what Strether and Britling see and hear—and what goes on "inside"—what each thinks.

Writing without a chip on my shoulder, I dared to suggest that James and Wells had much in common.

H. G. Wells and the Palimpsest of Time

> New lines are wreathed on old lines half-erased and
> those on older still; and so forever.
> The old shines through the new and colors it.
> What's new? What's old? All things have double
> meanings.
> —Conrad Aiken, "Palimpsest"

Bertie Wells had worked late into the night of August 5, 1914, completing an article, "The War That Will End War." By the time he had turned out the lights in his study and gone upstairs, the man whom the literate world had come to know as H. G. Wells had every reason to expect he might have trouble sleeping. During the day events had occurred which would complicate the pace of his domestic life in Easton Glebe, the pleasant old rectory in the countryside northeast of London, and also that of the larger world which, since the publication of *The Time Machine* two decades earlier, had become, in a sense, his private domain. One hundred miles away, in furnished lodgings, Rebecca West (an aspiring actress turned writer who had changed her name from Cicely Fairfield to Rebecca West to honor an Ibsen heroine), nineteen years old and unmarried, had given birth to their son, Anthony Panther West. Just twenty-four hours earlier—at midnight, August 4—England's ultimatum to the German government had expired. The two nations were at war.

The Great War produced the most profitable novel Wells ever wrote. *Mr. Britling Sees It Through* (1916) in its first eighteen months earned Wells £50,000, a sum equal to about $275,000 in 1986. The relationship with Rebecca West, which was no less a war, outlasted World War I and dragged out for a decade (1913–23). Moreover, its repercussions are still being felt. The offspring of this passionate liaison of literary geniuses, Anthony West, became an important writer. In 1984 he published a long-awaited biography of his father.[1]

Had Anthony West become, say, an eminent biologist like G. P. Wells, one of H. G.'s two sons within wedlock, rather than the author of a novel (*Heritage*, 1955)—a vivid, often comic account of what it was like to grow up as the bastard son of famous parents—his identity might have remained largely concealed. Rebecca West did all she could to conceal Anthony's identity. She obtained a legal injunction that prevented her son's writing anything in Britain about the circumstances of his birth. Thus *Heritage* could not be published on her side of the Atlantic. With Dame Rebecca's death in her ninetieth year in March, 1983, Anthony West put the finishing touches on the biography of his father that he had been working on intermittently for thirty-five years. With *H. G. Wells: Aspects of a Life* came the first publication in London of West's thirty-year-old novel and its return to print in the United States with a new introduction by its author.

Heritage leaves little doubt as to why Rebecca West might have wished it suppressed. In it young Dickie Savage draws a merciless portrait of the insipid, selfish Naomi Savage, the actress-mother who suffers by comparison with the father, Max Town, a writer-journalist of world fame. It covers Dickie's life from age six through his public school days and beyond to a maturity that finally allows him to come to a truce with his warring parents. A fairy-tale ending that West regrets in his 1985 introduction, Dickie Savage's happy maturity did violence to what actually happened in life. From his adolescence onward, he wrote, Rebecca West's aim was "to do me what hurt she could, and she remained set in that determination as long as there was breath in her body to sustain her malice." According to him, she blocked his career, made public scenes, tried to break up his marriage, tricked him out of his financial inheritance, and wrote hundreds of letters to people denouncing him.[2] The Wells biography *Aspects of a Life* makes everything explicit. It pillories Dame Rebecca as woman, mother, writer. Balanced judgments and fairness of comment are usually considered staples of the best literary biographies. *Aspects of a Life* draws a kind of venomous strength from its bias.

Anthony West has set out to even the score against everyone he deems to have done his father wrong. No one should be surprised at the force of the undertow.

2

   Lying awake with thoughts of the child he had sired by a woman not his wife—not the first such—and the crumbling civilization he was trying to reinvent, if H. G. Wells had taken time to think of his enemies—and his friends—he might have stolen out of his bedroom to his study to read the press cuttings that had been piling up. He might have been excused for looking again at the announcement of a forthcoming book from the publisher Mitchell Kennerley, New York, by a young American critic, Van Wyck Brooks. He rather liked the title, *The World of H. G. Wells.* Had any other imaginative writer, before or since, claimed so much of the planet—of the cosmos, really—for a literary playing field? H. G. might have been excused if he glanced rather quickly at the item on top, just received, "The Younger Generation," by Henry James in the *Times Literary Supplement.* James surveyed not only the middle generation of novelists—Conrad, Bennett, Galsworthy, himself—but the younger—Hugh Walpole, Gilbert Cannan, Compton Mackenzie, and a newcomer from the Midlands named D. H. Lawrence. No one, not even James's esteemed protégé Conrad, escaped his scythe. For Wells, James's courtesy and syntactical deviousness—failed to conceal the master's disapproval of the kinds of novels Wells and his close-friend, Arnold Bennett, were writing:

We confound the author of *Tono-Bungay* and the author of *Clayhanger* in his imputation for the simple reason that with the sharpest differences of character and range they yet come together under our so convenient measure of value *by saturation.* This is the greatest value, to our sense, in either of them, their other values, even when at the highest, not being quite in proportion to them; and as to be saturated is to be documented, to be able even on occasion to prove quite enviably and potently so, they are alike in the authority that creates emulation.[3]

Had Wells read further that early morning of crises, he might not have been put off when James wrote of Wells's "penchant for absorbing knowledge at the pores." Yet the drift became plain enough: "Where," asked James finally, is any "centre of interest or . . . sense of the whole?"[4] Their correspondence had been unfailingly polite until recently when James rebuked him for his novel *Marriage* (1912). At one time James had even expressed admiration for the *Tono-Bungay* (1909) that he now scorned. Just thinking about the guarded discourse that was now about to turn into an open literary quarrel could lead Wells away from his present tract, "The War That Will End War."

So it may have been on some such night as this that Bertie Wells determined to dust off an old manuscript he had conceived of as long ago as 1901 and returned to periodically during the dog days of *Ann Veronica* (1909) and *The New Machiavelli* (1911) and their stormy aftermath. He and a stunning nineteen-year-old Cambridge graduate, Amber Reeves, were perceived by the reviewers to be flimsily disguised prototypes of the principals in those two novels about human politics, suffragettes, free love. The critics, Wells complained, were always doing that with his novels these days—insisting his characters were based on actual people. Beatrice Webb had not forgiven him for making her into Altiora Bailey, with heart of cactus, in *Machiavelli*.[5] As now with his Rebecca, he and Amber had conceived a love child, a child whose coming had prompted him for the only time to consider leaving his devoted wife Jane. But Amber Reeves had married instead a barrister named Blanco White, who agreed while she was still pregnant to wed her and adopt the child.[6]

Years later, in a book he instructed G. P. Wells to publish only after all the principals had died, H. G. Wells would write of his major indiscretion: "Both Amber and I clung most desperately to the idea that we were sustaining some high and novel standard against an obtuse and ignoble world. . . . We ought to have gone on meeting as lovers and saying 'You be damned' to the world. . . . The child was an extraordinary irrelevance."[7] G. P. Wells published his father's book in 1984 under the title of *H. G. Wells in Love*.

The matter between himself and Henry James belonged to a different order of things. He might have settled this latest score by dropping in to see James at Lamb House, at Rye, for tea-talk in the garden. He had been an occasional visitor to Rye ever since he and Jane had built their "treasure house on the seashore"[8]—Henry James's very words—at nearby Sandgate. H. G. could recall when things were jollier between them. Once he had come to Rye with a car to fetch William James and his daughter to Sandgate and Spade House. The brothers had had a characteristic spat. Henry had caught William climbing the gardener's ladder to get a peek at Henry's guest, the vast G. K. Chesterton.[9] It was the sort of thing that, for Henry, just wasn't done.

That was the trouble between Wells and James. There were too many things one wished to do as a novelist which James placed off-limits as not being

H. G. Wells. *Photo courtesy of the H. G. Wells Archive, University of Illinois.*

appropriate for the Novel. Looking again at James's latest *obiter dicta* in "The Younger Generation," Bertie Wells may at some such moment as that have decided to fling the gauntlet back at his rival, even have some fun, too.

It would be on July 5, 1915, eleven months to the day after Wells's late-night vigil, before his "long and witty joke"—Leon Edel's words in the final volume of his monumental biography of James[10]—would come home to roost. Stopping at the Reform Club, James was handed a book parcel that had lain there for some time unforwarded. It had an elaborate title page: *Boon, the Mind of the Race, the Wild Asses of the Devil and the Last Trump.* Edited by one Reginald Bliss, who was mentioned as the author of *The Cousins of Charlotte Brönte, A Child's History of the Crystal Palace,* and a book on *Whales in Captivity,* it offered "an ambiguous introduction by H. G. Wells." In a crucial part of the fourth chapter ("Of Art, of Literature, of Mr. Henry James") a shocked James would find passages, which his detractors would be forever quoting, including Wells's description of a James novel as

like a church lit but without a congregation to distract you, with every light and line focused on the high altar, very reverently placed, intensely there, is a dead kitten, an egg-shell, a bit of string. . . . It is leviathan retrieving pebbles. It is a magnificent but painful hippopotamus resolved at any cost, even at the cost of its dignity, upon picking up a pea, which has got into the corner of its den.[11]

To Wells's badinage, James responded with a powerful letter upholding his commitment to Art as all that mattered. The letter, frequently quoted in manifestoes of the New Criticism, terminated their once-guarded friendship.[12] James died the next year. Long afterward, E. M. Forster unexpectedly came down on Wells's side when he called the James section of *Boon* "amusing . . . and perhaps profound."[13] Edmund Wilson, for whom James was a model for his own pursuance of a disappearing breed, the man of letters, once regretted in conversation with me that his hero had not replied to Wells in kind.[14] In 1914, however, with the Germans driving toward Paris, Wells could only think of recasting *Boon* to be not just his backlash at his critics but an effect of his deepening recognition, half derisive, half terrified, of the burgeoning peril of his affairs—political and personal.

3

Surely *Boon* and even Henry James were paltry issues compared to those which were prompting him in 1914 to write "The War That Will End War." Well's mind may have run on that night to his favorite preoccupation, the future. Surely it had been some such tendency in him that prompted Chesterton in 1904 to write, in fear rather than in praise, that he would wake up at night hearing Mr. Wells grow.[15] As Wells lay tossing, he kept coming back to the phrase he and he alone would make romantic: The Shape of Things to Come. When the war was over there would be a chance to create a new European order. "Order," in fact, had become his favorite word. That and "darkling". If you had an *order*—a New World Order—you would not have things that were *darkling*.

Thirty years later, at the height of the London Blitz, the aging Wells refused to leave the Regency house at 13 Hanover Terrace whose lease he had taken over in 1935 from Alfred Noyes. From a lecture platform in 1958, novelist Elizabeth Bowen would remember calling on Wells late at night during the blackout to the accompaniment of air-raid sirens. A trembling Wells came to the door. "But you shouldn't be frightened at this," Bowen remarked. "After all you invented it." Wells looked at her and said: "It's not the bombs, it's the dark. I've been afraid of darkness all my life."[16]

For a man approaching fifty in 1914, a man celebrity itself had already converted into the term "H. G. Wells," it might have been too much to expect a recollection of his first jousts with the darkness he feared. First, as with all of us, there was the mother. This little *black* figure of a woman was curiously suggestive in her later years, Wells would recall, of Her Majesty Queen Victoria. Sarah Neal Wells, viewed almost clinically in her son's autobiography that was twenty years away, committed the one unpardonable sin in his scheme: she had a "set" mind about religion, respectability, and her "place." She took for granted her Victorian world, the one Bertie would spend a lifetime exorcising from his soul. Not even her desperate single-handed battle to keep the family afloat made her sense for a moment, as her son would express it, that "her God in his Heaven was under notice to quit."[17]

Wells would recall his father Joseph Wells, undistinguished as he was in anything but cricket, both poignantly and also in terms of darkness. Where Mr. Polly in Wells's most endearing creation, a book done to honor his father, broke out in true Wellsian style from the bondage of circumstances, Bertie's father reserved his dreams for stargazing. Twenty-five years after his father's death, Wells wrote that if Joseph Wells "could look out of this planet and wonder about the stars, it may be he could also look out of his immediate circumstances and apprehend their triviality by stellar standards."[18]

How "stellar standards" won out over Sarah Wells's conviction that the best of positions for a young man lay in wearing a black coat and tie behind a counter is a story the novelist would never tire of retelling. In a moving segment of *Tono-Bungay*, Wells shows how George Ponderevo got up early one Sunday morning and walked twenty miles to Bladesover to proclaim to his mother, a lady's maid in the great house, that the latest experiment in drapery had to end.[19]

Wells learned firsthand about the Alfred Pollys, Artie Kippses, and Teddy Ponderevos. He came perilously close to living out the life of Mr. Polly without that little man's saving recourse to arson. He might have remained an underpaid teacher like his earliest realistic hero Mr. Lewisham, with a scheme for life that would have included marriage and children but not a lifelong chafing against convention. He might have had, with his Kipps, only vague intimations of the celebrity that elevated him to a kind of world statesmanship of letters: confrontations with Theodore and Franklin D. Roosevelt, Lenin, Stalin, and most of the other figures who shaped human destiny during the first third of the century. The body of work produced by Wells before his forty-fifth year was, as Orwell said, the fruit of a first-rate literary talent. When Orwell wrote an obituary[20] of his early hero, he claimed the years between *The Time Machine* (1895) and *The Outline of History* (1920) should bear the name Wells.

4

If he lay wakeful the summer's night that had been prelude to a war without and a war within, Bertie Wells was entirely too embattled to care that an age, as Orwell would claim, might one day bear his name. Within a few months, his mind entirely obsessed by the war that was supposed to end war, he would monitor the Great War novelistically even while British, French, and German soldiers were dying in the trenches.

Always a writer in a hurry, Wells would not wait, like Hemingway, Remarque, Cummings, and Dos Passos, for war to end. He would write *Mr. Britling*, a book that read like recent headlines. News flashes like this one:

At the very moment when Mr. Britling was saying these words, in Sarajevo in Bosnia, where the hour was somewhat later, men whispered together, and one held nervously to a black parcel that had been given him and nodded as they repeated his instructions, a black parcel with certain unstable chemicals and a curious arrangement of detonators therein, a black parcel destined ultimately to shatter every landmark of Mr. Britling's cosmogony.[21]

Midway through *Mr. Britling,* writing in the same sort of third-person solil-oquy that Henry James called the central intelligence and for which he said H. G. had no talent (writers like Wells, James had charged, gave in to "the *terrible* fluidity of self-revelation"),[22] Wells evoked the private Mr. Britling who in his darkest hours—his son would be killed on the Western Front—called up the memory of his (and Wells's) Victorian mentor-figure. It might have been on some such night as the one to which I have been referring that Wells wrote:

On those black nights, when the personal Mr. Britling would lie awake thinking how unsatisfactorily Mr. Britling was going on, and when the impersonal Mr. Britling would be thinking how unsatisfactorily his universe was going on, the whole mental process had a likeness to some complex piece of orchestral music. . . .

Was [Thomas H.] Huxley right, and was all humanity even as Mr. Britling, a careless, fitful thing, playing a tragically hopeless game, thinking too slightly, moving too quickly, against a relentless antagonist?[23]

If Huxley was not the creator of the theory of evolution, he was its earliest poet. Grandfather of Aldous and Julian Huxley, he was *the* teacher all of us wish we might have had. Bertie Wells escaped anonymity through a door few men of letters entered before him and only an occasional C. P. Snow or Kurt Vonnegut has since. Bertie began to pass examinations and to show unusual ability in science; when he was eighteen, he was offered a scholarship at the Normal School of Science (now the Imperial College), South Kensington, to train as a teacher.

At the time Wells arrived in 1884, Huxley was in his sixtieth year and exhausted to the point of illness by his brilliant campaign as Darwin's public spokesman and as a passionate battler for science education. Seventeen years later Wells recalled that he had only attended one course of lectures by Huxley and spoken to him but once, holding open the door and exchanging a simple "good morning."[24] Although Huxley died in 1895, the year of *The Time Machine,* what Wells drew from that year of study he would spend a lifetime dramatizing in story after story.

One can well imagine the impact on the young biology student of stories current among the older assistants about times only recently past when Charles Darwin had entered the lecture auditorium to hear his friend. Dar-win had been dead less than two years, and Huxley was still a decade away from delivering his famous lecture on "Ethics and Evolution" at Oxford.

Fifty years later Wells could write of his year in elementary biology and zoology under Huxley that it "was beyond question the most educational year of my life. It left me under that urgency for coherence and consistency, that repugnance from haphazard assumptions and arbitrary statement, which is the essential distinction of the educated from the uneducated mind."[25] More specifically, it was from Huxley that Wells drew the cosmic pessimism that marked his scientific romances from the beginning. His most reliable biographers, Norman and Jeanne MacKenzie, are particularly forceful on this point. Huxley's example and teachings, they declare, provided Wells with

the vital link between the evangelical beliefs in which he had been brought up and the scientific ideas which he absorbed as a student. For the remainder of his life he held these two systems together in a dynamic relationship. . . . Neither Darwin nor Huxley nor Wells after them . . . believed that progress was inevitable. . . . And both Huxley and Wells were plagued by haunting doubts whether in fact it would occur. . . . This dualism lay at the heart of Huxley's belief, as it was subsequently to run through Wells's scientific romances, his novels, and utopias.[26]

Huxley espoused a theory of evolution in which the world and the universe, society and nature, are viewed as operating at cross purposes, with man pitting mind against matter. If, as Huxley believed—I am here quoting from "Ethics and Evolution"—"evolution involves a constant remodeling of the organism in adaptation to new conditions, retrogressive change is both as possible and practicable as progressive. The course of earthly life is like the trajectory of a ball fired from a mortar, and the sinking half of that course is as much a part of the general process of evolution as the rising."[27]

H. G. Wells learned in Huxley's lectures and laboratory the dread potential for destruction held by forces outside man. This knowledge took shape in those cosmic phenomena so dear to his heart: colliding comets, invading Martians, monstrous creatures seen in the Time Traveller's kaleidoscope of the earth's dying. The convergence of the biggest idea of the nineteenth century—evolution—with a mind that was capable of grasping and extending it in all of its biological, philosophical, social, and poetical ramifications made possible Wells's earliest and best known writing. Although he subtitled his autobiography "discoveries and conclusions of a very ordinary brain," it was the cast of that brain—nurtured in the laboratory, yet tuned to the music of new spheres of possibility—that enabled its possessor to savor Darwin's ideas, then transform them into visions with untold vistas.

In his tour de force *The French Lieutenant's Woman* (1969), John Fowles realized something of the difficulty even the intelligent nonspecialist Victorian had in understanding that evolution was a scientific notion with implicit consequences for the worlds of ethics and social organization. Charles Smithson, himself unknowingly enduring a costly personal evolution, is an amateur paleontologist who keeps missing the point. Wells, of course, had wrestled mightily with the problems throughout his *oeuvre*. The leading French Wellsian J. P. Vernier recognizes the importance to Wells of translating *The Origin of Species* into the language of fiction. Many of Wells's later discussion novels, Vernier argues, elucidate the same view on evolution as the scientific romances; not regarded especially highly by Wells, they still retain the kind of fascination only literature can exert. The discussion novels are all but forgotten.

When the artilleryman of *War of the Worlds* observes that earthlings must seem to the Martians as alien and lowly as monkeys seem to his own species, Wells is dramatizing the notion that the process of natural selection provides a gauge for comparison between any two creatures. William Golding, among others, powerfully contested this idea of progress in his stunning novel about Neanderthals, *The Inheritors* (1955).[28] The notion that, after Darwin and Huxley, progress is an idea whose time has come is an article of faith that Wells extrapolates in book after book. What Golding applies to the animate in evolutionary theory, Wells, beginning with *The Time Machine*, applies to the spatial. Writing in their useful and enlightening *H. G. Wells: Early Writings in Science and Science Fiction* (1975), Robert M. Philmus and David Y. Hughes locate, by logical extrapolation, Wells's impulse to probe the future:

If the conceptual bridging of distances could be inferred from Darwin's theories, the telescoping of time was a necessity. Evolution enlarged human consciousness of time: most obviously, because for the theory to be true this planet must be older than anyone before Darwin had supposed it to be. . . . And once human consciousness opens itself to the possibility of conceiving the entire past of the evolutionary process, why not attempt to project the course of that process a . . . greater "distance" into the future?[29]

The important words, as always with Wells, are the last two. But if time and space lent buoyancy to *The Time Machine, The Invisible Man, First Men in the Moon,* and *War of the Worlds,* they were ballast for some of the later books. William Clissold, the narrator of Wells's most ambitious novel except for *Tono-Bungay,* looks out of the window and meditates about something he calls "flux universal." Instead of being tormented out of faith and, like Matthew Arnold before him, into seeking after some sharer of the human condition, the Wellsian spokesman in *The World of William Clissold* (1926) waxes mystical, messianic, and monotonous:

I see the nearness of an order . . . like the order of a garden, of a workroom, of a laboratory, a clean life and a direct life and a powerful life for men; the jungle and all its sufferings gone at last for ever.[30]

Fifteen years earlier, Benham, like Clissold, one of Wells's trademarked Men of the Future, searches for something he calls the "Life Aristocratic." He stands in the moonlight of the Bengal jungle, facing a tiger and lifting a hand to it: "I am Man," he intones; and the beast "vanished, became invisible and inaudible, with a kind of instantaneousness."[31] What is really instantaneous about scenes like this one—and they become common in what might be called his Great Man fiction after World War I—is their pomposity. For Edmund Wilson, the zeal of his youth set afire by the Wells of 1895–1914, the reading of that jungle scene in *The Research Magnificent* (1915) brought an abrupt falling-out and a determination to read Wells no more.[32]

The Traffords, Remingtons, Benhams, and Clissolds may indeed possess that wider grasp and vision with which Wells had endowed them. But their estrangement from the Lewishams, the Kippses, the Pollys, the Teddy Ponderevos—their standing apart from yesterday's men—makes them poor fictive company in any setting this side of utopia.

5

Utopia. World State. Universal Citizenry. The Mind of the Race. World Brain. Some or all of these slogans—surely others, too—may have coursed through the wakeful consciousness of Bertie Wells as he lay in the darkness of Easton Glebe the night and early morning of August 5–6, 1914. Perhaps he thought of tanks, the "land ironclads" he had invented in a short story of that title, or of the coming "war in the air," still another of his early titles.

What, though, of other thoughts? Had he not for a moment, as he labored long into the night to complete "The War That Will End War," stopped to consider the irony behind the confidence of that title? What war could end the warring forces within himself? Did he never wonder about the curious accident in time—a phenomenon unlikely in any other author—that nine years earlier *A Modern Utopia*, his clear call for a ruling hierarchy to consolidate one of his visionary utopias, and *Kipps*, his equally clear monument to ordinary human material, had appeared simultaneously in 1905. That the two conflicting tendencies gnawing at his soul should see the light of publication within six months of each other provides ample testimony to the early control with which Wells held the demands of the polemicist and artist. "No less than a planet will serve the purpose of *A Modern Utopia.* . . . World state, therefore, it must be."[33] But, of *Kipps,* hadn't Henry James written him in terms that were not the least ambiguous: "*Kipps* left me prostrate with admiration, a gem of such brilliancy, of *true* truth. You have for the first time created the English 'lower middle class,' without the picturesque, the grotesque, the fantastic interference of Dickens and George Eliot."[34]

Did Wells not see in a kind of progression a *loss* of control over his own "little wars"—books where the landscape not of order (that favorite word of his) but of *dis*order dominated? One could glimpse along with the spearhead ships from Mars a group of village urchins tossing stones at the cylinder that had fallen from the sky. One could hear the bark of a cart driver as he pulled up at Iping Village with the luggage of the Invisible Man. One followed Mr. Polly into a room of similarly dispossessed tradesmen after his "bit of arson" had destroyed the Fishbourne Hotel but also made a hero of him for rescuing his landlord's mother-in-law. The Brueghel setting of the early works, of whose humanity he would profanely remind the suddenly hostile Orwell in the late thirties,[35] was dwindling to that of a conference room. Could he not see—did he not care?—that in his zeal for utopia he was losing his distinction, as Gordon N. Ray would declare a decade after his death, as "the last English novelist to write from a sense of English society as a whole?"[36] Did he not see, finally, in the example of his own domestic wars that night of August 5, 1914, that such human factors would have to be taken account of in any consideration of a utopia, a world state; that even those most tuned to his universal citizenry could never rule out, as he was trying to do, all those others who by virtue of their human condition might never be so tuned?

6

In an auto-obituary, written when he knew he was dying, Wells discounted the "original freshness" of his romances. They had been destroyed, he wrote, by "the general advance of knowledge." Wells probably intended these words to bear a truth-telling writer's candor. Instead they demonstrate the grain of Wellsian thinking when it was directed, and the perversity of the Wellsian imagination when it was undersold. He believed that knowledge, born of the scientific spirit and buttressed by rational faith, would always mark advances and thereby redeem the future. In the same auto-obituary, he half joked about the impairment of his health "by a spell in a concentration camp under the brief Communist dictatorship of 1952." Certainly Bertrand

Russell, his old ally, was right when he speculated that confinement to a place like Buchenwald would have cost Wells his belief in the omnipotence of reason. "To the end of his days," Russell concluded, "Wells could not face the fact that sensible men have no power."[37]

Nor could he believe that the imagination *has* great power. Because his studies at South Kensington played like a monitoring palimpsest over the free flow of his imagination, he never credited the arming irony behind such truths as Auden's that poetry makes nothing happen. The coexistence of a glowing imaginative sensibility with a scientific rationalism betrayed him into a crippling messianism.

Yet the magic went out of Wells a lot more gradually than many of his detractors suggest. Arnold Kettle is certainly right when he says that Wells is a writer who is easy to dismiss until you read him.[38] Evelyn Waugh, in a memoir, quotes the opening words of *The Time Machine* and makes book that few contemporary critics could identify the voice of Wells. Walter Allen records in his recent autobiography the strongest of pluses for Wells with an implicit, if familiar, disclaimer: "I came on Wells, who I still think had the largest natural talent of any English novelist of the century. He did not, as we all know, always use it well, but he was a positive cornucopia of ideas, which he poured out in a ceaseless stream. And he had, too, an enormous capacity for fun. Almost certainly, he will look much greater in the future than he does now."[39]

The Wells that holds up is the Wells of the scientific romances, which some specialists say were the first science fiction; the poet fantasist of the short stories for which he has never received full credit; and the extraordinarily ordinary sage of that Edwardian trio, Kipps, Polly and Ponderevo. What one wonders, finally, is whether, in an age given to the premerchandised best-seller, it is possible for a young reader to come upon a book, like Orwell's George Bowling did with *The History of Mr. Polly*, and ask "if you can imagine the effect it had on me, to be brought up as I'd been brought up . . . and then come across a book like this."[40]

To the spiritually underfed young of post-Victorian days and ones much later, H. G. Wells introduced a priceless ingredient, one in short supply today: intellectual and imaginative exhilaration.

II.

The Anxiety of Confluence

In August, 1972, at the time of his eighty-third birthday, Conrad Aiken was made to appear ready for death. The *New York Times* quoted the old poet—"I'm running out of time. All things come to an end"—and invoked the final quatrain of his "Obituary in Bitcherel":

> Separate we come,
>   separate go.
> And this be it known is all
>   that we know.[1]

In October, however, I received a postcard written in the epistolary tone long familiar to me—that of a bookish hillbilly. It was far from detached. He inquired if my book on Malcolm Lowry had been published and hinted he would like a copy.[2] Five years before he had dismissed me in an interview for an essay that became the key chapter of the book. I had assigned him major roles in Malcolm Lowry's long gestation of *Under the Volcano*—as a vital influence, generally, and model for the Consul, particularly. If I were to go ahead and publish such drivel, he wrote just after the interview, "I fear you'll in the end be sorry."[3]

Had he had a change of mind? Now that he was invalided was he settling for less? Five years after he had demolished me, could he better accept my assignment of him as donor in a literary transfusion of Joyce to Lowry? I'll never know. Two weeks after his eighty-fourth birthday—August 17, 1973—

Conrad Aiken suffered a fatal heart attack. He never acknowledged getting my book, the first full study on Lowry. But as with Edmund Wilson, I had learned from Aiken a number of useful lessons in critical decorum. I shall note them in the pages ahead.

In his autobiography, Wells poses a question that looms more pertinent today, especially to commercial publishing, than it did sixty years ago: "Who would write novels if we could write autobiography—*all out?*"[4] This manifesto, a concession to Iago's definition of libel ("He that filches from me my good name . . . makes me poor indeed") also stems from Wells's late-career first-person harangues. However, a reading of the fiction of Conrad Aiken provides an object lesson for anyone who still thinks that narratives in the first person provide the surest door to the autobiographic.

Few writers of this century have been more obsessed by the "I" and have used it less than Aiken. It never occurs in any of his five novels, published between 1927 and 1940. Only eight of the forty-one stories in the Mark Schorer collected edition install it and never for disclosure of the speaker's inner world.

As we have seen, Henry James constructed fiction's most complex aesthetic out of ways to avoid "the *terrible* fluidity of self-revelation." Aiken drew from James an "I"-centered version of the third-person central intelligence. In James's use, the central intelligence is the solidly posed center which in *The Ambassadors* resides wholly in the consciousness of the principal envoy, Lambert Strether. Aiken, under the reign of Joyce's Leopold Bloom, is impatient with the usual means of narrative expression; he wants to give the reader a kind of third dimension. In his first novel, *Blue Voyage* (1927), whose conception, Aiken has said, owes everything to the appearance of *Ulysses* in 1922, the reader is required to follow the thoughts of Demarest (Aiken) through a crescendo of sensory impressions—a suggestive name hanging in the air of otherwise ordinary small talk but also capable of triggering an erotic fantasy or synthesizing a cluster of memories.

Aiken's masterpiece is his autobiography *Ushant*, which he published in 1952 when he was sixty-three but which he had worked over for twenty years. While it merits Malcolm Cowley's claim that it stands as one of the great American autobiographies, it can only be so classed in the sense that Nabokov thought of autobiography rather than as Henry Adams regarded it. All his writing life Aiken had anticipated Nabokov's notion that the best way of recapitulating a life is to identify its dominant metaphors and track them down through the years.

In *Ushant,* Aiken uses the image of the Great Circle: of a man circling back upon his youth, of being forced to swerve from it by the horror of its climax, and beginning once again the encircling passage. The forward movement in time is left to be reconstructed by the reader from nonchronological recollections concerning three conscious goals of the writer's life: literary excellence, women's favors, self-understanding.

There is no other autobiography in American literature remotely like *Ushant,* perhaps no book of any kind. Its sheer writtenness shimmers, passage after passage of Debussyan splendor, a painstaking but never labored stream-of-consciousness evoking memory. As the climactic work of a man and a writer who anticipated—and often experienced—what he referred to metaphorically as the "starfish turn"—betrayal—*Ushant* is Conrad Aiken's lamentation on graspable opportunities rendered demonic.

A graspable-opportunity-rendered-demonic may well encapsulate the curious friendship and tortured symbiosis between Aiken and his Harvard classmate, rival, and peer, T. S. Eliot, the friend he always referred to as Tom. Yet if they had not had the spur of a kinship born of rivalry for the distinction of best undergraduate poet of their time at Harvard, it is not certain they would have become close. As a student, Aiken was a gadfly who avoided Greek and most of the classics and would not be graduated in sequence. Tom Eliot from the start was what I once heard a "busted" doctoral candidate refer to as a member of the "cult of ultimate seriousness". Aiken barely finished; Eliot, coveted as a doctoral candidate, chose not to submit his thesis. Eliot deeply respected Aiken as a critic but thought him a facile philosopher. More to the point of "Conrad Aiken and the 'Tom' Catastrophe," the previously unpublished essay that follows, Aiken's subjective aesthetic produced in Eliot, putative father of the New Criticism, a lesion of hostility that never healed.

III.

Conrad Aiken and the "Tom" Catastrophe

Writing in 1989 in *The Yale Review,* James Merrill closes a brief essay on "The Love Song of J. Alfred Prufrock" with the confession that "even now I tremble when I open his books."[1] Merrill was writing in a special centennial-plus-one issue devoted to T. S. Eliot (1888–1965). If one of America's finest living poets can admit to "a sense of live menace and fascination" at even the contemplation of one of Eliot's poems, perhaps I can at last exorcise my sense for a quarter of a century that no one—not even his friends—had earned the right, especially after he published *The Waste Land* in 1922, to call T. S. Eliot "Tom."

Conrad Aiken always called him Tom, and, as I have been twenty-five years in the learning, he had earned the right. One often hears that early friendships have all the better of it. Partners have shared experiences; they have *done* things together. What I have learned about these two—friends from their Harvard days—was that, almost from the start, they *did* each other.

It was Stephen Spender who, in an earlier T. S. E.-tribute issue (this one by *Sewanee Review* in 1966, a year after Eliot's death), recalled that Eliot had told him in conversation of having always felt disturbed and unhappy that a contemporary and Harvard near classmate had had so little success as a poet: "I've always thought he [Conrad Aiken] and I were equally gifted, but I've received a large amount of appreciation, and he has been rather neglected. I can't understand it. It seems unjust. It always worries me."[2]

Recently published early correspondence points to the falsity of those words. What worried Tom Eliot was not Conrad Aiken's neglect but Conrad. In letters to his mother from London in 1920, he noted that the Harvard classmate of whom he had written earlier "is now quite a flourishing poet in America." While describing Aiken as "very nice," Eliot undercuts such faint praise with the damning comment that "in comparison with Englishmen [Conrad] seems to have had rather a soft and easy intellectual existence—not the hard knocking about that one gets among men of brains here." As if reference to Aiken reminds him of similarly unpleasant arrivals of other American poets seeking to follow the expatriate's lead, Eliot follows it directly with a pseudosympathetic account of

an odd American Jew here named [Max] Bodenheim; rather pathetic, although foolish. He is a vagrant poet. . . . [who] received his first blow when he found that no one had heard of him. I told him my history here, and left him to consider whether an American Jew, of only a common school education and no university degree, with no money, no connections, and no social polish or experience, could make a living in London. . . . I made him see that getting recognized in English letters is like breaking open a safe—for an American, and that only about three had ever done it."

Bodenheim, "though he has never been taught to write properly," has "a much better mind than Aiken, who gets on much better (he has an independent income too)."[3]

Writing to Ezra Pound in Rome, Eliot again juxtaposes Aiken and Bodenheim—now without kid gloves: the former is "stupider than I remember him; in fact, stupid." The latter "is not unintelligent, anyhow better than Aiken, and being Semites I suppose [the Bodenheims] will survive somehow" (*T. S. E. Letters*, 384).

Did Tom Eliot, who knew the importance of getting on Pound's good side, recognize it could do him no harm to hint at a kinship in antisemitism?

Actually, as is well known, Eliot had been on Pound's good side, artistically, for over five years. Pound had nagged Harriet Monroe into publishing "Prufrock" in *Poetry* (June, 1915), announcing it as "the best poem I have yet had or seen from an American." And, as I would learn at firsthand, it was Conrad Aiken, so often treated with merciless contempt, who first brought "Prufrock" to Pound's attention. Peter Ackroyd, the only biographer of Eliot so far, hints that Aiken's passionate commitment to his friend's poetry was crucial from the start. "Aiken . . . understood Eliot's poetry best. . . . Pound often missed its point [having] no real dramatic sense." Reviewing "Prufrock" in The *Dial*, Aiken described it as the work of a "bafflingly peculiar" man.[4] Just how baffling I have learned for myself and am still learning.

It has been twenty-five years since my two conversations with Conrad Aiken. I despair of ever coming to terms with them. I had journeyed to the charming city of Savannah, Georgia, its remarkable downtown then—Easter, 1967—in the process of being restored. Another restoration—that of the poet—would prove to be the project with which I would have to grope.

I had prepared for Aiken in a restricted sense only. The Eliot connection was the furthest thing from my mind. I was in the final semester of my residency for a Ph.D. at Purdue. To be sure, there was a thesis—in both academic and generic senses—to lay at the feet of the old poet, then seventy-seven. I should also have been prepared to discuss Aiken's long and varied shelf of books, some fifty and in all the major genres. It would have helped to have remembered a gloss by my teacher, Purdue's Professor Harold Watts, for five lines of Eliot's "Little Gidding":

> And last, the rending pain of re-enactment
> Of all that you have done, and been; the shame
> Of motives late revealed, and the awareness
> Of things ill done and done to others' harm
> Which once you took for exercise of virtue[5]

Watts speculated that such seemingly uncharacteristic lines from so unconfessional a poet might have been Eliot's attempt to assuage his guilt over his long-standing mistreatment of Aiken. But it would be years after my meeting with Aiken that I came upon my marked-up copy of *The Four Quartets* and spotted Watts's gloss.

I came to Savannah "prepared" in other ways, all of them destined to jeopardize the interview. I had asked Edmund Wilson, a summer neighbor in upstate New York, to write a letter of introduction to Aiken, who once had been *his* neighbor on Cape Cod. Edmund agreed but warned me that I was in for trouble.

"Conrad is one of those writers like Hemingway who are terribly vulnerable to what critics say about their books. But he is absolutely the most facile important poet America has ever produced. I do not mean to disparage him. He can churn out exceptional verse by the yard. I believe that is why T. S. Eliot is the greater poet. He had to work harder for his effects. When he got them they were worth having."

Then the Wilsonian catechism—the distillation you always waited for:

Conrad Aiken as I remember him. When I interviewed him during two days in his Regency apartment in downtown Savannah at Eastertime of 1967 (he was seventy-seven), he reminded me of the Chinese detective Charley Chan. *Courtesy Conrad Aiken Collection, Huntington Library.*

"They were classmates, you know—a year apart. At Harvard. Better not bring up Eliot. Conrad is paranoid on that subject."

Wilson wrote to Aiken as I had requested, but I did not remember his cautionary note. There would be no need to. My dissertational business had nothing to do with Aiken–Eliot; it had to do with Aiken–Malcolm Lowry. My timing seemed just right. That January, in response to a *Times Literary Supplement* leader on Jonathan Cape's publication of *Selected Letters of Malcolm Lowry*, Aiken spoke out[6] on his younger contemporary with whom, in the thirties, he had joined in a remarkable literary and personal symbiosis. I was especially proud of something I had written: "It is a multiple irony of modern literary history that *Under the Volcano*, a novel Conrad Aiken both *posed for* and helped *coach* into being, is often spoken of in the same breath as *Ulysses*, a landmark behind whose shadow Aiken's own long fiction has been relegated."

What I did not know, as I congratulated myself over his invitation to visit him in Savannah, was that Aiken would also come armed—armed with weapons brought to a fine sharpness by a half-century of defensive literary skirmishing. What I could not know, in my narrow-gauge academicism, was that I was invading private territory: that innermost domain which Dostoevski's Underground Man calls the place of secrets a man keeps even from himself.

I should have been forewarned, so badly did the interview start. I arrived on Good Friday, but Aiken could not see me until Monday. Allen Tate, I. A. Richards, people like that, were in town for Easter. "Noontime sessions are best, if that suits you. Better ring me up before you come, just to be sure." The voice on the phone was resonant Harvard, as I had known it would be from his Caedmon recordings.

Then, when Monday came, the interview almost blew up before it started. The Aikens lived in a brick-front Regency apartment next door, as an Aiken poem has it, to

> the house on Broad Street, red brick, with nine rooms
> the weedgrown graveyard with its rows of tombs

It was the house where the eleven-year-old Conrad in February, 1901, had heard the sounds of an early-morning quarrel, a half-stifled scream, his father counting three, two pistol shots; and then, furtively investigating, had found his parents dead after an act of murder and suicide. Broad Street had become Oglethorpe East and an apartment set aside for the famous native son by the financier-philanthropist, Hy Sobiloff, himself a poet. There the Aikens lived—he and "Lorelei Three" (Aiken, in writing, always referred to his three wives by Lorelei, plus the number), who was and is the artist Mary Hoover.

I could not find the number; I can *never* find house numbers. It was 230 Oglethorpe East but (I would learn later) the Aikens had had the number removed. I settled on the house between 228 and 232. I rang and waited. After what seemed a quarter of an hour—it may have been ninety seconds—I decided I had better enter. I turned the knob; the door was unlocked. I was standing in the Aiken parlor. Glaring at me from the head of a spiral staircase was an elderly man—heavyset, huge head, mandarin-looking, Charley Chan without moustache. There was no time to retreat.

"Are you in the habit of entering a man's house like a burglar?"

He motioned for me to ascend the stairs. I followed as he shuffled into a large drawing room and study. I noted a piano, tape recorder, microphone. Aiken hovered, not speaking, as I placed a stack of file cards on the table. I removed from a briefcase the R. P. Blackmur edition of his five novels, the 1960 *Collected Poems*—a volume of over one thousand pages, contrasted (I have since calculated) to T. S. Eliot's *Complete Poems and Plays* which come in well under four hundred pages.

What I did not bring out of the briefcase were the page proofs of my first scholarly publication, an essay trying to link *Ulysses* and Lowry's *Under the Volcano*, with Aiken's first novel, *Blue Voyage*, in the middle.[7]

From my newspaper days I ought to have learned to say nothing and await the main chance. Instead I tried for the lighter touch. "I guess I look like a book salesman which is just about what I am, when you come to think about it."

Chan didn't think about it. Only an inscrutable silence. Finally: "You wouldn't have needed that letter from Edmund Wilson. It was good to hear from him, but the fact is, Edmund and I no longer have anything to say to each other. He's a social and political historian, not a literary critic. And very unreliable about poetry. One time he was sounding off on the *symbolistes*. I interrupted by questioning his reading of those poets in *Axel's Castle*. 'That's *irrelevant*, Conrad!' he snapped. 'Irrelevant maybe, Edmund, but not incompetent!'"

He told of once suggesting a cartoon which would portray Wilson and *his* Lorelei Three—Mary McCarthy—then recently divorced but still publicly feuding. In the cartoon, McCarthy and Wilson would be sitting opposite one another, each reading the other's latest pillorying. Aiken's suggested caption: *The Shock of Recognition!*

(Two years after these talks, I asked Edmund Wilson if he had seen an interview on Aiken's eightieth birthday—1969—in which Aiken cast Wilson as the exemplar of a general decline in taste. "Of course," Wilson replied, "and I sent him a cricket." A "cricket," I learned, is a device which the offended, in retaliation, slips inside a letter to the offender and which erupts the moment the envelope is opened.)[8]

There is a rule about authors which I was bound to violate that Easter Monday in Savannah. Don't cast one writer as important mainly for his influence on another, especially if the first writer considers the second his inferior. Aiken had been quoted as finding Lowry's *Volcano,* at best, "inspired melodrama," and, at worst, "a literary accident."[9]

Undaunted, I plunged right into choppy waters. Why was he surfacing on Lowry after so many years of silence?

"I had a prolonged rassle with myself about that. I knew the risks only too well. I. A. Richards assures me I was exactly right in coming out with it although he wishes someone else had done it. So, by god, do I. But unhappily Malcolm's widow and disciples have been playing me down, and I felt that if I was not to go under, all meekly, I'd damned well better speak up."

Even in old age, with bald pate scarred both from a painful and chronic skin disease and a 1929 memento of a bibulous scuffle with Lowry for possession of a toilet seat, Aiken's complexion was that of a redhead. Now it was flaming, his private inventory of literary injustices having been triggered.

"I suppose you've read what Anthony Burgess has done to me. In *The Spectator* a couple of months ago.[10] Saying Malc wrote the kind of novel I wanted to do but lacked the architectonic skill for. My god, and I taught him all he knew. But I'm aware why Burgess writes that way. His publisher keeps sending me his novels for review, and I ignore 'em. And I'm about to get it from Louis Untermeyer again. 'Our best-known *unread* poet.' That's the sort of thing I've been reading for years from Untermeyer. We've had this love-hate thing for half a century."

In an effort to move Aiken back on the main track, I tried a placatory tactic. I produced Stephen Spender's memoir on Eliot, who had died two years before—the one recalling Eliot's ranking of Aiken's and his own gifts as about equal.

I overshot the mark—badly. Aiken's tirade now had a new target. He droned on, his rich baritone cracking at all the right places:

"Oh I've lots to forgive Tom Eliot for. We were rivals at Harvard and afterward. Ezra Pound always said it was I who discovered Eliot. I still have his letter. I brought "Prufrock" to Pound's attention, you know. Somebody—I forget who—reading my *House of Dust* has written that they were astonished the way I anticipated certain parts of *The Waste Land* and several years before Tom Eliot got around to them—right down to the tarot cards. Of course Tom knew *House of Dust* . . ."

(Brief interpolation: Not only did Tom Eliot know *House of Dust,* he registered his detestation of the poem in a letter to *Dial* editor Scofield Thayer which I shall get to shortly. My ready reference here to T. S. Eliot as "Tom" should not disclaim how uneasily Aiken's informal reference lodged in my consciousness. How dare even a classmate—even an acclaimed poet— refer to as "Tom" a world figure on whose works whole graduate seminars, including the one I had just taken, were based?)

". . . But such borrowings were fair enough. I'd pinched wholesale from Tom, too."

All during his harangue, a question hung in the air. If Aiken "pinched" from Eliot too, why the bitterness? Aiken may have anticipated it. "It wasn't that Tom Eliot got a better press than I—I've never cared much about attracting a following, popularizing myself. It was just that, as majordomo of Faber & Faber, he could handle the reviewing of my work in England. I was unread in London until after the Second War. Tom killed *Blue Voyage* in England.

"Once I sent him *Changing Mind,* one of the best poems I ever wrote. Two actual dreams are embodied in the poem—it shows the stuff of poetry being examined while *becoming* poetry—mind working on mind. Tom discarded from *Criterion* all but the little hymn at the end—nothing more than a coda—and said he'd pay me three pounds. I needed the money so I accepted. It was that sort of treatment I got from Tom Eliot—all down the line."

My host flung out his charges like counts in an indictment. Only Mary Hoover's benevolent interruption for martinis—the most powerful in my experience—could stanch the bitter flow. He agreed to extend the interview a second day, promising to read my Joyce/Lowry/Aiken paper. The less said about the second day, the better. The invective was extended to include me. My notion—a kind of anxiety-of-influence synthesis—was "all wet". "Of course *Ulysses* was in the air when I began to write *Blue Voyage,* but Joyce simply doesn't come into Malc's regurgitations of my work in his. He memorized *Blue Voyage,* literally *memorized* whole passages. We never talked about Joyce."

Then Aiken said something incredible, something I have never forgotten and which overlies my recollections of him:

"Malc knew what went into *Blue Voyage*. It will eventually prove a more influential and truer work than *Ulysses*."

I sat and probably stared. Had the martinis worked overtime? I remember, too, Aiken's last words, which followed an hour of chastisements for being like all those other comparative-lit. commentators who wrote out of an imperfect acquaintance with his work. He put a trembling hand on my shoulder at the door. "Don't take it so hard. I've been treated much worse—and by experts."

In a posthumously published novella-length story, "Through the Panama," Malcolm Lowry's alter ego tells of desperately trying to understand what his fellow writers are driving at by diligently attempting nightly to read Empson's *Seven Types of Ambiguity,* although the only work of modern literature that has touched him is a poem by Conrad Aiken. That poem was *House of Dust.*

On the plane from Atlanta to West Lafayette, I tried for the first time to read *House of Dust.*

For purposes of looking at the two poets side by side, a famous letter of Pound's may provide a point of departure. On Christmas Eve of 1921, Pound wrote from Paris to Eliot in Switzerland in praise of *The Waste Land,* to whose final version he had contributed so markedly ("Complimenti, you bitch, I am wracked by the seven jealousies. . . ."). Pound noted that "the thing now runs from 'April' to 'Shantih' without a break. That is nineteen pages . . . *the longest poem in the English langwidge* [emphasis mine]. Don't try to break all records by prolonging it three pages further" (*T.S.E. Letters,* 117).

Pound's enthusiasm should not be held to include statistical precision. And yet, writing at the end of 1921, he should have known of the existence of an even longer poem published the year before by a poet he knew well. Conrad Aiken's *House of Dust* occupies seventy-nine pages in *Collected Poems* (1970). At approximately 2,400 lines, *House of Dust* is nearly six times the length, at 433 lines, of *The Waste Land.*

In a letter to *Dial* editor Scofield Thayer, published for the first time in the Valerie Eliot–edited correspondence to 1922, Eliot hints strongly that *House of Dust,* which Aiken told me anticipated *The Waste Land,* was derivative of his own work: "I have glanced through [*House of Dust*] and it appears to me the workmen called in to build this house were Swinburne and myself; the Dust being provided by Conrad. I trust that this criticism will not appear egotistic on my part, but I can point to a quotation on page 83 . . ." (*T.S.E. Letters*, 414).

Eliot refers to III, vii, 9–10 of Dust—"Sometimes, I say, I'm just like John the Baptist—you have my head before you . . . on a platter"—as deriving from "Prufrock," lines 82–83: "Though I have seen my head (grown slightly bald)/brought in upon a platter,/I am no prophet—and there's no great matter." Eliot assumes that the unsolicited package from *Dial* containing *House of Dust* but without cover letter "was a piece of naughtiness on your part at Conrad's expense. . . . [and] I shrink from straining [his] friendship by reviewing his book."

Aiken's borrowings from and parodies of "Prufrock" are commonplaces of the early poems. He had committed that poem not so much to memory, as Malcolm Lowry would do with much of *Blue Voyage*, but to *heart*. "Prufrock" had occupied Aiken's nerve ends.

As to *Dust*'s invasion of Eliot's nerve ends, it was not only the perceived borrowings—what Aiken "pinched"—but Aiken's brief introduction to his vast poem that the older poet would have been unlikely to endorse. Aiken elevates the "I" to holy writ by declaring "that in the evolution of man's awareness, and in his dedication of himself to this supreme task, man possesses all he could possibly require in the way of a religious credo."

House of Dust was published in 1920, the same year that saw *The Sacred Wood*, Eliot's first collected essays, into print. In that book's famous essay, "Tradition and the Individual Talent," Eliot gives voice to an impersonal aesthetic when he writes that with the poet, "the more perfect the artist, the more completely separate in him will be the man who suffers and the mind which creates."

Aiken biographer Edward Butscher credits Joseph Killorin, editor of *Selected Letters of Conrad Aiken*, with having found in the margin of Aiken's review copy of *The Sacred Wood*, beside the above words, the notation "This might be *exactly the other way*."

I am not suggesting that such early pronouncements defined each poet for the other, but they do provide portents of the guarded nature of the friendship. From the start, Eliot's eye was directed away from self-disclosure. If every poet and storyteller is at heart an autobiographer, how much direct confession is consistent with art's traditional distancing? The interplay between what the poet's eyes—inner and outer—reveal and how much of the

"I"—the self—the poet chooses to reveal forms one of the touchstones of literature. For Conrad Aiken, as the recently published first volume of Butscher's biography powerfully demonstrates, the only meaningful place to look for guidance in problems of life and death was in confessing them into typescript.

"Possessed of his dead parents forever," writes Butscher, "Conrad Aiken, the man and the poet, became frozen in a narcissistic phase that did not permit him to enter other consciousnesses."[11]

No passage in all of Aiken's writings so reveals his obsession with self as this from *Blue Voyage* (1927). Demarest, Aiken's self-persona, looks at himself in his shipboard mirror.

Everybody of course was like this—depth beyond depth, a universe chorally singing, incalculable, obeying tremendous laws, chemical or divine, of which it was able to give its consciousness not the faintest inkling. . . . A universe that contained everything—all things—yet said only one word: "I."[12]

He is at all times an "I" writer. This subjective aesthetic doomed him to an inside outsider's limbo in the age of the New Criticism, the dominant mode of judgmental scrutiny which, following the lead of T. S. Eliot, would not allow a poem or a story to be read in the light of either biography or psychology.

The centennial of Aiken's birth, a year after the Eliot celebration, brought no special issues by prestigious journals. I found myself remembering anew what I have come to call the wages-of-neglect interview in Savannah. That summer I visited the Huntington Library which houses the papers and letters of Conrad Aiken. I had hoped to find some clue to why Eliot and *Criterion* declined all but the final twenty-four lines of *Changing Mind,* the poem Aiken told me he considered one of the best he had ever written. Was it merely the exercise of an editor's prerogative? Might it have been limitations of space—*Changing Mind* contains 450 lines—that led to Eliot's decision to eliminate all but the final four sestets?

(Another interpolation may be in order. Aiken wrote *Changing Mind* in 1925 and added it as the final of six "symphonies" which run over 260 pages in *Collected Poems* and which he collectively titled *The Divine Pilgrim*. Written well after the other five, all of which were separately published between 1916 and 1923, *Changing Mind* was the poem that introduced the specific "I". It is, as Frederick J. Hoffman notes, "the artist looking at Forslin, at Festus, at Senlin"—the invented personae of the earlier poems—"and at himself."[13]

After *Changing Mind,* in effect, Conrad Aiken would step outside his masks and be himself. The poem served as Aiken's manifesto that his art from then on would be wholly based on the theory, first expressed in the introduction to *House of Dust,* the poem so abhorred by Eliot, that consciousness represents a deified goal.

In his memoir, from which I have already quoted, Stephen Spender recalled that Eliot once told students at Oxford that he could not imagine an aesthetic without God.)

The only "lead" I found among Aiken's letters at the Huntington regarding the devastating excision of *Changing Mind* in *Criterion* may be buried in a letter from Tom to Conrad, dated winter of 1924, the same year Aiken submitted the poem: "The answer to par. 3 of your ltr is that I did not think it was good enough and that it did not seem to fit in with the rest." I could not find any trace of the Aiken letter that would determine what he had asked in "par. 3." No doubt Valerie Eliot's second volume will contain it.

Edward Butscher leaves no doubt as to his view of the importance of *Changing Mind.* Late in his first volume, which concludes with the fateful year 1925, Butscher declares that the poem "overtly challenged Eliot's domination of their competition. As his answer to *The Waste Land,* the poem committed [Aiken] forever to an autobiographical exploration and deifying of consciousness" (*Butscher,* 451).

My own view is close to Butscher's. Aiken's lifelong impulse to "come clean"—his oft-used words—and, in doing so, to unravel the mystery of identity was less an aesthetic than a wound-and-bow credo. The double catastrophe he endured in his twelfth year left the poet in the throes of a permanent quest for identity in an extraordinary array of writings which, paradoxically, stand as a refutation of the Sophoclean thrust, "Know Thyself!"—a failed quest that is confirmed in the lines T. S. Eliot did publish from *Changing Mind:*

> My father which art in earth
> From whom I got my birth,
> What is it that I inherit?
> From the bones fallen apart
> And the deciphered heart,
> Body and spirit.

> My mother which art in tomb
> Who carriedst me in thy womb,
> What is it that I inherit?
> From the thought come to dust

And the remembered lust,
Body and spirit.

Father and mother, who gave
Life, love, and now the grave,
What is it that I can be?
Nothing but what lies here,
The hand still, the brain sere,
Naught lives in thee

Nor ever will live, save
It have within this grave
Roots in the mingled heart,
In the damp ashes wound
Where the past, underground,
Falls, falls apart.[14]

Aiken mounts in the coda to *Changing Mind* something Eliot could not help but have recognized; namely, the fundamental necessity, not only of poets but of all of us in the face of the death of our parents: Now that my father is in the earth, my mother in her tomb, *what is it that I can be?*

Of T. S. Eliot, Cynthia Ozick wrote in her centennial-plus-one essay in the *New Yorker:* "The young who gave homage to Eliot through the Modernist era were ready to fall on their knees to a god. A god, moreover, who despised free-thinking, democracy, and secularism—the very conditions of anti-authoritarianism. . . . It is almost impossible nowadays to imagine such authority accruing to a poet."[15]

Conrad Aiken imagined it—and lived it. His devotion not only to his friend Tom Eliot but to other fashionable gods—Freud, Jung, Nietzsche, Ferenczi, Adler—almost anyone who was in vogue. He proceeded from one god to another, but mostly Eliot, always trying to harness other voices to his own narcissism.

The poet can only write about the *felt* world, Eliot wrote to poet John Gould Fletcher in 1920, and

experience without emotion (of *some* kind) is almost a contradiction. I think there is an important distinction between the emotions which are in the experience which is one's material and the emotion in the writing—the two seem to me very different. But I do not believe that my view is very different from yours. It differs much from Aiken's. (*T.S.E. Letters,* 410)

And so it did. The most pronounced trend not only in poetry but in fiction as the century draws to a close is the author as vessel. The confessional poem and the first-person novel—these and their many variations—comprise today's dominant genre in which autobiographers gather their evidence from the self and leave it at that. If T. S. Eliot had not lived to spearhead the New Criticism as the dominant analytical tool by which poems entered the sacred canon during Conrad Aiken's most productive four decades, he—Aiken—rather than Robert Lowell would be wearing the diadem as the father of modern confessional poetry. Today he would feel right at home.

IV.

Ground Rule for "Marginal" Memoir:
Being Heard But Not Seen

A close friend wrote in a recent letter his belief that I make too much of my single interview with Somerset Maugham and not enough of my good fortune in having known Edmund Wilson for ten years. If the remark had not come from my oldest and best friend, I would think the comparison disingenuous. I never locate the glorious one shot with Maugham in the same part of memory as the extended and "neighborly" relationship with Edmund. The first was the event of a lifetime, wholly unexpected. I was not ready for Edmund Wilson.

When I met him in 1963, I was still mourning the loss of my local column in the *Utica Observer-Dispatch*. During the previous fifteen years my reading had been undirected, spontaneous as it is once again in retirement. Until I boned up, the only Wilson work I had read was his *New Yorker* essays, one of which savaged my man Maugham as little better than Louis Bromfield, whom Wilson had earlier savaged. I had been more receptive to the urbane reviews of Clifton Fadiman, who preceded Wilson at my favorite magazine. Little did I know that it would be Edmund Wilson's essays on *Finnegans Wake* that I couldn't read in the *New Yorker* which would help me through graduate school. By the time a former *Observer-Dispatch* colleague arranged for me to join him for an interview with Wilson in Talcottville, I was working on a book on Wells. I came to know Edmund Wilson as upstate neighbor for nearly ten springs and summers. But it was not until two years after his death that I began to think of writing about him.

By this time I had been at Texas A&M for four years and been promoted to professor largely on the bases of the Wells and Lowry books. A summer grant in 1974 enabled Jo, our son Phil, and me to return upstate. We made Rome, New York, our base, but I ranged widely. I went to Toronto to talk to Edmund's old friend, Morley Callaghan, and to renew my friendship with a hostile Earle Birney, who had bristled over being omitted from Wilson's book, *O Canada*. I called in a decade's worth of letters to my friend J. F. Hopkins, the perfect partner teachers of writing rightly advise neophytes to visualize as an audience. Hop has savored nearly every word written by and about my subject. I had daily chats all summer with Mary Pcolar, Edmund's amanuensis and my student at Utica College. But my book would not "write." A memoir is a special genre. It requires a special voice.

All memoirs are self-serving. In the extended form of autobiography, they often claim to set the record straight while actually attempting to mitigate guilt. In *A Life*, Elia Kazan defies the reader to throw the first stone. Given my choices and opportunities, he asks the reader, would you have acted any differently? A memoir about somebody more important than the writer should not veer into a personal vendetta. Mary Lee Settle's *Yale Review* memoir of Maugham and Angus Wilson fails its promise when it becomes just another vehicle for her bitterness against reviewers.

Memoirs are personal biographies of the great by the ungreat (although *ingrate* might not be amiss here). The former can never count on how they will be remembered by the latter. The main rule for what James Atlas calls the "marginal memoir" is that the memoirist should be heard without seeming to be seen. A corollary rule is never to forget that the value of such a memoir as I was writing rests with—depends on—its built-in limitations. I should make no pretense of being an intimate. But the Edmund Wilson I knew was offguard. Inaccessibly accessible in Talcottville and only occasionally obliged to perform as resident celebrity, he could devote himself to the effort of self-reformulation to which he was dedicated in old age.

What follows, while not an exact fit for a section devoted to literary quarreling, belongs nevertheless. It deals not so much with any of his many quarrels with others as with his quarrels within. I make no claim to verbatim fidelity to his words, but I do claim trueness to the remembered *spirit*. His legendary command of the periodic sentence carried over to his conversation. It is that very quality—Wilsonian periodicity—that I wish to mark in the next pages.

V.

The Sentence(ing) of Edmund Wilson

In an imaginary interview conducted with himself and published in the *New Yorker,* Edmund Wilson, asked by his alter ego to what he attributes his success as a writer, questions back, "Am I a success as a writer?" and then answers: "I attribute such success as I have had to my mastery of the periodic sentence." The *New Yorker* published Wilson's self-interview in June of 1962.[1] It was the same summer that I wrote him a note asking if I might see him for a chat about H. G. Wells, on whom I was writing a book. He answered promptly, mentioning the mock self-interrogation. His note, typewritten on *New Yorker* stationery but mailed from Talcottville, Lewis County, New York, observed that he was leaving the old stone house for his main residence at Wellfleet, Cape Cod, Massachusetts: "I don't like to give interviews anyway, unless I can play the straight man myself, as the one you saw in the *New Yorker.*"

When a year later I finally met Edmund Wilson and saw him frequently during the course of eight springs and summers, I always intended to ask him about his crediting of the periodic sentence, but I never did. Somehow, even if he did mean it with entire seriousness, Wilson's tribute to the periodic sentence has remained in my consciousness for over twenty years. When I first read it, I had just shifted professions—from newspaper journalism to college teaching—and I did not know exactly what a periodic sentence is. So I looked it up.

periodic sentence: a usually complex sentence in which the principal clause comes last or which has no subordinate or trailing elements following full grammatical statement of the essential idea. As in: YESTERDAY WHILE I WAS WALKING DOWN THE STREET, I SAW HIM. [Compare, Webster suggests, with the *loose sentence.* So I did.]

loose sentence: a complex sentence in which the principal clause comes first and the latter part of which contains subordinate modifiers or trailing elements, as in: I SAW HIM YESTERDAY WHILE I WAS WALKING DOWN THE STREET.[2]

Without making any attempt at "transforming" grammar—that is, at converting the rules of syntax into rules of life, I should like to suggest another perspective from which to view the *periodic* as against the *loose,* a vantage from which to view Edmund Wilson, both generally and, specifically, as an upstater. The periodic sentence *withholds* its principal element; the dependent element functions like a signal—a promise—of something important—even vital—to come. The maker of such a sentence builds to a commitment that cannot be fulfilled until the end. The maker of the *loose* sentence is less certain of priority; he announces the main element but keeps sticking on appendages. Such a creation never accepts the fact that the main statement has already been made. The periodic sentence waits until all the returns are in to complete itself.

It was, I believe, upstate—those annual late springs, summers, and early autumns in Talcottville and environs—that rendered the life of Edmund Wilson periodic rather than loose. Just as, syntactically, a main clause anchors the periodic sentence, tactically, upstate New York anchored Edmund Wilson.

Like Thoreau, one of his heroes who came to know himself even as he "travelled a good deal in Concord," Wilson had known upstate as spiritual home since his childhood. The region captivated him. It was a place where he felt the first intimations that, if he was not destined to become a poet, he would, as he put it, be "something of the kind."[3]

Upstate New York was the place where as a youngster he "felt excitement" summers fleeing his native Red Bank, New Jersey, for Talcottville, where "there is nothing between me and the widening pastures, the great boulders, the black and white cattle, the rivers, stony and thin, the lone elms, like feather-dusters, the high air which sharpens all outlines, makes colors so breathtakingly vivid, in the clear light of late afternoon. . . ."[4]

And where, in old age, he returned summers, an international literary figure, but in Talcottville (population 80), a neighbor.

Somebody else's genealogy is much like somebody else's vacation slides—

largely uninteresting. I shall neither tax these pages with even a summary of what Wilson has done fully in the first seventy pages of his *Upstate: Records and Recollections of Northern New York* (1971) nor risk inevitable errors in so detailed a family tree. I wonder, though, if any other major American writer, who was also a world traveller, turned as completely, at the end of a full and controversial life, to the pastoral.

In his sixty-fifth year, he devotes a long diary entry to the job of "discovering" with Boonville friends a sylvan retreat at Dry Sugar River where he had picnicked many times as a youngster. And he—not unintentionally, I suspect—pairs the entry with a description of the verve with which he reads English memoirs of the late eighteen hundreds and early nineteen hundreds, the period in which he feels most at home. He gives exactly twice as much space to the "Discovery of the Showy Ladyslipper" at age seventy as he gives to the the "Death of Hemingway" four years before. Wilson uses the incidence of such a discovery for bucolic relief. No one of the blessed dares reveal where they grow naturally.[5]

When upstate, he had an upstater's interests, some those of a gentryman—benevolently squirearchical—and some a regionalist's. On those occasions when he would take long drives with Mary Horbach Pcolar, his Hungarian-American amanuensis from West Leyden, he often sought to satisfy his insatiable curiosity—about such as the origin of Sodom, New York, a village east of Speculator in a remote part of the Adirondacks; about the nature of the place, Palmyra, where Joseph Smith was supposed to have been visited by his angel. In Sodom, he met an old woman who told him that nothing was amiss in Sodom, but "what I call Gomorrah is down the road." Gomorrah proves to be a house whose new owner had allowed it to run down. At Palmyra, the self-described atheistical Wilson asked just the sort of questions one would expect. Working as he was on revising his *Dead Sea Scrolls,* he was especially interested in the shrine at Palmyra. Could Joseph Smith actually have found on the side of a hill, in Wilson's own upstate New York, new Bible scriptures that an angel from Heaven gave him? At the Mormon information desk, Wilson approached a woman missionary. "Where are the Plates?" he asked. She was ready for such questions. "They are in Heaven," she replied, explaining that the angel who had "loaned" them to Joseph Smith had taken them back. Edmund, Mary Pcolar told me two years after his death, was still chuckling when they arrived back home.[6]

Of special importance to the author of *Apologies to the Iroquois* (1960) were the tours of the Iroquois Confederacy with New York State anthropologist

Edmund Wilson at 70, responding to a question in my journalism class at Utica College, fall, 1964. "He drew his hand across the back of his bald and noble head in that way he had of signalling an announcement." *Photo by F. Kurt Rolfes.*

William N. Fenton of Albany. He witnessed ceremonials at the Cattaraugus, Allegany, Tuscarora, and Onondaga reservations. His final public appearance upstate was at a symposium on the Iroquois, October, 1968, when he shared the stage at Utica College with Fenton. He put on a false-face mask, carved by a Cayuga out of basswood and given him by an anthropologist friend. Edmund informed his audience that he had been assured the mask had not been blessed with magical powers and need not be kept covered for fear of its bringing a curse.

"The Old Stone House" is one of Edmund Wilson's most anthologized essays.[7] The thirty-eight-year-old newly hired staff critic of the *New Republic* writes of returning north, after many years away, on the Utica-to-Boonville milk train, seeking renewal and rebirth "up in the country." Instead, the journey he chronicles is to limbo, caught as he is between the upstate world of the Bakers and Talcotts—his maternal ancestors—and the making-it maelstrom of Manhattan and the Village which is inclining him, as it did his friend John Dos Passos, toward a vast leftward leap over his shadow.

During the 1930s, Wilson's interests were more political than literary. The Depression, the New Deal, the Soviet experiment absorbed him. His posthumously published notebooks of *The Thirties,* edited by Leon Edel, reveal him in the early part of the decade as a fellow traveller of the American communists. He spoke and in his letters wrote what an admirer, Joseph Epstein, calls "the standard Marxian gobbledygook of the day [and] took up the conventional radical animosities against his own country . . . supported William Z. Foster, in 1932 the Communist Party candidate for President."[8]

So it was that in 1933, in the return to the upstate country of his childhood summers, Wilson tries to renew and refresh himself. For him, nearing forty, neither the disillusioning path of left-wing causes in New York City and the *New Republic* nor the conservative life he remembers from his childhood relieves his severe depression. During his misery, he reads anew of Lincoln, understands empathetically the identity agonies of the transplanted president. For Edmund Wilson cannot, in early middle age, go back any more than could Lincoln, to the backwoods America of his ancestors. He cannot go forward either to the "old wooden booth . . . between First and Second Avenues," to the city of "sordid and unhealthy neighbors, who howl outside my window day and night." He ends the essay in the belief that he has left the old for the new, in which he has not succeeded.[9] His ambivalence, here reflected in an imperishable essay, revealed itself in a memory I retain of him when he was ill and old at his upstate refuge.

One summer's night, when he was seventy, Edmund was rebuking me on one of my missing circuits: he could not understand how anyone could be so wholly wanting in ties to family and origin. He spoke in words similar to those I would read in *Upstate:* "There is all the difference between a place in which one feels the fibers of family and a place in which one is totally unaware of other peoples' similar fibers."[10] I will never forget his next words, for whose exactness I cannot vouch but whose sense I have indelibly. "You, Dick, don't appear to know or care about such things, but the fact is that my life would have been altogether different if my mother had given me the house in my forties instead of my sixties. I'd have settled upstate here as a landowner, a family man, and the entire direction of things would have been different."

We had been talking, I believe, about Dos Passos and that writer's sudden veer in middle age to the right. Most accounts charge disillusioning experience with Communist-front activity in the Spanish Civil War for his disenchantment with the left.[11] But that night in the old stone house Edmund Wilson attributed the shift to Dos Passos's inheriting of a large estate in Virginia. Suppose, however, that Edmund Wilson had inherited the house well before 1951 and become a gentryman. How would his life have been different? Could ownership of land in his remote corner have quieted that restless intelligence? And how better for the man who, as Daniel Aaron puts it, was "the moral and intellectual conscience of his generation"?[12]

George Orwell notes in "Inside the Whale" (1940) how by 1934–35 it was considered eccentric in literary circles not to be more or less leftwing in politics and how the Communist Party had an almost irresistible fascination for young writers.[13] Wilson continued to write for the *New Republic,* but he differed with his Marxist colleagues Michael Gold and Granville Hicks in crucial ways. As the country moved out of the Depression into war, his briefly held revolutionary expectations dwindled and by the mid-1930s he had lost whatever hope he entertained in the possibility or the desirability of a communist system. George H. Douglas writes that Wilson was one of the first American liberals to turn away from the actual system of communism in Russia; indeed, he was denouncing it just about the time his colleagues on the *New Republic* were becoming enchanted with it.[14] By mid-1935, Wilson was writing from Moscow and reassuring Dos Passos that the Soviets "had never had any kind of working democracy and they are having a hard time getting it even under socialism. We have had; and I agree with you completely that whatever is to be accomplished in reorganizing American society, will have to be accomplished in our way and not in the Russian way."[15]

The book that emerged from the deep split between his America-Firster instincts and his learned—and lost—Leninist/Marxist sympathies was *To the Finland Station*. Writers as various as Lionel Trilling and George Steiner, in print, and, in conversation with me, Walter D. Edmonds and the Canadian poet Earle Birney say they consider *Finland Station* Wilson's most important book. Looking into the new edition published a few weeks after its author's death, one still finds Edmund Wilson's faith in some kind of humanitarian socialism as appealing and convincing as in 1940 when the book was first published.[16] "This book of mine," he writes in 1971 for a new introduction, "assumes throughout that an important step in progress has been made, that a fundamental 'breakthrough' had occurred, that nothing in our human history would ever be the same again." He still regards the book as a "basically reliable account" of a revolution aimed at "a better world."[17]

To the Finland Station is a monument to a kind of idealism that could not work in twentieth-century American society. Lionel Trilling, shortly before his death, wrote of rereading *Finland Station* and finding it enormously impressive in its coherence and sense of the drama of developing revolutionary ideas. Significantly, however, Wilson concedes that his hopes for the Soviet system were myopic. "I had no premonition that the Soviet Union was to become one of the most hideous tyrannies that the world had ever known."[18]

In the 1940s, the "unreconstructed isolationist"—Mary McCarthy's phrase for the man to whom she was married from 1938 to 1946—took over. As revealed in his *Forties* notebooks, Wilson viewed Hitler as a threat only to the nations of the European continent and refused to lend his pen to the American war effort. He remained natively chauvinistic. It was during this time that he made the statement, frequently viewed as heroic, that he considered war a cause he didn't consider worth devoting himself to but that literature was one he did. For him both world wars were the sorts of wars that Americans have readily accommodated; in neither case were the purposes or the national involvement questioned by the populace. In both cases, the opposing sides were made to appear as calculated villains. It was Wilson's belief that we were "furtively brought into [the Second War] by President Franklin D. Roosevelt, who had been making secret agreements with the British but pretending, in his public statements, that he had not committed himself." As for the war with Japan, it was one secretly hoped for because the Japanese were threatening our commercial interests in China. These quirky notions are contained in the introduction to his monumental *Patriotic Gore: Studies in the Literature of the American Civil War* (1962) in which he shows similarities among Lincoln, Bismarck, and Lenin; gives a short history of United States imperialism; and likens the United States and Soviet Russia to voracious sea slugs preying on smaller organisms. I leave to the reader's judgment, however, the accuracy of the following—from the same introduction, written at the start of the 1960s—as a prognosis-in-the-form-of-a-diagnosis of the shape of nuclear jockeying and policing of small nations by the two major powers as the 1980s were ending:

The Russians and we produced nuclear weapons to flourish at one another and played the game of calling bad names when there had been nothing at issue between us that need have prevented our living in the same world and when we were actually, for better or worse, becoming more and more alike—the Russians emulating America in their fanatic industrializing, and we imitating them in our persecution of nonconformist political opinion, while both, to achieve these ends, were building up huge government bureaucracies in the hands of which the people have seemed helpless.[19]

In the forties, too, his personal life came apart. Not only had his friend from Princeton Days, F. Scott Fitzgerald, died in early middle age, but his third marriage—the one to Mary McCarthy—collapsed. In Wellfleet, on long walks with no one but a dog named Pal, he paused beside a pond and observed his image in the mirrored water. There was, he wrote, "a darkness into which I sink and a clear round single lens, well guarded and hidden away."[20] That sentiment is a far cry from his mood, at sixty, when he could write that at the house in Talcottville "I may find myself here at the center of things since the center can only be in one's head."

In 1946, Wilson, just over the hump of fifty, divorced Mary McCarthy and entered his fourth—his lasting—marriage to Elena Mumm Thornton. The marriage to Elena, as *The Forties* shows, while dictated by an intense passion, also marked a significant change. Leon Edel credits Elena's Europeanness—she was of German and Russian parentage—as the main factor in their rapport. Elena, Edel notes, was more conscious of her husband's needs than were her three American predecessors. In the years I knew him, Edmund always stressed that it was Elena who made it possible for him for the first time to straighten out his relations with his three children and with his friends.[21]

The fifteen years from 1946 to 1962 comprised his golden period: 1946, *Memoirs of Hecate County* (his favorite of his books, the one he believed most strongly to have been critically undervalued); 1955, *The Dead Sea Scrolls;* 1959, *Apologies to the Iroquois;* 1962, *Patriotic Gore.* But the years between 1946 and 1955 were also the years in which he did not file any income tax returns. In the first of his two polemics of his final decade, *The Cold War and the Income Tax* (1963), Wilson explains why he did not pay his taxes. He had never made much money. He was genuinely ignorant of tax laws. His attorney in New York City had died. In 1946, when *Memoirs of Hecate County* was published, his income doubled. Then the book was suppressed by court order and the income stopped. What with one thing and another, he never got around to filing a return.

When through an accident of geography and the generosity of a former journalist colleague I met Edmund Wilson, his tirade against the income tax was about to be published. In the summer of 1963, he expressed a determination to settle in Switzerland. Wasn't Switzerland the place where film stars settled to avoid tax problems? But Edmund Wilson—with Mencken, perhaps, America's best cultural critic between the end of World War I and the start of the sixties—this man about to move to Switzerland! At his door, end of August, he dropped a hint about matters that would color his conversation for several years. Going to Switzerland would be "like taking it on the lam." His already high-register voice would go even higher at such times. Of course Helen, his teenage daughter by Elena, would be enrolling in a Swiss private school. He had these other reasons for emigrating. Still . . . "You see, I'm bringing out a tiny book, a pamphlet, really. It's all about the income tax business and the outrageous things the federal government is doing. Arthur Schlesinger, my neighbor at Wellfleet, thinks it's my book that's outrageous. But lay people simply don't read the fine print in the *New York Times.* I've spent the whole summer going over federal tax statutes, mountains of clippings. I'm sure my living abroad will look as if I'm trying to avoid the repercussions."22

He, of course, did not emigrate to Switzerland. The income-tax crisis interrupted but did not alter the course of what Joseph Epstein calls "Edmund Wilson's second adolescence in the 1960s."23 The 1960s, which were his seventies, were also the years when Edmund came closest to breaking out of his fate of being "sentenced to the sentence." What he rarely articulated in conversation, but what he manifested in noble efforts at accessibility upstate, was his attempt to deal with the other claims of his personality: his absorption in the people who were his forebears and, above all, his desire for human links. If his bookishness was his salvation in earlier years, it was his intensifying sense of community in his late years that tempered that bookishness and enriched our lives.

It was Edmund Wilson's uniqueness to be obsessed by the America of his lifetime and detached from it at the same time. In conversation, he would wave aside his critics, who saw in the 1960s only a faded curmudgeon who scorned America, and say only that he was enjoying himself as "old-fogeyism is settling comfortably in."

If Edmund, as Dos Passos charged in one of their lively political arguments when both, now solid gentrymen, were nearing seventy, lived in an "in between world—between for and against,"[24] it was the character of the sixties that often reduced him to limbo. Professor Douglas puts it well:

But it was Wilson's tenacious grip on the American past, his never-ending attempts to dredge up the values of his forebears and the ambiance of the old America that make his views on the new so refreshing and invigorating. If Wilson was irritable and contemptuous of the world around him, it was not because he had given up on his homeland, but because he was struggling desperately to find in it permanent values that could make life worth living.[25]

Edmund Wilson, rooted in the Puritan tradition, always had a sense of America as something special. His despair over what he regarded as the faded promises of the Soviet experiment foreshadowed his despair at the end of his life over America, where for him, as with the Soviets, forms have outlasted their use. What kept Wilson going was a sense of the contradiction of things, of the sheer excitement that stupidity can cause in a professional watcher of his fellow countrymen. It was Edmund Wilson, it should not be forgotten, who edited the posthumous book of F. Scott Fitzgerald's last writings. In *The Crack-Up*, Fitzgerald observed that his collapse came when he could no longer keep in counterpoise the opposed notions that all was hopeless and that it was necessary to go on. Wilson quotes his friend on how difficult but requisite it is to live with contradictions.

Edmund Wilson's was never a household name, although *Esquire* magazine, shortly before his death, classified him as one of America's fifty—or was it one hundred?—most influential persons. The ironic error with Wilson is in classifying him at all. He resisted classification. He was never widely read, not because he is difficult to read—he is the simplest of writers. He does not fit any of the academic categories. He wasn't an eighteenth-century man who would then be read by other eighteenth-century men. He wasn't a Victorian specialist, although he wrote one of the best essays on Dickens. He wasn't a certified Hebrew scholar, so that when he wrote about the Dead Sea Scrolls such scholars didn't pay much attention—until later. He wasn't a Marxist; he wasn't an anti-Marxist. His books, his publisher has said, were difficult to package because they belonged to no visible category.[26]

What Edmund Wilson did was to write essays, fiction, verse, and plays out of a civilized interest and inquisitiveness about human affairs. Even Dwight MacDonald, who didn't much like him—and Edmund returned the disfavor with gusto—said Edmund Wilson was a man who was always on duty. He was a major critic—literary and cultural and political—who also wrote in all the categories. The interesting mind is always on duty, whatever he writes. He had, as George Steiner puts it, a formidable appetite for difficulty and saw as his job the making of the inaccessible accessible.[27]

And he, in his redoubt upstate, was the most accessible of all.

Thus Edmund Wilson's life, a seventy-seven-year-old periodic sentence, paid off its promissory note. When he came up to the country for five or six months annually, especially when he came to the old house in June, 1972, a dying man wearing a McGovern button, it was to drop anchor once again, to settle in, and be, as he wrote in *Upstate* (it is my favorite Wilsonian periodic sentence) that person who, "although I embody different tendencies and remember that, in early life, I was sometimes in doubt as to what kind of role I wanted to play, I have never had much real doubt about who or what I was."[28]

VI.

The "Burrowing" of Literary Moles: Turgenev and Flaubert

At eight o'clock on a November morning in 1868, the most famous of Russian novelists boarded an express train in Paris bound for Rouen, some seventy miles to the northwest. At 10:40 he was met at the station by the most famous of French novelists, embraced, and conducted by carriage to the latter's house at Croisset, just outside Rouen, where over wine and cheese he read to the Russian excerpts from *Sentimental Education,* his novel-in-progress.

The Russian, who knew French almost as well as his native language, expressed pleasure over what he heard but thought the title should be changed. At parting, he promised to send an inscribed copy of *Smoke,* his own just-published novel.

The two world figures, both middle-aged and single, had not seen each other since their first meeting nearly six years earlier—February 28, 1863—at a literary dinner in Paris. They had kept in touch over the years, either by letters to one another or via communications to mutual friends.

When the reunion was a certainty, Gustave Flaubert wrote to Ivan Turgenev: "Ah! At last! We are going to see each other, dear friend!" Afterward, Turgenev wrote a thank-you note to Flaubert for "the delightful day." He spoke of their "real affinity," a confirmation of more colorful language he had put in another letter that spring, honoring their first meeting: "It seems to me that I could talk to you for weeks on end, but then we are a pair of moles burrowing away in the same direction."

One of the many joys of the correspondence between the author of *Madame Bovary* and the author of *Fathers and Children* (*Flaubert and Turgenev: A Friendship in Letters, the Complete Correspondence,* edited and translated by Barbara Beaumont [New York: Norton, 1985]) is to be able to infer a subtext that tells us a great deal about the possibilities and limitations of a relationship between coeval literary geniuses.

Did Turgenev, based on that first afternoon at Croisset, decide that he could only abide so many readings by Flaubert, who *always* read to his guests?

It might appear so because, for every encounter between the peripatetic Russian and the stay-at-home Frenchman, there were a dozen missed connections, often apologies from the traveller for still another attack of the gout that caused him to repair to a watering-place in Germany.

A notorious hypochondriac, Turgenev didn't merely imagine he was a chronic sufferer from gout, an affliction seemingly endemic to sedentary writers from Dr. Johnson to Edmund Wilson. Certainly the letters do indicate that gout often happens *for* Turgenev as well as *to* him. Flaubert, whose father had been a surgeon, advises the sufferer that "all remedies are dangerous. There's only one that I trust, and it's atrocious. I'll tell you about it." But he never does—at least not in the letters.

There is also evidence that Turgenev, the author of *A Sportsman's Sketches,* played the athlete to Flaubert's aesthete.

In summer of 1871, Flaubert's letter to Turgenev in London ("I beg you to answer *straightaway* to let me know which day I should expect you at Croisset. . . . I'll expect you . . . *next Saturday*") caught up with "the notorious bird of passage" in Scotland ("I am shooting grouse at a friend's place. . . . I wish you were in Paris that day and I didn't have to go to Croisset."). Flaubert, who detested the literary life of Paris, found himself stood up ("No, my dear friend, I am not cross with you, but I felt disappointed. . . . I forgive you on condition that you will devote *several* days to me in October").

Throughout November, Turgenev wrote from the Baden and Paris houses of his French patrons—the Viardot family—with excuses that range from the dependable gout ("But on the *very day* of my arrival I was *seized* with an attack") to personal problems ("I'm becoming more and more snowed under by life's events").

Their suffering without quite bowing under to "life's events" produces the most moving letters. By the time they met, Flaubert, forty-two, and Turgenev, forty-five, had become inured to crisis.

His characterization of Bazarov, the nihilist hero of *Fathers and Children*, left Turgenev with hardly a friend when he returned to Russia in 1862. *Madame Bovary* brought down on Flaubert civic prosecution throughout the late 1850s for outraging religious morality by his portrait of Emma.

The debacle of the war of 1870–71, the defeat of France by Germany, the ensuing fall of Louis Napoleon, and the scarifying interlude of the Commune offered fullest scope to Flaubert's inherent pessimism. For a month and a half of the occupation, Prussian officers were billeted in Flaubert's ivory tower at Croisset ("I kept silent as one does in a railway carriage when entering a tunnel: the infernal noise overwhelms one and makes one's head spin.").

In *Smoke,* Turgenev is bleaker even than Flaubert. He reveals a full sense of the abyss, an outrage at his own class: "We educated people are poor stuff. . . . But . . . look at that peasant. . . . That's where it will all come from."

Although Flaubert addresses him as "My Old Muscovite," Turgenev was neither a Slavophile like Dostoevski nor a worshipper of the *muzhik* like Tolstoy. He was a civilized man of the world who was never above exploiting a convenient life: so fast a study as a translator that Flaubert trusted him with all his Russian versions in the 1870s.

Before our era of clipping services, Turgenev would placate the disappointed Flaubert by sending him reviews—only the favorable ones—from Russian, German, English, and Italian sources that were closed to Flaubert. He would agree to do the Russian translations, never accepting a fee but often using them to jockey for position with editors and publishers. Professor Barbara Beaumont, this book's fine scholar-editor, presents evidence for their inadequacy.

For students of world literature, the book is a treasure.

The pragmatic Turgenev chides the perfectionist Flaubert against stylistic over-refinement. Both laugh bitterly over their failures in the theater. Turgenev withholds, one feels, his admiration for the rising Zola's naturalistic stories in deference to Flaubert's uncompromising hostility. The emotional Flaubert writes of "blubbering shamelessly" at the funeral of George Sand in 1876 ("poor old Mother Sand"); Turgenev, a regular beneficiary of her patronage, urges a stiff upper lip.

They gossip—Flaubert about his pupil Maupassant whose "ladies" can no longer cheer him, Turgenev about a distressful breaking off of a marriage of his patroness's second daughter.

During the two years before Flaubert's unexpected death at sixty in 1880, the letters accelerate but grow shorter. Turgenev promises to send Count Tolstoy's *War and Peace* in three volumes. Flaubert deflects that effort. He appears to prefer talking about caviar which he now eats like jam, without bread.

Although she refers to her book as the "complete" correspondence while acknowledging that some letters have not survived, Barbara Beaumont has rendered a service to reader *and* scholar. For those who don't care to read letters alone, her thirty-four-page introduction is a liberal education in the lives and writings and times of the two masters. For those who do, she makes us grateful that Alexander Graham Bell's invention, which has been the deathknell to letter-writing as an art, did not come to Europe until some years later.

VII.

The Triumph of Richard Ellmann

Many blockbuster literary biographies lose their subjects in the welter of minutiae. Elizabeth Hardwick, reviewing Carlos Baker's seven-hundred-page biography of Ernest Hemingway (*New York Review of Books,* Jan. 5, 1969), puts the problem well:

> We have been told that no man is a hero to his valet. Professor Baker's method makes valets of us all. We keep the calendar of our master's engagements, we lay out his clothes, we order his wine, we pack his bags, we adjust to his new wives, endure his friends, accept his hangovers, his failings. . . . We are often thoroughly sick of it, feel we need time off, a vacation, a raise in pay. We get the dirty work and somebody else, somewhere, gets the real joy of the man, his charm, his uniqueness, his deeply puzzling home life. Someone else gossips about him, turns over his traits, ponders the mystery of his talent: all we get are signed copies of his books for our grandchildren.

That Richard Ellmann could write an even longer and more detailed biography than Baker's, and do so without losing his man—James Joyce—remains a triumph of something Joyce said every writer should try every so often: a project seemingly beyond the writer's ability.

When Richard Ellmann, then at nearby Northwestern University, visited Purdue in 1966 for a lecture on Wilde and Yeats, I had not yet read as a book his biography of Joyce.[1] Becoming expert at the vulturism practiced by us English graduate students, I had found a single quote in the Ellmann that enabled me to complete the term paper for Maurice Beebe's fall, 1965, seminar on *Ulysses*. Ellmann records that Joyce once explained to Eugene Jolas, apropos of *Ulysses,* that "I am trying to build up many planes of narrative, with a single aesthetic purpose. . . . Did you ever read Laurence Sterne?" The notion that a landmark book like *Ulysses* could be even in small part derivative of an author—Sterne—writing 160 years earlier was a rich one. From Joyce's tribute to Sterne, I applied Aiken's to Joyce—he had credited the publication of Ulysses for giving him the courage to start *Blue Voyage*. I tried to demonstrate that it was Lowry's study of *Blue Voyage*—he committed much of it to memory—that enabled him to implement the lessons of Joyce and *Ulysses* more effectively than his mentor Aiken was able to do even though Lowry never read *Ulysses*. But on the evening that my mentor Maury Beebe held a reception in his living room for Richard Ellmann, I had neither the *chutzpah* nor the courage to express my debt to his book. I shook hands—once more an admiring suppliant—and determined I would read the biography one day. Twenty years later I made the book—revised and expanded by Ellmann in 1982—the key work in my seminar on literary biography. I have now read the 1959 edition once and the 1982 twice.

All that can be said with certainty is that Professor Ellmann's triumph has to do with his ability to make an electrifying narrative out of Joyce's preparation for, and agonizing writing and publication of, *Ulysses,* the book every literature student talks about but few have read. (As a sophomore English major, I brandished my copy of the Random House edition which followed by a year U.S. District Judge John M. Woolsey's historic ruling allowing *Ulysses* into the country. An attractive co-ed was impressed. "Oh Dick," she said, "may I borrow your copy of *Ulysses* so I can read it this weekend?")

Ellmann makes it evident that Joyce devoted much of his career to gestating the single book. He started by storing up memories for *Ulysses* during his childhood in Dublin, but began writing it only in 1914, when he was thirty-two and teaching at the Berlitz school in Trieste. The earliest version appeared in 1922. In loving but never stockpiled detail, Ellmann describes the origins of the characters, places, and events in *Ulysses* in the order in which Joyce experienced them as a child and young man in Dublin. When he reaches 1914, Ellmann begins a flashback technique that is not unlike film. Richard Altick puts his finger on Ellmann's book-saving technique: "Ellmann stopped the film [with 1914] and in a retrospective chapter reran the reels with a different filter, this time drawing out from the chaos of events a leading theme previously undiscussed: Joyce's artistic development, the emergence of peculiarities of technique which were destined to make *Ulysses* so revolutionary a work of fiction, and the slow formulation of an over-all plan for the book."[2]

Reading the biography, we are privy to watching Joyce putting his plans into execution. As many a doctoral student facing preliminary examinations came gratefully to know, Ellmann's twenty-five page twenty-first chapter ("The Origins of *Ulysses*") along with Edmund Wilson's forty-five-page chapter in *Axel's Castle,* could be life-savers.

Ellmann, whose puckish sense of humor was apparent even in a roomful of academics at Purdue a quarter-century ago, with his high forehead, heavy-rimmed eyeglasses, and soft-spoken Midwest manner, could be kindly even in his implied criticism of the competition. Writing respectfully of his major rival in the modern literary-biographical sweepstakes, Ellmann chides Leon Edel for a certain ingeniousness in applying the discoveries of Freud whenever Edel can: "Edel sometimes adopts Freudian techniques, sometimes not. That some of James's chills and fevers should be pronounced psychosomatic and others be just chills and fevers, is probably inevitable, posthumous diagnosis by biographers being as hazardous as diagnosis by doctors when the patient is alive."[3]

This remark appears in a reissuance of Professor Ellmann's inaugural address at Oxford when, in 1971, he was appointed Goldsmiths' Professor of English literature. At his death, in his seventieth year, he was professor emeritus at the English university. Fifteen months before his death he was stricken with amyotrophic lateral sclerosis (Lou Gehrig's Disease), a degeneration of the nerve cells for which there is no known treatment. Walter Goodman of the *New York Times* reports in his obituary (May 14, 1987) that Professor Ellmann's wit remained intact through his illness: "With speech difficult, he typed out repartee with visitors."

To anyone who was fortunate enough to have known him even so casually as in a queue to get a book inscribed, there could be no other way.

Ambiguity in relationships is one of Joyce's more fascinating aspects. Whether George Russell's version of Joyce's parting shaft after meeting Yeats can be credited—"We have met too late. You are too old for me to have any effect on you"—matters less than that Joyce acknowledged candidly to his brother and himself that he could never rival his countryman. Pound and Eliot, instigators with Joyce of literary modernism, could never tune in on Joyce the man, much as they supported him in word and deed. Even when notoriety overtook him in Paris in 1922 with the publication of *Ulysses* and world fame accompanied him throughout the 1930s, which were his fifties, Joyce attracted acquaintances rather than friends, helpers rather than soulmates.

It is unlikely that any major writer depended more on the favors of acquaintances or gave less of himself to them. As Nora said, "If God Almighty came down to earth, you'd have a job for him." He was punctiliously solicitous but rarely cut into his fulltime commitment to work-in-progress. However, his unstinting dedication to his hopelessly ill daughter Lucia stands as moving testimony to his devotion to a loved one beset. In frail health, generally, and with steadily deteriorating vision, particularly, Joyce required the ministrations not only of his wondrous wife Nora but of a network of doers in support of the ever tottering affair that was his career.

Perhaps of all Joyce's friendships, the one with Alessandro Francini in Trieste, nurtured in cabaret and *casa* equally, had the best chance. How it instead became a casualty of the larger destiny of genius is a story that can be read between the lines of a great biography and a poignant memoir. In "Friendship, Francini, and the Triestine Joyce," I have tried to tell that story.

VIII.

Friendship, Francini, and the Triestine Joyce

Fritz Senn reminds us that Joyce "fared better, on the whole, with friends in Trieste, international refugees in Zurich, or a mixed clique in Paris than with . . . Dublin cronies or English publishers."[1] Senn lists Italo Svevo, Stefan Zweig, Valery Larbaud, Louis Gillet, Ernst Robert Curtius, Carola Giedion-Welcker, Bernard Fehr, and Hermann Broch among perceptive foreign readers of the works. As to perceptive foreign readers of the *man,* I would lead off any list with the splendidly vocalic name of Alessandro Francini Bruni.[2]

Somehow, even in his definitive biography, Richard Ellmann has not done justice to this relationship. It was Francini who saw—often joined—an unadorned Joyce in countless sprees at their favorite café, Trieste's Restaurant Bonavia, and steered him homeward to the apartments the Joyces and Francinis shared both in Pola and Trieste, Jim and Nora Joyce's first lodgings on the Continent after their departure from Dublin in 1904. It was Francini who early on made Joyce's "archaic" Italian serviceable in the city where Triestino ruled. If he was not Joyce's closest non-Irish friend, Francini of Trieste, by way of Florence, was the one who came to know him best. To know well the man whom Francini would call "inconceivable and absurd, a composite of incompatibles" (*JJII,* 187) took much doing as well as much being done by.

No one, excluding Nora and possibly his brother Stanislaus, saw as much of Joyce *au naturel* during the Trieste years, 1905–20 (except for 1915–19 when the two were separated by the fortunes of World War I). Francini, so far as can be inferred from his published memoirs, never laid claim to any such distinction. Perhaps, then, it must fall to a mutual friend to assess, in retrospect, Francini's informal privilege. Silvio Benco, Joyce's admiring editor, admits to a ready acceptance of the prevailing impression "of a mature, already decided [Joyce] . . . in his stiff, automaton-like bearing" while hearing about—but knowing nothing of—"his evenings drinking with Francini." Benco was privy only to the professional teacher "always hastening from house to house to give an hour of English to all the Triestines. . . . punctual in his work, devoted to his wife, his children, and his house . . . remarkable for his sobriety." But Francini, Benco writes in 1930, was perhaps the only one to know from the beginning "the poetic torment, the keen critical mind, the paradoxical *diablerie* of Joyce."[3]

Something of that Joyce—the Irish jester affronting a Triestine court, seeming in his excesses to encourage an alcoholic's doom—survives in the form of a published transcript[4] of a lecture delivered by Francini on the evening of February 22, 1922, to a large assemblage of Joyce's friends and pupils (the two were virtually identical): a spoken memoir which testifies at nerve-end level to a relationship that was engendered by mutual love of language, yet transcended it; flourished despite some discord between a fallen Catholic and a devout one; and finally fell victim to burgeoning literary fame which was becoming a *fait accompli* for Joyce in Paris even as Francini was lecturing in Trieste.

Behind Francini's fervent memoir lies the unspeakable terrain of which Dostoevsky wrote in *Notes from Underground,* slightly amended. The Underground Man observes that there are those most crucial of reminiscences which a man is afraid to tell even himself. Francini concerns himself with matters about his friend to which he scarcely dare give voice—even to himself.

The lecture, titled *Joyce intimo spogliato in piazza,* is usually translated "Joyce Stripped Naked in the Piazza."[5] *Spogliato,* the past participle of *spogliare* ("to cast off," as of skin or clothes) makes the best sense in Francini's context only if we assume it is *Joyce intimo*—the *innermost* Joyce—that he wishes to expose *in piazza,* in the marketplace, *in public.*

For his public stripping of his friend, Francini might well have chosen to speak in Triestino. With help from Francini, Joyce had mastered the corrupted Italian that was spoken in the streets of Trieste. He invariably concluded his letters from Paris to Francini, Svevo, and other friends he had left behind in

Trieste in the dialect. However, for his talk on Joyce—in effect, his farewell to the Joyce persona he had known and supported through ceaseless adversity for fifteen years—Signor Francini Bruni chose what Richard Ellmann calls "extraordinarily colloquial Tuscan" (*JJII*, 766). It was a fitting choice. It had been Francini who recognized from the start in Pola that Joyce spoke "a dead language that had come alive to join the babel of living tongues" (*JJII*, 187) in the old port city; and it was Francini who taught Joyce Tuscan, both in its formal aspects and in its character of a local dialect with special words and meanings. Francini spiced his colloquial Tuscan with smatterings of Triestino and even a Venetian dialect as well as numerous puns, double entendres, outrageous figures of speech, and digressions. The difficulty of its style, coupled with the rarity of copies, has prevented the memoir from being widely known, except for passages—although none of the scurrilous ones—quoted by Ellmann, who required the help of three translators.[6]

Willard Potts, in his illuminating collection of recorded impressions of Joyce by Europeans, finds Francini's style in *Joyce intimo* significant in other respects:

> It reveals an antic humor that helps explain Francini's strong appeal to Joyce, who worried that domestic life was making him too solemnly conventional. It also suggests the linguistic daring and caprice of Joyce himself. Although the first impulse would be to conclude that he had influenced Francini, Nora thought the influence flowed in the opposite direction, to the detriment of her young husband's verbal manners. "Since you've come to know Francini," she told him, "I can't recognize you anymore."[7]

The reports on Francini's lecture were mixed. Benco called it a "delightful" book with an ugly title. Ellmann defers to the lecture with a three-page translated excerpt (*JJII*, 216–18) and credits it frequently–six endnote citations–but only once are Francini's words included. At all other times we read only Joyce's words as quoted by Francini. When Ellmann, with seeming full assurance, writes that Francini "did not mind Joyce's irreverence" (*JJII*, 187), none of the three translators drove home to the biographer the impassioned statement of devout belief that Francini expressed on the final page of *Joyce intimo*. Given the difficulties of Francini's words even for native speakers, Ellmann's ambiguity is not surprising. That ambiguity is best illustrated in Ellmann's report on Stanislaus Joyce's report on *Joyce intimo*.

So far as I can determine, Stanislaus was not only the first but the only correspondent who both attended and reported Francini's lecture to Joyce. He considered the performance an outrage. Given his humorlessness and an understandable antipathy toward one whom he could not help but have associated with his brother's café-hopping, Stanislaus can be expected to have cried "foul!" He wrote to Joyce that Francini "swore to me before the lecture that it was a caricature in good taste and 'worthy of the subject.' Instead it was vulgar and silly. . . ."

Stanislaus infers betrayal and implies that the audience agreed:

> Francini has read a conferenza-caricatura on you. . . . You may easily guess that he has been out of a job for some time and was trying to turn an honest penny. He goes to Florence to-morrow to take up a job on the "Nuovo Giornale". The hall was about half-full. Anybody to whom I have spoken about it was dissatisfied, but I am sending you the booklet so that you can judge it for yourself.[8]

At first Joyce laughed it off, remarking, "I'm sure it was very funny and quite suited to the distinguished audience" (*Letters III,* 61). But after reading it he came to agree with his brother's verdict. Joyce's sense of betrayal was always acute. It is ironic that Herbert Gorman's 1939 biography, coached by Joyce, includes not only Francini and other Trieste friends as doers of slights he will avenge, but Stanislaus as well.[9]

Ellmann believes that Joyce was "egged on" by Stanislaus to believe his friend Francini was debunking him (*JJII,* 481). I would go further. In the context of their Trieste rapport, it could be said that Francini's earthy profile was true to life if not to art. The emergent literary figure in Paris bore little resemblance to the man Francini both cherished and lamented in Trieste. Almost none of Joyce's Italian friends, except Italo Svevo, really understood what was happening to their teacher-friend. The first publication of *Ulysses,* not quite three weeks before Francini's lecture, launched an era in literary history. In a sense, possibly subliminally, Joyce, as Stanislaus observed ("God protect me from my friends," he had written to his brother in Italian) had to protect himself—his new persona—from friends like Francini. Prince Hal's discarding of Falstaff upon ascending to the throne as Henry V provides a relevant literary analogy here.

Joyce and Francini kept in touch, however, until Joyce's death two decades later. That Joyce softened his attitude to the memoir is indicated by a comment Joyce made (in French) in a letter to Swiss critic Jacques Mercanton in early 1940, a year before his death: "I shall write to Francini when I recover his letter. Is he going to reissue his booklet in a de luxe edition, on Japanese paper?" (*Letters III,* 463). Perhaps the only apparent betrayal lay in Francini's assuming the right to caricature Joyce, who preferred reserving that right to himself.

Such jauntiness about his sorely misunderstood profile would have pleased Francini, especially if it had come in 1922 instead of 1940. The truth is that the spirit of Francini's recollection is Proustian, an attempt to rescue from oblivion the Joyce that he remembered from before the war, the Joyce that Francini sensed had been superseded by the Paris celebrity.

Writing twenty-five years later—it is 1947, he is seventy, and Joyce has been dead six years—Francini recalls sadly that he and his wife hardly knew the Joyce who returned to Trieste in 1919 after taking refuge in Zurich. "Times had changed and Joyce was obviously no longer the same man. He seemed serious, almost conventional now."[10] Once Joyce departed a year later for Paris, there would be no reunions with Francini and, Joyce insisted, no bitterness.

Joyce was not unmindful of how their final months in Trieste together threatened the friendship. He wrote (June 7, 1921) from the rent-free Paris flat Valery Larbaud had provided to permit Joyce physical comfort while completing *Ulysses:* "It is unbelievable. Behind the Pantheon, ten minutes from the Luxembourg . . . , absolute silence, great trees, birds (not, mind you, the sort you're thinking of!) . . ." (*Letters III*, 44).

And then, this implicit apology to Francini which stands as at once a rueful glance backward and a prophecy: "Is it possible that I am worth something? Who would have said so after my last experience in Trieste? Larbaud says that a single episode, *Circe,* would suffice to make the fame of a French writer for life. But oh! and alas! and ugh! What a book!" (*Letters III*, 45–46).

What a book, indeed; yet among his intellectual friends in Trieste, almost none other than his fellow novelist Svevo had major clues about the great-book-in-progress. It was Svevo whom Joyce, anticipating Leopold Bloom, probed for lore on European Jewry. It was Svevo who answered Joyce's S.O.S. and delivered in person in Paris a packet containing notes made in Trieste for the *Ithaca* and *Penelope* episodes. For most of his Trieste friends, including Francini, the first substantive knowledge of *Ulysses* was a four-page promotional prospectus that Sylvia Beach mailed to the famous and un-known alike (*JJII*, 506). Joyce complained in a letter to Francini just before New Year's, 1922, that, among Triestines, only his Greek patron Baron Ralli had subscribed: "When you find a Triestine . . . who will pay 500 lire for a book of Zois light a candle to Saint Anthony the Worker of Miracles" (*Letters III*, 56).

This bantering letter about Triestine parsimony was apparently the last Francini received before presenting his *Joyce intimo* lecture.

If, as Stanislaus reported, Joyce's friends walked out on the lecture in droves, the reason may have had less to do with any perceived pillorying of "Il Professor d'Inglese! Mr. Joyce, professor *honoris causa* dell-Università di Cambridge," as Francini refers to him early on, than it did with the mounting tedium induced by devastating hyperbole aimed at the Berlitz operations in Pola and Trieste. Francini was the director of the Berlitz school in Pola when Joyce arrived as a teacher of English. Shortly after Joyce was summoned to the larger school in Trieste, the Francinis rejoined the Joyces. The two men along with their wives spent many evenings together, for a time even sharing an apartment, first in Pola and later in Trieste.

Francini's lecture begins with a long, indulgent description of the Berlitz school. It drones on for seventeen pages about the officials, teachers, methods, and general incompetence of the system. Surely little of this diatribe, which resembles in spirit the jocularity with which World War II recruits enjoy reminiscing about army snafus, could hold much interest for an audience that consisted of students to whose homes Joyce went to give his lessons. While making the grim side of the school perfectly clear, Francini shows that there was a great deal of laughter and joking in which Joyce participated fully.

Except for a vivid description of how understandably forlorn the Joyces appeared upon disembarking at Pola in early November, 1904 (they were not met by Francini at all but by Almidano Artifoni, owner of the school, whose name Joyce later used in *Ulysses* for Stephen Dedalus's Italian teacher), Francini appears to have lost his man temporarily in the din of his ravings against Berliz. What remained, for anyone who stayed, was Francini's straight-man recital of Joyce's seeming indifference to it all.

Who has not known a co-victim of an intolerable job situation whose forbearance, even occasional prosperity, hasn't proved irksome? So, hints Francini, did his friend Giacomo prosper. It was clear that the rebelliousness of his young Irish friend, freely given voice in matters of Irish and Triestine politics, did not include, apropos of Berlitz, *non serviam*. After all, he had signed a contract.

Richard Ellmann, especially in his comparison of James and Stanislaus, has prepared us well for his subject's refusal ever to wear himself down in open revolt. Francini, reviewing nearly two decades, recalls in what can only be assumed to be mock wryness—one easily taken for unqualified hostility by his audience but a spirit fully in keeping with the often black candor of their wine-fortified aggressions—his colleague's survival tactics.

Once Francini takes himself—and Joyce with him—out of the Berlitz classroom and forgets the zoo that they found there, his tone changes. Earlier, he characterized his friend as a vagrant wandering from tavern to tavern singing in a bleary tenor songs in Triestine and Florentine dialects. Herbert Gorman writes vividly of the wild domesticity of the two friends:

There were evenings in the house on the via Giovanni Boccaccio when Francini-Bruni would get into the infant Giorgio [Joyce's] carriage, suck at a milk bottle and cry, squeal and regurgitate like a baby while Joyce trundled him about the place. This would be at midnight. And after the clowning was over Joyce would sing Gregorian chants and the excitable Francini-Bruni, who had a high shrill laugh like a goat, would kiss the singer in an ecstasy of joy. Many a bottle of Triestine wine was emptied over the midnight table. (*Gorman*, 159)

Almost unexpectedly, seven-eighths of the way through his lecture, Francini reveals his compassion for a desperate friend who often, as a last resort, played the clown. He excuses—forgives—Joyce whose excesses were always played against disaster.

His artistic reversals had a disastrous effect on his animal spirits. His self-destruction was cold and premeditated. He would plunge recklessly when the world treated him badly.
 I had great respect for the genius who was my friend, and it tormented me to observe the cynicism of a man consciously bent on suicide and darkness.
 I knew better than anybody else. (*Francini I*, 32)

What Francini knew, although he may have overstated the case, was something of 1914, the year *Dubliners* was finally published, marking "the first step to fame . . . the critical year of his life . . . when *Dubliners* was born, this jewel for which a Calvary had been reserved."

Francini presents a voluntary exile whose thoughts like his writings were never far from Ireland. Joyce was "a man discoursing on the heartrending state of his land, all the while showering it with scorn, his moist eyes gazing at some point in the void. In an outburst of weeping he would speak of the tears cried from thousands of tormented [Irish] souls over the course of centuries, trying himself to drown those tears in a river of eloquence" (*Francini I*, 33).

Between binges, Joyce had convinced Francini that he was "a born gentleman . . . from a very noble family in the West of Ireland, a region that bears the name of his ancestors—the Joyce Country. . . . Excesses are one thing: true nature is another" (*Francini I*, 33).

Francini's sense of Joyce's "true nature" provides the most incisive portrait we have from a European. Willard Potts declares that "the Joyce Francini recalled closely resembles the Stephen Dedalus of *A Portrait* and *Ulysses*, only now seen from a comic perspective as the young husband in exile" (*Francini I*, 6).

In effect, Francini draws on Voltaire's notion of God, suggesting that if Joyce did not exist it would be necessary to invent him. The sheer improbability of the man becomes the theme for the lecture's strongest insights. What Francini says about the incongruent parts of its creator has frequently been applied to *Ulysses*. Francini, lecturing a few weeks before the first subscription copies were available in Trieste (*JJII*, 529), could not have anticipated any such analogy. "Joyce is all discordant. His head is a hive of discordant and disconnected ideas. All the same, there is a perfect order in it. If there is chaos, it is in his soul. You have to take him as he is. . . . He is an alloy composed of elements which, according to the laws of physics, should repel one another but which instead hold together through a miracle of molecular aggregation" (*Francini I*, 34).

Joyce's constant shiftings of taste and viewpoint are not seen as capricious but traceable to the quickness with which intellectual elaboration works in him. Francini finds in puzzling tandem an admiration for Dante as well as the "ephemeral" Verlaine, a thorough knowledge of the church coupled with a total lack of faith, a powerful intellect in the service of denial. No idol is sacred. He is no longer uncritical of Ibsen, the inspiration of his youth.

Finally, with an honesty unusual among those who have written about Joyce, Francini admits that he cannot understand his friend. He is equally candid about his feelings, which range from love and admiration for Joyce to disgust, to a religiously based note of disapproval and concern.

We do not know how well Francini could have known *Portrait* and *Dubliners*—he could only have read them in English at the time of his lecture—but he knew well Joyce's double-barreled genius for expanding language and contracting tolerance. "He would be a complete enigma if he weren't a terrifying dialectician. He stretches language to express commonplace vices in a desolate and pitiless way that sends chills up the spine. Tongue ever turns to aching tooth" (*Francini I*, 35).

How "fallen" a Catholic Joyce was may not have been known by many in his predominantly Catholic audience. Perhaps many of those who Stanislaus claimed departed the hall early would have been surprised by Francini's rage to bring Joyce's soul into the church's fold. In closing a talk which filled forty-one pages in its printed version, Francini puts into words what his actions had shown for two decades—his remarkable understanding of, and tolerance for, his friend's often-expressed apostasy.

> Joyce is not irreligious. He is without religion. There is a difference. He doesn't even believe the bread he is eating. He is so consistent in his unbelief that his children have not been baptized. I, bonehead, without being asked never tired of telling him what I thought of this arrogance. And every time he would answer with the same argument: "Shut up, melon head!" Then the conversation could continue without difficulty. (*Francini* I, 35)

Richard Ellmann devotes only one paragraph in his massive biography to Joyce's attendance—for aesthetic, not pious, reasons—at church during Holy Week. He notes that Joyce remained "too fond of the liturgy and music to forgo them" (*JJII,* 310). Francini doubts that Joyce partitioned off the aesthetic from the pious so neatly.

> In his house there is no religious practice, but on the other hand there is much talk of Christ and religion and much singing of liturgical chants. I can go even further. You had better not look for Joyce during the week before Easter because he is not available to anyone. On the morning of Palm Sunday, then during the four days that follow Wednesday of Holy Week, and especially during all the hours of those great symbolic rituals at the early morning service, Joyce is at church, entirely without prejudice and in complete control of himself, sitting in full view and close to the officiants so that he won't miss a single syllable of what is said, following the liturgy attentively in his book of Holy Week services, and often joining in the singing of the choir. (*Francini I,* 35–36)

It would not do, however, for the believer to let off the apostate so easily, and Francini doesn't. He cannot understand how anyone with so superior a religious education could so distance himself from the "Supreme Good." He must somehow qualify Joyce's fallen state. His friend has made himself a master of "Jesuitical casuistry [which means] that he has the ability to confuse an opponent in a mesh of dialectical subtleties, make him skid on the pavement of the discussion, or lose him in a perverse labyrinth with an ambush around every corner" (*Francini* I, 36).

After twenty years of contemplating the enigma who is his friend, Francini will not label him a Voltairean—an intellectual anarchist—for he knows Joyce would reject any such categorization. Rather, he finds, it is the prerogative of his individualistic temperament to be attracted to intellectual arrogance—a Dionysian contradiction—just because he knows that to be the unpardonable sin. For Francini, Joyce rests, politically, in similar contradictions, favoring neither constitutional monarchies nor republican governments.

Once, confessing his heresies (Francini reports), Joyce demanded to know if his friend believed in "the sun of the future." "I believe," Francini answered, "in Jesus . . . the Man-God. Of course, Joyce doesn't; never mind, I still like him" (*Francini* I, 38).

After an apostrophe to Italians ("It shouldn't be so, but it's a damned law of the Italian people to destroy idols and rebuild them again immediately afterwards in their hearts," *Francini I,* 38), Francini concluded his lecture on the one note for which Joyce would be least likely to forgive him. He asks, for Joyce, divine forgiveness.

Joyce from Paris, Francini from Florence continued to write to each other fairly regularly. In a letter to Dario deTuoni, a Triestine poet to whom Francini had introduced him before the First World War, Joyce at sixty-two reports that his old friend, four years older, has returned to teaching and is an instructor of the Scalopi Fathers in Florence (*Letters III,* 467). This was on February 20, 1940, less than a year before Joyce died.

Ellmann interviewed Francini extensively in 1953–54, five years before the great biography appeared. Joyce's first Italian friend in his exile was seventy-six. He would live another decade.

The biography makes no mention of Francini's later memoir, "Ricordi su James Joyce," published twenty-five years after *Joyce intimo.* It was no loss. Now a professor of Italian in his native city, Francini dismisses the colloquial mode that so enlivened the best parts of the earlier piece. His new delivery is essayistic, even slick. Joyce has been dead nearly seven years, his position in the vanguard of modernism already secure. Francini writes a *pro forma* essay as no doubt befits a senior academic—he is seventy—who by an accident of geography came to know a man who was destined for world fame. Familiar phrases recur but never any of the wryly comic ones that showed *Joyce intimo* to be not the hostile remembrance Stanislaus reported but an extension of a unique friendship. Francini notes—snidely, possibly grudgingly—that his friend published *Ulysses* at a propitious time when Paris "propaganda" and several clever women combined to make him and his book famous.[11]

It is as if Francini still prefers to believe he "lost" his friend less to literature than to a kind of international self-promotion. Francini has recently learned—he is appalled—that manuscripts of *Ulysses* are being sold at auction in London. He devotes about one page each to summaries of that book and of *Finnegans Wake*. He closes by recalling an aspect of the sometimes child-like man he remembers. No amount of greatness of mind could help "Giacomo" during a thunderstorm. He would run to a corner or, late at night, pull the covers over his head: "Each time [of thunderstorms] he would say that Italy was a country of cosmic revolutions and that he wanted to go away. But he stayed."

To the end, the memory of the heart is the longest.

PART THREE

The Serious Business of Comedy, Innocence, and Homage to the Hemingways

Prologue
Lucky Jim and Johnny Come Lately

There is a story I read somewhere about the character actor Edmund Gwenn. Near death, he is said to have replied to a hospital visitor who asked him if he had ever experienced anything of comparable difficulty to dying. "Yes," Gwenn whispered. "Every time I played comedy."

It is a commonplace to say that comedy is serious business. It is hardly surprising that the bibliography for theories of tragedy is endless while that for comedy contains relatively few staples, of which Henri Bergson's "On Laughter" is my favorite. Although the essay deserves a more serviceable translation for students, Bergson's key notion is that comedy results whenever "something mechanical is encrusted on the living." The basis of laughter is the undercutting of the natural by effecting in human actions, attitudes, and speech some form of the mechanical. To illustrate, let me offer a brief comedy of classroom manners. For an early-in-semester seminar on Milton, all twelve of us arrived early. A professor, new to me, entered, strode to the lectern, and began lecturing on phonemes. Had he looked up from his notes he might have seen the Milton man, who was late, standing in the rear holding his finger to his lips. We read his signal and obeyed. The linguistics scholar, face still buried in script, droned on. Was it his peripheral vision that eventually called attention to the many empty seats in his large lecture section? As soon as he gave full attention to this contradiction, laughter exploded.

In James Thurber's story, "The Catbird Seat," the formula works overtime. When the officious Ulgine Barrows arrives to impose a new order at F&S, her reforms threaten the comfortable inertia of chief clerk Martin. He makes an out-of-character night call on Ulgine intent on "rubbing her out." But before he can bungle the job, his heretofore untested imagination concocts a fiendish plan to undo his harasser nonviolently. Martin will convert his most disabling trait—his sheer ordinariness—into his most potent weapon. By deft manipulation, Thurber represents the mechanical as the clerk's deadly routine on which the efficiency expert's killjoy acts are encrusted. However, in an ironic twist, Martin demonstrates that he is not the old stick everyone at F&S—and no one more than Ulgine—had taken him to be. To unseat her, Martin relies on just this perception of himself as dull but honest. When Ulgine protests that Martin, of all people, has rigged the case against her, no one believes her.

Forces necessarily dehumanized have been loosed against rigidity in the interests of restoring the human. This is comedy's charge. Its moral function, in Bergson's terms, is to ridicule the mechanical whenever it obstructs freedom, and to praise the flexible, which allows us to survive and grow.

When W. C. Fields sees his cue-stick literally turn against him at just the projected moment of triumph, we are at the crossroads of two minds in the matter. Charlie Chaplin, enslaved by the machine while tightening bolts for eight hours, encounters a lovely object for his affection, only to find himself programed to his assembly-line ritual which he enacts on the buttons of her frock. The Tramp's chivalric dreams turn instantly to humiliation. Empathy lets us laugh at the human comedy the very moment we share the anguish of it.

Lucky Jim is the fictional quintessence of comedy à la Bergson. Kingsley Amis's academic picaro falls squarely in the British tradition—Shakespeare to Fielding to Monty Python—that, however beastly the social horror, it can be handled. Jim Dixon is a basket case whose only claim to his job as a university lecturer rests in his having none of the disqualifications. Although shelved with novels and plays of the angry-young-man persuasion, *Lucky Jim* more properly belongs with comedies of manners, generally, and, specifically, among the first books to speculate with wit the consequences of a particularly British stiff upper lipness when confronted with the gamesplay of *muddle, sham, cheek,* and *I'm all right, Jack.*

Appearing only a few years after *The Catcher in the Rye* and sharing that novel's preoccupation with phoniness, *Lucky Jim* never projected the direness of Salinger's statement. If heroism is impossible in the modern world—

and Jim Dixon, typically, is no better but much less worse than any of the other male figures—*Lucky Jim* speaks for everyone who has felt enslaved to empty forms. His plight provides an early, admittedly caricatured, reference for nearly every graduate student's defenses in the face of utter dependence on forms. In fact, his rituals of publish-or-perish, as enacted in all of the English departments with which I had any acquaintance from the sixties through the eighties, stood as testaments to academia's mandates to publish even the most obfuscatory drivel, illustrations of a kind of Bergsonian encrustation of mechanical theorizing on living literature.

Perhaps this is the place to acknowledge that *Lucky Jim,* while my own favorite comic novel, cuts a narrower swath than, say, a work like *A Handful of Dust* (1934), whose remorseless wit cuts to the heartless core of British high life. Evelyn Waugh's Tony Last anticipated Amis's hero-as-loser by two decades. Unlike Jim Dixon, who wins on all fronts, there could be no recovery for so terminally shaken a victim as Waugh's. Betrayed by everything and everyone he's been foolish enough to believe in, Tony Last reminded me of the toughest editor I ever worked for. Late one night, once the edition had been put to bed and after many beers, this merciless red-penciler confided that the world had lost most of its allure after he learned in mid-teens that *King Arthur* was not a true story. Tony Last's undoing is his belief, despite assault from all sides, in his castle called Hetton and all it Arthurianly stands for.

Waugh allows decency no quarter. He displays Tony Last's rectitude under siege, betrayed by the ironies of modern rites—rites of visitation, both host and guest; of kissing, infidelity, concubinage, and separate domicile; of gossip and the predatory; of churchgoing and, above all, of bereavement. These are familiars in most experience of passage. However, I did not read the earlier book—the Waugh—until much later, as a tenured professor teaching doctoral students in a seminar on the British comic novel. I had survived.

I read *Lucky Jim* at a time when I had just changed careers, faced the serious illness of my wife, and, at thirty-five, did not even have lack of the disqualifications in my favor. I have been seriously out of sequence all my life. I learned to drive at thirty, again changed careers at forty, learned to swim at fifty, took up disco dancing at sixty, and am trying golf at past seventy.

My early history is such as to make Jim Dixon a confrere.

The only time I have ever been ahead of the game was midway into infantry basic in Georgia the second spring after Pearl Harbor. My final semester in college had been interrupted by a callup of the enlisted reserves. The rhythms of wartime—patterns of start-and-delay, hurry up-and-wait— were for me the shape of things to come.

Halfway into the thirteen-week training cycle, notification came courtesy of the Commonwealth of Pennsylvania that I and other last-term seniors had been granted our degrees in absentia. However, rather than a passport to officer candidate school, the degree proved a false start. I was rejected for "lack of military bearing."

Bearing notwithstanding, removal from orders to a combat outfit came providentially: a high score for the only time in my life in an exam and with it assignment to study Italian to become an interpreter with "cobelligerents" (euphemism for prisoners of war after Italy's surrender in 1943). After two pleasurable months, I was banished to a year's limbo of wasted, though gratefully safe, stopgaps in ordnance, quartermaster, signal corps.

Only heavy losses in the Battle of the Bulge ended my no-man's-land status and provided me, after two years, a number and a name: *745; casual replacement; rifleman.* There was nothing casual about my fourth basic-training stint—this one a "refresher"—and prompt introduction to the Rhine Valley, foxhole vantage. Besides learning for myself that few in combat are *scared shitless*—it is just the opposite—my infantry assignment provided me my first stripe (outside a pfc's; inside, a coward's). My small stature endowed me with my only perquisite in the military. I wasn't considered for our squad's Browning Automatic Rifle team. That required brawn as well as bearing.

My discharge came just a few days too late to start a graduate course in journalism. I lost six months without ever thinking of them as time lost. I found a night job in an oil refinery monitoring thirty-two huge vats to make sure oil and clay met without overflows. One night I fell asleep on the graveyard shift and woke to an oncoming river of steaming lava. I rang the emergency bell twice—the signal for sand to be dropped from a conveyor onto the spillage—but I neglected to ring three times to stop the sand. In a few minutes the oil-storage building was like the Red Sea parting to admit the Sahara. After I had spent the rest of my shift, plus the next, cleaning up the mess, the foreman, a soft-spoken Texan, was gentle but direct: "Leave your locker keys at the office and pick up your pay. You might consider another line of work."

When Jim Dixon goes to sleep with a lighted cigarette and burns a rug, a table, and the bedclothes in the Welches' guestroom, I could relate everything to the oil-filter caper.

A respected and older friend once counseled me that a man should program nothing until he reaches thirty and everything thereafter. His advice did not allow enough room for habit. I had certainly followed the first part of his prescription. On the job front, fortuity ruled. I spent the decade of my thirties without showing the least inclination for what is now called *upward mobility*. When, closing in on forty, I was assigned to write a semidaily column with no lessening of other duties, I was so grateful I didn't even ask for a raise. Within a year I found myself famous—locally, that is—and so heady was the wine that for nearly four years I measured out my life in four double-spaced pages three times weekly. Just visible on the friendly horizon we call "in due time" loomed the expectation of syndication. It never came.

Meeting invariable deadlines, as a way of life, distorts time. Newspapering makes it cyclic, temporarily disposable only to be plotted again the next day. Time, when one is young, should be an ally, not the enemy. It took an offstage theater-of-the-absurd incident to convince me.

I was sitting in a cigar shop at ten to twelve (our paper had a noon deadline), waiting for a hand signal from the police reporter on the second floor of the building across the street. Later that day our paper would have its banner headline—a murder-suicide—but now, ten minutes to deadline, neither *de facto* victim would expire and become *facto*—for P.M.s (evening) release. I could hear the voice of the managing editor screaming into the receiver: *"Dammit, what-duh-yuh mean they're both dead but we can't say so? Have we got a ribbon or haven't we?"* My colleague's semaphore—right hand raised for the slain, left for the slayer, both hands for both—never flashed, or at least not in time for the edition. We had "2 Men Near Death After Double Shooting," but our nightside brethren could shout, "2 MEN DEAD; POLICE SAY MURDER-SUICIDE!"

At noon I dictated into the phone as much as I knew while awaiting my partner's confirmation of the cessation of one or both pulses. As had been happening every working moment of my life for years, acute gastritis hit me in the pit of the stomach. Only at mid-afternoon, when we left the wrapup for the night staff, could I slow down and ponder the imbecility of the latest panic. At some such moment, I may for the first time have faced up to myself. I was forty and a hack: an accessory or maybe slightly more animated appendage to the routinized gadgetry that was churning out, not "miraculously," as I had once written, but inevitably, a daily newspaper.

I gave notice—sheer fortuity again—on my first working day after the Sunday at the beginning of July, 1961, when Ernest Hemingway, once himself a fugitive from newspapers, managed from an awkward position to fire a shotgun into his mouth. Neuterized at sixty-two by electroshock therapy, Hemingway had denied time—now his enemy—its due course. Even for the less talented, time in that sense must have a stop.

I quit journalism for teaching for an array of irritations and one overriding consideration. I was afraid to grow old in that setting. Greyness did not confer eminence. The aging men I knew had ulcers or smoked and drank too much. For years I had downplayed my lifelong love of books and fascination with writers, reduced them to an occasional review disguised as a column. With Jo's encouragement I determined to return to graduate school—in English. I was forty-four.

I completed my doctorate at Purdue during the fall semester of 1968. Maury Beebe, who had moved on to Temple University in my hometown to launch the *Journal of Modern Literature,* graciously returned to West Lafayette to preside. The years at Purdue were the most focused and rewarding of my life. While Jo pursued an M.A., I tried hard—without success, of course—to fill the huge gaps in my reading. Fortunately, I did not have to teach while taking courses. I had received an editorial fellowship with *Modern Fiction Studies* and wrote unsigned book reviews for the journal's newsletter. Thus, for two years, I had only to read books and write about them. Both at Purdue and at Texas A&M, I was fortunate to find others for whom literature was holy writ. It was at a monthly meeting of colleagues, all of them younger than I and most having recently, like myself, completed their degrees, that I presented, in much shorter form, the essay on Kingsley Amis that follows. "Laughing with the Early Amis," which deals with novels that look on the comedic side of academe, had built-in sympathy that evening. I never tried to place the paper.

I.

Laughing with the Early Kingsley Amis

In a long and generally loving essay published some twenty-five years ago in the *New Yorker*, "One of the Family," W. H. Auden called Max Beerbohm "probably the finest [parodist] in English." He regrets that it is only Sir Max's "visual" parodies—his caricatures—that have reached a wide audience. "Unfortunately," Auden writes, "literary parodies can . . . be appreciated only by a reader who is intimately acquainted with the authors parodied." Then, in an about-face that had excised from my memory any of the praise, Auden concludes:

Greatly as I admire both the man and his work, I consider Max Beerbohm a dangerous influence—just how dangerous one must perhaps have been brought up in England to know. His attitudes both to life and to art, charming enough in him, when taken up by others as a general cultural ideal, become something deadly, especially for the English, an intelligent but very lazy people, far too easily bored, and persuaded beyond argument that they are the *Herrenvolk*.[1]

Auden's essay appeared in late 1965. A decade earlier, one of the *Herrenvolk*, W. Somerset Maugham, writing in the Christmas, 1955, issue of the *London Sunday Times*, faintly praised a first novel by Kingsley Amis entitled *Lucky Jim*. Maugham's review may have been the first to call attention to the book's significance as a social document—a significance he regarded as "ominous":

I am told that today rather more than sixty percent of the men who go to the universities go on a government grant. This is a new class that has entered upon the scene. It is the white-collar proletariat. Mr. Kingsley Amis is so talented, his observation is so keen, that you cannot fail to be convinced that the young men he so brilliantly describes truly represent the class with which his novel is concerned.

They do not go to the university to acquire culture, but to get a job, and when they have got one, scamp it. They have no manners, and are woefully unable to deal with any social predicament. Their idea of a celebration is to go to a public house and drink six beers. They are mean, malicious and envious. They will write anonymous letters to harass a fellow undergraduate and listen in to a telephone conversation that is no business of theirs. Charity, kindliness, generosity are qualities they hold in contempt. They are scum. They will in due course leave the university. Some will doubtless sink back, perhaps with relief, into the modest class from which they emerged; some will take to drink, some to crime and go to prison. Others will become schoolmasters and form the young, or journalists and mould public opinion. A few will go into Parliament, become Cabinet Ministers and rule the country. I look upon myself as fortunate that I shall not live to see it.

The review was widely quoted, responses usually disparaging. C. P. Snow asked, two issues later: "Why is it so contemptible to go to a university on a government grant? Why is it so bestial to celebrate by drinking pints of beer?" Maugham was to live another ten years—into his ninety-second year—during which, had he been disposed to read about them, he would have observed the ominous become realized—in fiction anyway—in a profusion of beer-drinking provincial students, schoolmasters, or university lecturers, surrounded by a philistine affluent society, which is utterly indifferent to the job they are doing and implicitly denies the values for which such jobs stand, mocking their own earlier emblems of high culture, and settling for the roles of court jesters or provincial cynics.

Both the Auden and Maugham commentaries suggest that life, after all, is a serious business; that it is folly, in literature, to adopt Beerbohm's sly suggestion that minor artists may look down their noses at major ones and that "important" work ought somehow to be left to persons of lesser caliber; that, in life, it is better to be dead than follow any fashion that relegates charity and generosity to the backseat.

The effect on me of these warnings is characteristically unheroic. It is to feel at most a tinge of shame while laughing again over Sir Max's parody of Milton's epic style when applied to a description of Adam and Eve's toothbrushing habits; and to take refuge in the truism that parody is the tribute nonpareil to the original. And what better tonic after a bad day, week, month, semester than to reread *Lucky Jim* and the early episode where the masquerading medievalist Jim Dixon, after an overdose of culture, sneaks out to a pub, later falls into a drunken sleep with a lighted cigarette, burns a rug, a table, and the bedclothes in the spareroom of his hated sponsor's family? It is easy, in the general hilarity, to forget that Jim, after all, was a guest.

This year—1994—marks the fortieth anniversary of the original publication of *Lucky Jim*. Since then, Amis's production has included eighteen novels, a book of stories, five essay collections, a popular biography of Rudyard Kipling, two books of his own light verse, and another—the New Oxford—of other people's light verse. Not to be overlooked are Amis's aficionado interests in science fiction and in crime/spy thrillers. These can be said to join two popular genres which I have always believed are mutually exclusive; that is, I've observed that the science-fiction person comes to these stories from almost any point of view—literary, sociological, psychological, political, even anarchistic/misanthropic/dystopian. The reader of thrillers is apt to be the more attractive conversational partner, one who values entertainment and "entertainments" foremost. Kingsley Amis brought science fiction to the Christian Gauss Seminars in Criticism at Princeton in spring, 1959. A year later his lectures became a sci-fi survey, *New Maps of Hell*.

"I am not that peculiarly irritating kind of person," Amis writes in his foreword, "the intellectual who takes a slumming holiday in order to 'place' some 'phenomenon of popular culture'. . . . Science fiction is not tomfool sensationalism, but neither is it a massive body of 'serious' art destined any moment to engulf the whole of Anglo-American writing."[2]

The significant words are "popular" and "serious". Amis surely is implying the same dichotomy that Auden used to deflate Beerbohm: the peril to the "greater" at the hands of the "lesser". In "A New James Bond," Amis states his case for the latter: "Our cultural puritanism does not encourage the writer of thrillers or adventure stories, any of the genres, unless it can be maintained that the genre in question is being used as no more than a vehicle, a metaphor, and that the author is really going on about modern society and the human heart with the best of them." He goes on to decry the trend against the genres; to aver that "a clumsy dissection of the heart is so much worse than boring as to be painful"; and that "John D. MacDonald is by any standards a better writer than Saul Bellow, only MacDonald writes thrillers and Bellow is a human-heart chap, so guess who wears the top-grade laurels?"[3]

Some of his claims for science fiction and Ian Fleming foreshadow Amis's decline in critical esteem. Harold Orel writes ("The Decline and Fall of a

Comic Novelist," *Kansas Quarterly* 1 [Summer, 1969]) that "it has been a long time, alas, since Kingsley Amis in his rapid slide downhill into commercial success has cared about our caring." Richard J. Voorhees ("Kingsley Amis, Three Hurrahs and a Reservation," *Queens Quarterly* 74 [Spring, 1972]:38) finds that, "although Amis's range and vitality are admirable . . . he has perhaps dissipated his talents as well as developed them." I stopped trying to keep up after *Jake's Thing* (1976), a novel to which one might with justice apply Wells's comment in his glowing review of Joyce's *A Portrait of the Artist as a Young Man* that it is a work by an author with a "cloacal obsession." *Jake's Thing* is 276 pages built on a single joke which is not so jokeful to some of us older parties. A thrice-married Oxford University reader in early Mediterranean history is treated by a quack for declining libidinal prowess. Part of the therapy includes a complicated but thankfully imaginary instrument called a "nocturnal mensurator". During sleep this device somehow hooks up to the relevant part and records on discs significant nighttime didoes.

Anthony Burgess, in a review of *I Want It Now*, comments that with that novel, Amis's seventh, a moral philosophy begins to emerge, hinting that there was none in the first six, including *Lucky Jim*.[4] To determine the validity of Burgess's implication, it is necessary to examine the moral/ethical footprints of Amis's nonheroes, not only in his first novel but in the two that followed—*That Uncertain Feeling* (1955), which ironically won the Somerset Maugham prize for that year, and *I Like It Here* (1958). In the background I hope to reserve Amis's apparent antipathy for any cult of ultimate seriousness and in the foreground his corollary notion that the pursuit of laughter— particularly of laughter-at-self—may be the only way some aspects of the serious can be borne. For related themes I wish to draw on quotations on comedy and laughter, respectively, from George Bernard Shaw, where one would expect it, and from Emerson, where one might not.

First, Shaw (in his preface to a 1934 collection of his plays) writes that he is "a classic writer of comedies" and that his purpose is "to chasten morals with ridicule."

Second, Emerson, who in 1843, defining our need for laughter, wrote: "All our plans, managements, houses, poems, if compared with the wisdom and love which man represents, are equally imperfect and ridiculous. But we cannot afford to part with any advantages. We must learn by laughter as well as by tears and terrors; explore the whole of nature, the farce and buffoonery in the yard below as well as the lessons of poets and philosophers in the hall."

My first engagement, however, will be with Auden's faulting of Beerbohm as it might be applied to Amis in the matter of disrespect for his betters.

Writers—real and fictional, the living and the dead—fare poorly in the early novels. Among those multiple masks Jim Dixon wears to hide his self-contempt are an Edith Sitwell face and an Evelyn Waugh face. Finally, on the last page, triumphant and no longer requiring a face to face the face in his inner mirror, Jim encounters the Welches, his former tormentors, now in disarray and retreat. On Jim's arm is "the Callaghan girl," the prize he has won from Bertrand Welch in a matter-over-mind class struggle; and in hand the good job that has become his by virtue of having, along with none of the qualifications, none of the disqualifications either. Symbolic of the shift in fortunes, Welch senior wears his son's characteristic beret and Welch junior wears his father's fishing hat. Amis writes: "In these guises, and standing rigid with popping eyes, they had a look of being Gide and Lytton Strachey, represented in waxwork form by a prentice hand."[5]

But it is another writer—one who novelist Frank Tuohy, in conversation, told me "probably had the last complete literary career, moving from strength to strength"—it is Graham Greene—the name, the themes, the productivity—who is Amis's persistent butt in his first novels. In the midst of a self-destructive liaison with Margaret Peel, a fake-suicide compulsive of a type probably recognizable on both sides of the Atlantic to anyone who has been a graduate student in English, Jim remembers "a pity moving in him like a sickness, or some such jargon. The parallel was very apt: he felt ill" (*Lucky Jim*, 190). This disdainful allusion can only be to the Graham Greene of *The Heart of the Matter* whose hero, Major Scobie, is the exemplar of Greene's self-humiliating saints, a man corrupted by pity. Jim Dixon forces himself to feel responsible for Margaret because she is not pretty. Curiously, his sacrifices in behalf of Margaret Peel are not unlike those in the Greene book against whose "jargonized" sicknesses Amis scoffed. They are similar to the ministrations of the married Scobie who imagines himself in love with Helen Rolt until he realizes his feeling is a false effect of his pity. Jim Dixon also gives in occasionally to self-pity. He tells Christine Callaghan that "I can't help minding [about Margaret]. Minding isn't a thing you can do anything about. I can't help going on with it" (*Lucky Jim*, 221). He is saved only when a former suitor of Margaret's—significantly named Catchpole—counteracts his pity by revealing that Margaret has been practicing emotional blackmail on both of them. Finally Jim realizes the futility of "trying to save those who fundamentally would rather not be saved. To go on trying would not merely be to yield to pity and sentimentality, but wrong and, to pursue it to its conclusion, inhumane. It was all very bad luck on Margaret, and probably derived, as he'd thought before, from the anterior bad luck of being sexually unattractive." (*Lucky Jim*, 247)

In his second and third novels, Amis makes Graham Greene the prototype of the fashionable best-selling novelist who writes too many books. John Lewis of *That Uncertain Feeling,* an assistant librarian in a Welsh town, receives an invitation to the home of Mrs. Edith Rhys Protheroe, one of the premier hostesses thereabouts. She is actually the wife of the big local butcher and Lewis notes "the latest Graham Greene and Angela Thirkell lying, still in their jackets, on a copy of *Vogue.*"[6] In *I Like It Here,* a nonwriting novelist who barely keeps himself and his family going on the proceeds of journalism and a bit of lecturing, is about to board ship for Portugal for some commissioned literary sleuthing (about which, more later). Amis stations his man, Garnet Bowen, in the ship's lounge where his eyes are assaulted by a book, "the new Graham Greene." In the earlier novel the latest Graham Greene merely tags the bourgeois Rhys Protheroes as part of the buying-but-not-reading-current-best-sellers set. The new Graham Greene allows Amis to fire depth charges in the direction of Greeneland: "He had nothing against that author personally or aesthetically, but wished he would die soon so that his lectures on him would not keep on having to have things added to it every eighteen months or so. Perhaps it would be better in the long run to set his teeth and make the switch to E. M. Forster. The New Graham Greene, like most of the old Graham Greenes, was about abroad. Extraordinary how the region kept coming up."[7]

Although his insecurity about "abroad" and being there keeps turning up and although almost everything non-English keeps getting put down in *I Like It Here,* it is foreign locutions applied to the names of his country's authors that give Bowen (and Amis) a chance to snipe Beerbohmishly at his contemporaries. He recalls hearing the novelist's name mangled by "some foreign persons" into *Grim-Grin* (*Like It,* 45). When his Indian students asked him about another writer whom they called *Edge-Crown,* Bowen

searched his brain frantically. *Grim-Grin* he had been ready for, together with *Ifflinn-Voff, Zumzit Mum* and *Shem-Shoice.* This was new. "Could you amplify that a little?" He ran through the possible variants—Adj-, Each-, Age- . . . . Some foreigner? But no; it had been *his* Edge-Crown.

"*Sickies of Sickingdom,*" the woman explained, irritably.

"Yes . . . of course . . . Well . . . He began nodding his head with little hope of ever having reason to stop.

After a brief explanatory uproar he was enabled to wonder aloud what had led his questioner to detect a resemblance between *The Power and the Glory* and *The Keys of the Kingdom*, by A. J. Cronin. . . ."

The answer: ". . . There is a priest in both." (*Like It*, 46)

Amis devotes most of the first two-thirds of *I Like It Here* to Bowen's Peter-Sellers-as-Inspector Clouseau-like difficulties with abroad. Some are vintage Amis, as when Bowen "fancied that he had a long history of lower-middle-class envy directed against the upper-middle-class traveller who handled foreign railway officials with insolent ease, discussed the political situation with the taxi-driver in fluent argot, and landed up first go at exactly the right hotel." (*Like It*, 23)

He concluded that things could be worse. Abroad will at least give him a chance to behave like a Somerset Maugham character. (*Like It*, 35)

Something which, happening near the end of *I Like It Here,* at the tomb of Henry Fielding in Lisbon, at once caps the donnée of the novel and provides a fuller perspective on the seeming irreverent-young-man attitude to the great old men of English prose literature. First, the fictional situation:

A London publisher takes his seemingly permanently blocked novelist to lunch to discuss the latter's impending trip to Portugal. "I've got something rather interesting to tell you, but you must promise to keep it under your hat. Let's try a little experiment. Wulfstan Strether. What's your reaction?" "Boredom, chiefly," Bowen replies, perhaps not only for himself but for his creator too. "I never seem to get on with great novelists." (*Like It*, 14)

The publisher reveals that Wulfstan Strether—to whom he refers as "the one indisputable major talent to have arisen since the death of Conrad" (Later Bowen will refer to Conrad as "that crazy Polish scribbling sea-dog")—after publishing five brilliant and brisk-selling novels, has gone down, Salinger-like, without a trace. Strether, in fact, had always kept his identity and whereabouts a secret, but now his agent-executor has died after destroying Strether's papers. A typescript has been received in London, breaking a decade's silence. Its title is *One Word More*, but it will be referred to throughout the book as *One Turd More*. Its author, an expatriate living in Portugal under the name Buckmaster, claims to be Strether. Expert readers have deemed the work just possibly Bad Strether. Bowen's commission will be to go with wife and children, all expenses paid, to Portugal to determine if the claimant is actually Strether or pseudo-Strether. As in *Lucky Jim,* the matter of a steady job is crucial. That in combination with the money he will make from writing up the possibly not-so-late, great novelist makes for an offer Bowen cannot refuse.

Once arrived in Portugal, Bowen makes no progress in breaking through the Strether-Buckmaster curtain until the latter invites him on a visit to Fielding's tomb. Bowen finds himself standing with the mystery author in a churchyard, where they find a white stone sarcophagus with Latin inscriptions and everything so well tended that it might have been put up just then.

Bowen thought about Fielding. Perhaps it was worth dying in your forties if two hundred years later you were the only contemporary novelist who could be read with unaffected and whole-hearted interest, the only one who never had to be apologised for or excused on the grounds of changing taste. And how enviable to live in the world of his novels, where duty was plain, evil rose out of malevolence and a starving wayfarer could be invited indoors without hesitation and without fear. Did that make it a simplified world? Perhaps, but that hardly mattered beside the existence of a moral seriousness that could be made apparent without the aid of evangelical puffing and blowing. (*Like It,* 185)

But it is precisely the "evangelical puffing and blowing" of Buckmaster that convinces Bowen that he is really Strether. While Bowen tries to read some of the Latin on the tomb, Strether/Buckmaster "open[s] the floodgates of English Men of Letters Series eloquence." He pontificates on the inability of the "utterances of comedy" to move the reader to the extent of the "authentic voice of tragedy. . . . [speaks] of the loneliness and dignity of man." Posterity will not place "this assured master of the picaresque . . . this colossus of the eighteenth century . . . [beside] the colossus of the twentieth."

Like Jim Dixon before him, Garnet Bowen cannot fully suppress his own authentic gesture in the face of this "prancing phoney" who elevates himself above Fielding: "A monosyllable of demented laughter broke from Bowen before he had time to arrange a coughing fit." (*Like It,* 186)

Characteristically in Amis's nonheroically heroic audibles, the noises outside never drown out cerebral activity within. Instead of sticking to the way he would assume everyone, including Bowen, would expect "great writers" to behave— that is, with "humility, reverence and what-have-you"—Strether/Buckmaster has acted the way Bowen knows that people of the "great-writer period" act. This period he designates as "roughly between *Roderick Hudson* and about 1930, death of Lawrence and the next bunch all just starting off—Greene, Waugh, Isherwood, Powell" (*Like It,* 200). And the way people of the great-writer period act is to think they are better than Fielding.

For Bowen, "prancing, posturing phoniness" is the way in which writers of the great-writer period perform. Buckmaster must indeed be Strether. Curiously enough, however, Strether's being locked into the great-writer syndrome does not prevent Bowen from liking him almost from the start; liking him well enough to resolve sentimentally not to do anything to damage his claims. As it turns out, Strether is less important to Bowen as a mystery to be cracked than as a human being to be helped. Bowen, in fact, becomes protective of him. He defends him from an attack by his chauffeur and, although it presents the frightening prospect for him of driving a car in Portugal, Bowen fetches a doctor to treat Strether's injured leg. Before that, however, Bowen does the ultimate in the Amis benevolence repository: he adjusts Strether's false teeth that had been half knocked out in the assault.

Throughout the novel, Garnet Bowen desires virtue before profiteering. His self-disgust and confusion are evident in his reflections on his passport photos: "The lad in the 1936 one . . . had seemed on the point of asking Bowen why he wasn't a pacifist or what he thought of *Aaron's Rod.* The 1956 Bowen . . . had . . . the air of a television panelist. . . . It was odd how the two of them could differ so much and yet look exactly the kind of man he would dislike to meet or be." (*Like It,* 36) He detests having been dispatched to the never-never land known in Amis country as "abroad" as a spy on and potential blackmailer of Strether. His final guide to self-credibility is that his wife could not be a blackmailer's girl—something Bowen had never put to himself before—and that that was the most important thing about his wife.

Richard Voorhees is right when he writes that, although they are not equally unified and formally disciplined, Amis's first three novels constitute a clear enough period. I believe that what truly links them is the presence of moral moments, moments in which the flawed heroes make their problems bearable by trying to be funny about them.

Having already written a good deal about *I Like It Here,* I shall limit these few concluding remarks to the Margaret theme—or, if you will, the Peel amendment—in *Lucky Jim* and the Elizabeth caper in *That Uncertain Feeling.*

What, other than his belief that she is suicidal, keeps Jim, whom Margaret alone calls "James," from giving her the old heave-ho? In the last of their many painful scenes, Jim tells Margaret without bitterness that "the point is I've got to stick to you." "You're throwing her [Christine] away for a scruple," Margaret replies, no doubt in the theatrical way that has been her book-long manner. "That's the action of a fool."

Amis makes it clear that Jim acts not from scruples but as a reflex action.

He felt more than ever before that what he said and did arose not out of any willing on his part, nor even out of boredom, but out of a kind of sense of situation. And where did that sense come from if, as it seemed, he took no share in willing it? With disquiet he found that words were forming in his mind, words which, because he could think of no others, he'd very soon hear himself uttering . . . .: "It isn't a matter of scruples; it's a matter of seeing what you've got to do." (*Lucky Jim*, 191)

Early in *That Uncertain Feeling*, Amis monitors the contemplations of John Lewis, a married assistant librarian in a Welsh town. "That I'm not one of those to whom the reprehensible automatically becomes pleasant is one of my finest beliefs about myself," muses Lewis self-satisfiedly. Still he finds himself liking the very thought of an affair with Elizabeth Gruffyd-Williams, an attractive but venomous member of the "anglicized upper classes" Lewis despises. As he sips a cup of tea from what he barely notices is a too-heavy teapot, he momentarily wishes Elizabeth were clairvoyant just to see the expression on his face. In this instance, unlike a parallel scene in *Lucky Jim* when Jim does his automatic self-parodying ape imitation, it is life that administers the rebuke:

Immediately I brought out a loud gargling cry. I began giving an incredible imitation of a man whose mouth has been invaded by a swarm of small flies or midges and who now wants to expel them. Spitting, choking, hecking, retching, making a noise at the back of my mouth like one saying "Aagh" to a doctor, I stumbled misty-eyed to the washbasin and began ridding myself of the thousands of tea leaves I'd taken in with the draught of tea. (*Uncertain*, 102)

Lewis gags on the tea leaves just as he is considering taking on the double-barreled self-deception of an affair with the hoity-toity and promiscuous Elizabeth who, because of her husband's power in the town, can get Lewis the library promotion which like Jim Dixon's tenure he only thinks he wants. He does commit adultery—once—with Elizabeth, but its chief consequence is to make him penitent. Moreover, he is unwilling to get promoted through influence. To avoid listening to Elizabeth's advice on the phone about how to handle the library board, he reads a story in a science-fiction magazine about a man who has reproduced himself by fission. "[T]here were 512 personages, all identical, considering the situation likely to arise when they became 1,024 in ten minutes' time. They were travelling in a small space ship which by now they filled to the air locks . . ." (*Uncertain*, 168–69).

Richard Voorhees puts well the final disposition of Lewis: "Lewis's brief and clownish frolic with Mrs. Gruffydd-Williams reveals to him that his very nature is disposed to licit love. His fundamental need is a conservative one for a wife and children, not a revolutionary and romantic one for love affairs. His strongest instinct which he had thought to be centrifugal turns out to be centripetal." (*Voorhees,* 45)

I once had a friend who complained that he suffered from what he called "compulsive fidelity". If we extend "fidelity" beyond its domestic connotation and use it to mean keeping faithful to one's self, to one's true nature, it is the theme of these earliest Amis novels. Their heroes detest fraud and cant in themselves. Then, instead of whistling in the dark, they laugh at their own self-entrapments to keep from crying. Finally, when they find they can neither laugh any longer nor find manners to accommodate their self-deceptions, growth begins. But the moral focus has been there all the time, only slightly disguised in the many faces of Lucky Jim.

II.

Dorothy Parker: Nothing Sacred

"During that winter, mourning one pregnancy and trying to achieve another, Dorothy Parker worked on a comedy and did her best to produce amusing dialogue."

This sentence, which appears innocently halfway through Marion Meade's *Dorothy Parker: What Fresh Hell Is This?* (New York: Villard Books of Random House, 1988), the biography of perhaps the most continuously amusing writer in American literature, encapsulates in twenty-five words the sadness at the heart of the jester. Even the title of the comic film she was working on in 1936—*Nothing Sacred*—has the right sound.

For nothing was sacred in her seventy-four years: certainly not in her writings. Her detractors said she wrote "flapper verse." Meade is kinder, noting that, like her friends Robert Benchley and Ring Lardner, she was a "sprinter," not a writer of short takes.

Certainly not her love life. Preferring the company of men, she always chose lovers with whom there could be no second act. She was quoted, after undergoing an abortion, as saying the experience served her right "for having put all her eggs in one bastard."

Certainly not the way she lived her life, a frenzy, controlled by liquor and occasionally mediated by the imagined insult given life by the perfect squelch. Born reluctantly half-Jewish, she felt obliged to invent herself as she went along, effacing Dorothy Rothschild ("We'd never even heard of *those* Rothschilds"), daughter of a garment-industry businessman, for Dorothy Parker of the Algonquin Round Tablers. Both her mother and stepmother were gentiles, and Dorothy referred to herself as a "mongrel," a word doubly rich for her because of a succession of housepets, the only creatures she never turned on or eventually alienated.

An earlier, much less talented Sylvia Plath, except that it was not her father but her mother "who went and died on me," she wrote poems that were redolent of necrophilia. Later, she would make her despised first husband, Edwin Pond Parker, II, the butt of blackly humorous stories. She would regale her fellow Round Tablers, who were all fellows, with the various pickles Eddie Parker blundered into.

Had they heard about so-and-so's funeral? Since she and Eddie arrived early at the mortuary, he decided to pay his respects to the deceased. Kneeling before the coffin, he inadvertently brushed against a knob, gears whirred, a door popped open, and before either of them could react both casket and corpse had disappeared into the flames of the crematorium. They ran out a side door before anyone noticed. It had been a ghastly experience for poor Eddie.

Only in her penchant for black humor was Parker ahead of her time. In all other literary matters, she was a product and victim of Prohibition and the unprohibitive 1920s. If she had been of the next generation she would probably have been a well-paid Hollywood gossip reporter like Sheila Graham, her friend Scott Fitzgerald's last flame. As it was, she supplied Franklin P. Adams's famous column "The Conning Tower" with clever fillips—usually for free.

Adams was a charter member of the Algonquin Round Table, named for the Manhattan hotel where he, Parker, Aleck Woolcott, Heywood Broun, George Kaufman, Marc Connelly, Robert Sherwood, Harold Ross, and Robert Benchley became famous for being famous. The acclaimed fare of the group was great talk but their serious business was drink and slander. No book more dramatically illustrates the desperate camaraderie of the Round Tablers than this one. They leaned on one another for support when they were tippling and toppling in their marriages, their mistresses, their unfulfilled dreams of literary fame.

Baltimorean H. L. Mencken, who—like Edmund Wilson ("who would want to sit around with that crew?")—was an occasional visitor only, called the efficacy of the Algonquin a matter of propinquity: "The distance from the front door to the elevator is only forty feet, an important consideration to a man whose friends all drink too much, and sometimes press the stuff on him."

Between her marriages especially, Dorothy Parker "quickly discovered that the simplicity and lack of responsibility connected with hotel living suited her taste perfectly. The limited space also pleased her. Among institutional furnishings she felt free and organized. The Algonquin was her second home."

But where Parker really lived was behind the meat-cutter's counter where her portions were always generous. She knew everybody and few were left unscathed. Her literary betters were unmercifully savaged. Although she gained from collaboration with playwright Elmer Rice, she labelled him much later as the worst bed partner of her life. She always played up to novelist John O'Hara to his face but called him repulsive behind his back. William Faulkner fled from her early, a vulnerable country boy she saw as in desperate need of her protection.

The one great love of her life was Robert Benchley, but she needed him more as a protective brother than lover. His preference for ingenues and for continuing an unstable marriage wrecked her chances.

She reserved genuine affection for her canines (she once spiked her Dandie Dinmont's food with sleeping pills so they could both sleep) and perhaps for Gerald and Sara Murphy, who seemed to live with style and grace, impressing the communist-leaning Parker even though they were extremely rich. But she knew them only as an eager guest on the Riviera knows a lavish host.

She claimed to have had affairs with everyone who counted and some no-accounts. Of the former, the one with Charles MacArthur, who cowrote *Front Page* and married Helen Hayes, was the most passionate; of the latter, the one with John McClain, who used her to obtain introductions to the literary community, was most devastating.

After her divorce from Eddie Parker, Dorothy married writer-actor Alan Campbell and converted him from a too-pretty young man into a too-frequent boozer. They formed a successful team, wrote for the movies, divorced, and remarried. Campbell's major feat was in maintaining the marriage and remarriage despite the same sort of slander—this time directed at his sexual ambivalence—to which she had submitted her first husband.

Only Ernest Hemingway appears to have scored on her without living to regret it. She played Desdemona to his Othello, being enchanted by his tales of how American writers were living and working in Paris. Hemingway characteristically pilloried her at a party by reciting an antisemitic poem she never knew about in her lifetime. It was published only after both were dead.

Recent reviews of this biography charge Meade with underestimating

Parker's pain and sense of loss. The abortion, the several miscarriages (one well into her forties), and botched suicides may indeed seem to be chronicled almost matter-of-factly. One reviewer even suggests that Meade actually disliked her subject.

I believe Marion Meade has followed Dorothy Parker's own lead and deliberately wisecracked her way through the catalog of horrors as a means of preventing the narrative from crumbling away in abjection. The biographer turns to a kind of nonjubilant laughter to keep from crying on the page.

Perhaps the best balance would be to read this lively and unlovely book and then go back to its subject's classic short story, "Big Blonde." Hazel Morse ("a large, fair woman of the type that incites some men when they use the word 'blonde' to click their tongues and wag their heads roguishly") is Dorothy Parker, who was not a blonde but whose fictional portrayal forever vindicates the lives of the created and creator.

III.

The Custodianship of Mary Hemingway

I have already made the briefest of mentions of Ernest Hemingway's suicide on the morning of July 2, 1961. I had resigned from the *Utica Observer-Dispatch* the previous week. My fortieth birthday beckoned on the fifth of July. Being the frustrated columnist and would-be novelist that I was, it was inevitable that I made a spiritual connection. Hadn't Hemingway's creative side come to the fore only after he had shaken the dust of the *Toronto Star?*

Ernest Hemingway was the most admired writer in the world among the newspaper people I had known throughout the 1950s. Everyone knows that if you scratch a newspaper reporter you find an aspiring novelist. One of them never stopped talking about how he, like Hemingway, was doing newspapers only until he could finish the novel in progress. Although he had read all of Hemingway's books, he never took to heart something Papa once said in conversation. What you talk about you don't write.

To this day I have never, except to my wife, talked about wanting to be a fiction writer. I simply didn't have the stomach—was much too vulnerable— for that. Still, under the surface, I was no different from my colleague. Hemingway was the model. It did not hurt either that his deceptively simple style did not appear all that difficult to imitate.

But that illusion had long since been dispelled. I knew I could never write like Hemingway. Jo and Philip, who was five, were still asleep the Sunday morning of Ernest Hemingway's death. It would be several hours before the suicide would be confirmed. I began typing within a few minutes, the first time I can recall doing that (although I did set up my portable at an open-air café in Nice to make notes on everything I remembered within an hour of our departure from Maugham's villa two years before). Here is what I wrote in one take and without revision (also a "first") that morning:

It was not always easy with Ernest Hemingway to separate the artist and the legend. The latter sold books for the former but, in the end, damaged him irreparably.

So the good part about Hemingway's dying is that there will be no more *New Yorker* profiles by women journalists who interviewed Papa with the famous actress he called the Kraut; interviews where they took down every ill-considered word in shorthand so they could tell their editors how many drinks Papa consumed and exactly what profanity he used.

The good part is that there will be no more *Time* magazine inventories about Hemingway's 237 World War I shrapnel scars, the shot-off kneecap, the two plane crashes in Africa and the ruptured kidney, cracked skull and compressed vertebrae.

There will be no more warmed-over *Life* magazine exclusives on Don Ernesto and the bull fights that always purported to be his greatest masterpiece since *The Old Man and the Sea,* that previous *Life* exclusive.

There will be no more news pictures of the great white hunter on safari with the beard and the cap and the fallen rhino and the latest wife.

The good part about Ernest Hemingway's dying is that the legend, lacking fuel, may start to die a little too.

The bad part about his dying is that the pure line in American prose literature that started with Melville and continued with Mark Twain and took on new dimensions with Hemingway is now either broken by forfeit or, worse, left to dangle and be snapped up by the "great-god-I" writers who scribble defiantly from the psychiatrist's couch or decadently from a plantation hammock.

The bad part is that there will be no more stories like "The Killers" and "Fifty Grand" where in a few pages set between quotation marks he gave us more of the feel of violence than lesser writers were able to do in hundreds of pages of lavish narrative.

There will be no more novels like *The Sun Also Rises, A Farewell to Arms* and *For Whom the Bell Tolls*—titles whose mere mention brings saliva to the mouth.

There will be no more books from a man who never thumbed a dictionary or Thesaurus but wrote every word from the pit of his stomach.

The bad part about Ernest Hemingway's dying is that the ore is gone and the alloys remain.

Pretty overheated, I admit. Still, after a Ph.D. and thirty years of teaching literature, I still believe that about Hemingway. One sentence proved prophetic: ". . . the legend, lacking fuel, may start to die. . . ." It has. But I'm getting ahead.

In 1976, Ernest Hemingway's widow and fourth wife, Mary Welch Hemingway, came to College Station to give a lecture and autograph copies of her autobiography, *How It Was,* which had just come out from Knopf. She was the guest of David and Diane Stewart. Dave, chair of English at Texas A&M and my boss, had known Mary Hemingway as a near neighbor in Montana. I wrote to her. Might a couple of former reporters get together for a chat?

Like the boy I become again every time I read or hear anything by or about Hemingway, I brought along to her suite the fat file of clippings, reviews, and pictures I've been saving in an unscholarly way since he won the Nobel Prize in 1954. What I was really trying to do was impress her that I was not just another academic feeding at the trough (which, of course, I was).

To break the ice, I pulled from the file some color pictures from her own magazine piece ("Hemingway: A Personal Story by the Great Writer's Wife, Mary Hemingway," *Look,* September 12, 1961). The spread contained five pictures, all handsome and no doubt posed, especially a two-page shot of Ernest congratulating Mary on bringing down a kudu on safari in Kenya, 1953–54. The caption describes the shot as "lucky" and quotes from Mary's diary: "The kudu was too young and too handsome and too full of life to die by a lucky shot from a stranger in his country." As the great white hunter and wife look adoringly at each other, a native appears to be examining the horns. The kudu appears to be enjoying all the attention until you notice blood flowing from the mouth. With the humans in the familiar Hemingway tableau, not a strand of hair is out of place.

"Why," I began, "of all the deaths of famous writers over the last twenty years does the death of Hemingway always seem to have happened yester-day?" I had prepared that question, but it was not meant to be rhetorical. Like most of Papa's favorite women—Dietrich, Bergman, two of the three previous wives—Mary is fair (she would say later, in her lecture, that Hemingway would have been ecstatic in a world of dandelion). Her blue-gray eyes were playful; they fix on you unwaveringly. When she did not answer my question, merely smiling, I went on: "Had you read his novels and stories before you met him?" She had. "What is your favorite?" "Does a grand-mother say which child? . . ." Mary did not finish the sentence, her voice trailing off.

I was getting the feeling that I ought to say something about *her* book. It has 537 pages, and I still had 150 to go. It is her story mainly, not Heming-way's, and if the book is not as pleasurable as other books about him, it may be because she lets the frame do the job of the picture. "I am impressed by the restraint with which you wrote the book," I heard myself saying. "Were you aware of holding back, perhaps, to protect the privacy of the dead?" I

The Hemingways—Ernest and Mary Welch—about to debark from the *Ile de France* for a two-day stopover in New York enroute to Cuba in early 1957, a "son of a bitch of a year" for the depressed writer. *Courtesy Associated Press/Worldwide Photo.*

winced inwardly at that phrase, but she took it in stride. "No, I was not aware of holding back." There have been so many false accounts (later, in the question period after her talk, she would come down hard on A. E. Hotchner's *Papa Hemingway* because of the impression it left that he and Ernest were close). "My goal was to set the record straight. Accurate reporting is what I did best, and it's what I have tried to do in this book."

I quoted from page 117: "I had never before been catapulted into the role of whipping boy, a part I would play, unexpectedly, from time to time for years. I never learned to play it as gracefully and dispassionately as I should have liked." Would she care to elaborate?

"We had lots of fights. They were generally quick-fuse, over quickly. There were always others around; one stayed seven years. At one stretch, in Cuba, there was at least a third for lunch for fifty-four consecutive days. Something would get Ernest going, and there would be nobody that night or next morning to take the rap. So he'd light into me." I remarked that the book gave an impression that one or the other was always getting maimed. "It's true. Ernest never really recovered from the brain concussion he suffered in the Africa crash. To get out of the burning plane, he had to force his head through the cabin. That was in 1954, and he was never the same. I married him in 1946. I was thirty-seven and had never so much as broken a bone. I must have broken just about everything at least once in our sixteen years."

We talked about the reported instances of cruelty—I didn't use that word—to anyone who ever helped him. "I can't speak, of course, for the years before I knew him, but it was like this: he enjoyed shattering poses. Once John O'Hara showed Ernest a walking stick which he said was unbreakable. All part of a pose, and Ernest knew it. He took O'Hara's stick and broke it over his own head." She acted out the gesture. I mentioned F. Scott Fitzgerald and the picture Hemingway gives in *A Moveable Feast* of a man (Fitzgerald) whose masculinity is under siege. "Ernest apparently couldn't take the combination of Scott and Zelda—they were so competitive. In those days he had a biting wit, and Scott was an easy target. By the way, have you read Morley Callaghan's *That Summer in Paris?* It was published just after Ernest's death—about all those people in 1929."

Through an old friend, the poet Earle Birney, I had had lunch with Callaghan in Toronto two years before, in 1974, when Callaghan was seventy. On that occasion we talked not about Hemingway but about Edmund Wilson (see my memoir, *Edmund Wilson: Our Neighbor from Talcottville* [Syracuse University Press, 1980]).

It was curious that our associative memories should join forces. Mary Hemingway began talking about Wilson and perhaps the only time she ever, in print at least, answered slurs on her late husband's memory:

"In his *New Yorker* review of *That Summer in Paris*—it was sixty-one or sixty-two, I think [a check revealed it was early 1963]—Wilson commended Callaghan for the gift of moral objectivity which enabled him to portray unpleasant traits in Hemingway and Fitzgerald without indulging in malice. It's too bad the same could not be said of Mr. Wilson." She proceeded to display a resentment against Wilson, little diminished after fourteen years, for describing Hemingway as an "exhibitionist," a jokester whose jokes were sneers, a ribber who always lapsed into the insulter, a humorist (although never about himself), an "insufferable" man, altogether an "improbable human being." The *New Yorker* published her letter, and Wilson never responded.

If Edmund Wilson did not care for Hemingway the man, he cherished, from start to finish, the artist. His review of *In Our Time* in the twenties was the first major praise Hemingway ever received, and his review of the post-humous *Islands in the Stream,* shortly before his own death, found more to praise than had any other critic. Wilson records in *Upstate,* the last of his books published during his lifetime, that "Hemingway's death has very much upset me. Absurd and insufferable though he often was, he was one of the foundation stones of my generation, and to have him commit suicide is to have a prop knocked out." And it was, rather. Despite early signs to the contrary—such as the letter at nineteen to his father from Milan in 1918 when he was recovering from his war wounds ("And how much better to die in all the happy period of undisillusioned youth, to go out in a blaze of light, than to have your body worn out and old and illusions shattered")—the so-called code hero of his best books was always a good man who became better the worse things became.

My impression was building, as the interview went on well beyond the allotted half-hour, that the wife of Ernest Hemingway, the girl from Bemidji, Minnesota, had had, with Frederic Henry of *A Farewell to Arms,* to grow "strong in the weak places." Her answer to the last question from the audience later that day may have caught the essence of the relationship. Had Earnest ever commented on her writing? "*My* writing?" she replied, her deep, melodious voice by then on the verge of cracking. "I was a hausfrau, a hostess, a fishing-hunting partner, a cook and bottle-washer, a nurse. A few times, when I'd write something, Ernest would boast to anyone who'd listen: 'Look what our Mary has done. Isn't it wonderful!'"

As I gathered together my notes and the Hemingway file, the interview at an end, I looked again at the picture of Ernest and Mary on safari, standing over the bleeding body of the kudu, "too young and too handsome and too full of life to die by a lucky shot from a stranger in his country." How like that was to the life and death of Hemingway: a life generated by the exuberance of youth, the contesting for championship of games and books; a death hurried by a lucky shot when jouster had become old for games or craft, a stranger in his country.

IV.

Edith Wharton's Age of Innocence— and Mine

Recently, at a reunion in my adopted hometown of Utica, New York, Jo and I dined with a small group of survivors from the 1950s when I first taught at Utica College. We were of the generation whose professional lives started after the Second World War. Four in our group were widows of onetime colleagues, a fifth had just lost his wife. The lively talk turned to the prevalance of divorce among younger couples in the wake of the sixties. "It's all so easy now," someone said. Another quoted the usually quoted statistic for the nineties: one of every two marriages ends in divorce. We were all smug in our shared monogamy. Although listening keenly, I had not spoken. When I found an opening, I plunged in:

"We are all alike. We got married, stayed married, brought up our kids in two-parent homes. I won't ask if any of us ever contemplated divorce. Some of your kids not only considered divorce but have gone through it. But I, alone, can speak as a *child of divorce* . . ."

I felt self-conscious using that phrase. The truth is that my youth as a child of divorce contained so many qualifications that I rarely talk about it even to my wife. And I acted no differently now. It had been silly to raise the issue; I muttered something about the bark of divorce once having been worse than its bite. The idea of divorce was too awful for adults in the thirties even to contemplate. Shaming. So shaming that if it couldn't be avoided it ought to be kept as quiet as possible. I rang off with a vague reference to how much I still wished my folks had levelled with me about what, with some of the finality of death but none of its conclusiveness, had remained their dirty little secret.

My mother told my sister and me that our father had died in the 'flu epidemic that swept cities like our native Philadelphia at the end of the second decade of this century. By 1921, when I was born, the scourge had abated. My sister and I were too young to make anything of the disparity between these dates. I grew up in a household of Hauer women: a working mother, loving grandmother, and stunning blonde sister—a year younger, also named Jo. Despite the absence of a father, ours was a patriarchy ruled by my grandfather who had his architect's business upstate. He came by his patriarchy naturally—big brother among four younger sisters. Grandpa was used to being obeyed. When he wasn't, he was not above resorting to corporal punishment. I usually escaped his justified wrath by crawling beneath the grand piano. Grandpa was *in loco parentis,* but we never hit it off.

In "Abiding Gods," I alluded to the loneliness I felt among my mother's people, respected and caretaking though they were. My puberty years included the Great Depression. Mother devoted her life to trying to give my sister and me all the signifiers of WASPness the name Costa belied, and she largely succeeded. We were barely aware of her struggle. Yet I wallowed in self-pity. In the houses of my neighborhood—even in that of Bill W. whom we nicknamed "bankruptcy" without knowing what the word meant—there were men who took their sons to baseball games or pitched quoits on summer evenings. Nothing could take the place of what all my classmates had by birthright.

I was sixteen years old when I learned we had had a father all along. He had not died of the flu, but he had flown. It all came out at once. My sister and I happened upon old letters stored in the attic—letters from our father to our mother that postdated by years the time of his purported death. We read about his insolvency, his inability to contribute to our support. Mother made an apparent clean breast of it. Rather than have to tell us our father had bolted without a trace when we were three and two years old, respectively, why not just consign Leonard A. Costa to the grave where, so far as we three were concerned, he would always be anyway?

Later in that very year of discovery—1936—our father materialized. Mother spruced up the house and us two teenagers for his visit to the wife and children he had not seen for thirteen years. He had been living not on the other coast, in California, as mother said she had been led to believe, but in the same state as we—in Pittsburgh. It would be hard to say who of us was the most overwhelmed. He was enchanted from the start by what a beauty his infant daughter had become at fourteen. He and I talked baseball. I had caught the fever two years earlier when my Sunday school teacher took the class to see the Babe Ruth–Lou Gehrig Yankees play the Athletics. The game has been a passion of mine for sixty years. My father, a man who could sell anything, convinced me that he had been quite a pitcher in the amateurs. Now, at forty, he knew he would never achieve his ambition to pitch in the big leagues. Sister Jo found him less handsome than the early photo we had dug up. In the thirties, facial hair connoted villainy, and our father wore a moustache. Recovery of the father whose existence had been denied me lasted less than an hour. By that time I knew the real reason for my father's visit. He had fallen in love with a woman in Pittsburgh and wished to start a second family. For that he needed a divorce.

I did not see my father again for a decade. He was, however, a charming letter-writer. My habit of correspondence started when he began writing to me during the war years. He remembered my love of baseball and persuaded the then manager of the Pittsburgh Pirates, Hall-of-Famer Frankie Frisch, to write to me while I was an infantryman in Germany the final weeks of WW II. He visited us in Texas the last year of his life. We saw a game at the Astrodome. With the members of his second family, I was at his bedside when he died.

I wish things had been different in those early years. My life would have been much fuller for knowing I had a living father. Yet attempts to uphold at any cost the sanctity of marriage must have been taken as much for granted then as divorce is now. It is an ideal whose time has thankfully passed.

When Isabel Archer returns to the perfidious Gilbert Osmond in Henry James's *Portrait of a Lady* (1881), it is largely out of an ideal of self-sacrifice. That ideal, espoused by an even earlier New England heroine named Hester, may have begun to fray with Penelope Lapham in William Dean Howells's *The Rise of Silas Lapham* (1885). Penelope refuses to give up her requited love for Corey in favor of her sister, Irene, who happened to meet Corey first. The Laphams' minister praises Penelope for putting into practice an "economy of pain." He demands that Silas's rigidly conventional wife Persis explain why it is better for three to suffer than one. "We are all weakened by a false ideal of self-sacrifice," this wise cleric sums up.

It is easy to overlook Howells's early plea not to repress passion for mere social forms; the novel, after all, belongs to Silas Lapham and his moral rise in the crucible of his economic fall. It remained for Edith Wharton, writing in 1920, the year of Howells's death, to dramatize what novelist Francine Prose calls "the impossibility of following one's heart beyond the brick-wall barriers of social custom and class." Recalling the New York City of the 1870s, Wharton deals in *The Age of Innocence* with a version of the same problem my mother and her people surely faced in the 1920s—the conflict between duty and freedom.

My turning to Wharton and *The Age of Innocence,* a novel I had somehow missed, was not happenstance. Now that I am retired, I had no excuse not to read the book before seeing the Martin Scorcese film version here, as I write, in early autumn, 1993. How much easier to do the opposite and somehow never get around to reading the book. Slow reader though I am, I read it in four sittings. I found myself so fascinated that I am fearful of seeing the movie.

The Age of Innocence (Random House/Modern Library, 1948; quotations are from this edition, noted by page numbers) is the story of a love triangle whose drama rests not in how the three interact but in the charades to which they resort to suppress any interaction that would involve passion. Wharton, influenced by the final novels of her late friend Henry James, focuses all the action through the discriminating intelligence of Newland Archer, a rich, well-born young lawyer. His betrothed is May Welland whose family, as we now often hear, "networks" widely. The Welland circuitry contains no shorts and her engagement and marriage to Archer will complete a distinguished connection. The problem is that to be happy Newland would require a "miracle of fire and ice to be created"—if not a Beatrice to his Benedick, at least a partner with some of the worldly wisdom of "the married lady whose charms had held his fancy for two mildly agitated years." Instead he realizes, even before the decision favoring a short engagement is exhaustively rendered, that May's "training" rules out, by definition, any sort of freedom of judgment or any other "freedom," a word beyond May's ken.

On their European honeymoon, Newland fully confronts his dilemma of having married a woman on whom everything is lost. Yet he will neither try to reverse the arrangement nor change its terms:

It was less trouble to conform with tradition and treat May exactly as all his friends treated their wives than to try to put into practice the theories with which his untrammelled bachelorhood had dallied. There was no use in trying to emancipate a wife who had not the dimmest notion that she was not free. . . . Whatever happened, he knew, she would always be loyal, gallant and unresentful. (156)

It is the indissolubility of marriage that cannot be questioned. The testing of the knot that binds is provided by the worldly Ellen Olenska, May's first cousin, who has recently returned to New York as a countess after leaving her Polish husband. We learn little about the count beyond his preferences for fine china and other women. Ellen rarely emerges as more than a shadowy presence. Far from resenting the impalpability of her mystery, as I did that of the misty heroine of John Fowles's *French Lieutenant's Woman,* also a book of the 1870s, I was carried along by Archer's deep feeling for her, fueled as it was by May's inadequacy and Ellen's unattainability. Having lived so long abroad, and having abandoned her husband, Ellen is under a cloud, initially regarded as a woman who has done the unspeakable. She is welcomed back, reluctantly, only after Newland and May's families see to it that she is invited for dinners at the right houses. Ellen, who for the social record has said that all she wishes is to be again among her own people, finds, as the saying goes, that she can't go home again, at least not as a married woman without mate. She is surprised when the members of her family rise up to denounce her plans to divorce. Only Archer demurs from the received social gospel. "Our legislation favors divorce, but our customs don't" (91), he concludes in perhaps the novel's wisest commentary. Appearance is all. People can do whatever they like as long as they don't allow it to become public knowledge.

(It was convenient that my maternal grandparents moved from Philadelphia to the suburbs after my father abandoned us. The elders could take the three of us in with them. No one need know about our previous life. My father was a foundling. His Italian-born parents died within months of landing on Ellis Island in 1896. There would be no one on his side to intercede. Our relatives were all pledged to keep the secret. Widowhood had the advantage of violating no rules. Although it was never discussed, why wouldn't my improvident father not be content to remain out of the picture? *Let the dead past bury its dead.*)

For Newland Archer, Ellen's past is part of her fascination. Chosen by the family to convince Ellen she should not divorce the count, Archer succeeds, only to fall deeply in love with her. The "affair" that follows is hardly that by contemporary terms: a few covert meetings in which hands are held and kisses stolen. Ellen is the realistic one. When he suggests she devise a plan "for us," she reminds him of the societal frame into which no picture involving them can ever fit:

"For *us*? But there's no *us* in that sense! We're near each other only if we stay far from each other. Then we can be ourselves. Otherwise we're only Newland Archer, the husband of Ellen Olenska's cousin, and Ellen Olenska, the cousin of Newland Archer's wife, trying to be happy behind the backs of the people who trust them." (231)

She sees paradox at the heart of their relationship ("I can't love you unless I give you up"). The conjugal code conquers. She could not love him if he dishonors it.

Once the system has closed escape routes—once Newland marries May and she announces her pregnancy and once Ellen returns to Europe, although not to her husband—Wharton wisely telescopes the action. For her final chapter, Wharton has allowed twenty-six years to pass. Archer is fifty-seven, widowed two years before ("May had suddenly died—carried off by the infectious pneumonia through which she had nursed their youngest child"), and in Paris with his soon-to-be-married son Dallas. Looking out of his hotel window, Newland muses over his son's choice of Fanny Beauford, the orphaned daughter of notorious parents.

[She] had appeared in New York at eighteen, after the death of her parents, had won its heart much as Madame Olenska had won it thirty years earlier; only instead of being distrustful and afraid of her, society took her joyfully for granted. (279)

He cannot help the bitterness that creeps into his thoughts. Young people like his son take it for granted that they're going to get whatever they want—how different from a generation ago when "we almost always took it for granted that we wouldn't." Later, feeling "shy, old-fashioned . . . a mere grey speck of a man compared with the ruthless magnificent fellow he had dreamed of being," he is joined by his son who announces that the Countess Olenska expects them that very afternoon at her apartment. Then he stuns his father:

"Wasn't she—once—your Fanny . . . the woman you'd have chucked everything for: only you didn't . . ." (282).

Dallas has learned about the Olenska affair from his mother on her deathbed: "She said she knew we were safe with you, and always would be, because once, when she asked you to, you'd given up the thing you most wanted." Father and son walk across Paris until they approach Ellen's apartment. Archer asks his son to go up on the elevator; he needs the exercise and will follow on foot. But he rules out reunion: "It's more real to me here than if I went up" (287).

Edith Wharton's triumph is the skill with which she develops the unsaid as Newland Archer's uncompromising familiar. By the time we have left him walking back alone to his hotel, no assignation at fifty-seven with the woman he once loved to mar his perfect correspondence with the age of innocence, we understand the unstated premise of Archer's class. No dalliance would be allowed to sway him from his appointed fate. From the vantage of the age of licence—the start of the twenties—Wharton looked back on the tired-out world of her youth. With hindsight, she realized not only that its strictures were dying but that with round-the-clock vigilance, helped by the tacit consent of reluctant strayers, sacrifices were the order of the day.

(I shall always believe my parents were still in love when they decided to split up. My mother never said a word about that nor ever bad-talked my father for a moment. Everyone else did. "Grandpa thought our father would never be able to support us. All he saw ahead were more kids and poverty for us all. He had to save Mom from a fate like that." This was the way my sister summed up the decision to sacrifice a marriage. It was a version of Howells's theory of the economy of pain with which I began.)

PART FOUR

The Consul and
Other Notations from
Underground

I.

How I "Discovered" *Under the Volcano*

There were, of course, the professionals who will lay claim to the distinction. John Woodburn wrote a stunning review in the *Saturday Review of Literature* (February 23, 1947). These were the latter days of that publication before it dropped *of literature* from its name; while it was still concerned for literature rather than forced into the care and feeding of kitsch. Near the close of that review, long portions of which I committed to memory, Woodburn wrote: "I have never before used the word in a review, and I am aware of the responsibility upon me in using it, but I am of the opinion, carefully considered, that *Under the Volcano* is a work of genius."

Albert Erskine, who died recently (I am writing in February, 1993, the forty-sixth anniversary of my "discovery"), was Malcolm Lowry's editor at Reynal & Hitchcock, the original publisher of *Under the Volcano*. Erskine could make a valid case for having discovered the book. After all, he accepted it.

Conrad Aiken, who was Lowry's mentor and influence, might have put in his claim when, during a visit to the Lowrys in Cuernavaca, Mexico, he read the first version of the novel that would not be published for eleven more years.

Margerie Bonner Lowry, a former actress and herself a writer of detective novels, lived through the *Volcano's* decade-long gestation as Lowry's second wife. Without her loving care and protection, the "contemporary classic" (Alfred Kazin's tribute in 1969) could never have been completed.

Finally, there was at least one college professor, Leonard Brown of Syracuse University, who was telling his students about a new novel he had read in page proofs that he thought was the greatest work of fiction in English since *Ulysses*. Leonard Brown was a legendary and, by his own choice, an un-Ph.D.-ed teacher whose students had included Shirley Jackson and Stanley Edgar Hyman.

These people all had a fervent but nonetheless vested interest in *Under the Volcano*. But in the sense that I, a police reporter for the Syracuse *Post-Standard*, had on the bases of John Woodburn's *SRL* review and the passed-down praise of Leonard Brown, gone out and bought the book, read it, and immediately set about reading it again, I discovered that book.

For it was a *reader's* discovery and, although no special credit is due me, I don't believe it is possible to discover a new book the way one could fifty years ago.

To do so requires freedom from the New York-based media gristmill which merchandises even bad books into best-sellerdom months before publication. (One remembers the case of Peter Benchley's *Jaws*.)

To do so requires ignorance of an author's previous books and of his/her name itself. In North America, at least, Malcolm Lowry and *Under the Volcano* met all the terms. His only previous book, *Ultramarine*, had been published fourteen years before and only in his native England. It had long since been remaindered.

The name could only have been known to me if I had read more regularly than I did a magazine called *Story*, owned and edited by Whit Burnett. *Story* published two Lowry stories in the early 1930s, his only appearances in print in America before *Under the Volcano*.

It is still possible to recall what in the book caught me up from the first word, sped me through it in a single sitting, and prompted me for the only time in my life to begin a book again immediately. The opening chapter, considered in terms of conventional fiction all wrong—an epilogue in the place of a prologue; an opening in which the fate of the two main characters is revealed; a chapter which is itself a series of intricate flashbacks and where Mexican local color, as an unsympathetic reader put it, is "heaped on in shovelfuls"—struck me as *right*.

If the opening chapter denies the suspense of impending catastrophe, Lowry provides something equally dramatic and more in keeping with the mood of the book: a sense of dread at what has already occurred, a thing so shattering that it has left the survivers no peace during the intervening year.

In those first readings it never occurred to me to ask such interlocking questions as why Goeffrey Firmin, an alcoholic ex-British consul in *Quauhnahuac* (Indian name for Cuernavaca), drinks, or why, given the kind of desperate love for his estranged wife Yvonne that an unsent letter reveals (in itself a love-sonnet sequence in prose), the Consul rejects her throughout the long day of Yvonne's return. After chapter one—forty-two pages, a kind of overture—the rest of the book—eleven chapters, 332 pages—covers just twelve hours.

The novel requires the reader to follow, always from the inside, the mind wanderings of four characters whose futures have passed. A pall of *former* -ness hangs over this book. A *former* British consul, whose *former* film-actress wife is the *former* lover of both the *former* consul's half-brother, Hugh, a *former* would-be fighter for the Republic in the Spanish Civil War, and a French *former* film director named Jacques Laruelle. It is as if Lowry has set out to prove that none of us can overcome our history.

Readers who believe that they can—and should—determine their own fates in life-affirming ways may find the Consul an unfathomable antihero. Geoffrey Firmin, who turns up in fiction directly between Hemingway's Jake Barnes and Heller's Bob Slocum, is the supreme practitioner since World War II of self-knowledge that is cut off from the ability to act. Reading *Volcano* at a time when, although I had survived it, the war had shattered my confidence, I warmed to the Consul who hovered between the "either" and the "or". The Consul knows what he must do for redemption, but never really doubts that even the letters of his name should be transposed—Firmin is *infirm*. With the Underground Man, he understands the most advantageous advantage is to be able to assert his own identity. The Consul's last remembered words to Yvonne, whom he loves, and Hugh, the half-brother who has cuckolded him with Yvonne, are about his verdict for death over life.

After the opening chapter, which takes place on the Mexican Day of the Dead (All Souls' Day), 1939, the action proper begins in chapter two, when Yvonne returns to Mexico from the States to attempt a reconciliation. Arriving by taxi outside a cantina, she sees the man she has divorced but still loves making a supreme effort "to build himself to his feet." The reunion scene—a drunkard's tableau—never changes. Malcolm Lowry's major triumph lies in making forceful the attempts of the other principals to save the Consul while also assuring, with the inevitability of Greek tragedy, the Consul's rejection of those attempts.

For the book to "work," Lowry must convince us that the Consul is much more than a theatrical drunk flinging himself at destruction (as John Huston wrongheadedly directed Albert Finney to be in the disappointing 1984 film). The character must rise from the page as a tragic, real, rounded man of mind and emotion etched from the inside.

When *Under the Volcano* appeared, the world was still digging out of the ruins of the Second War. The malaise of alienation that was to carry the name *existentialism* was not yet a large enough subject, except in France, where *Volcano* was considered a classic from the start, for other than melo-dramatic treatment in the "entertainments" of Graham Greene or the tough crime stories of Dashiell Hammett or Raymond Chandler.

After a few weeks of middlingly brisk sales (I found lots of people in those days talking about the book but few who had read it), the book slipped quickly out of bestsellerdom, giving way to *Forever Amber.* Lowry, in the decade of life left to him after the book's publication, often expressed the feeling that Charles Jackson's *Lost Weekend,* published two years earlier, had spoiled the psychological moment for his own. But could the mass of readers who had made a bestseller of an alcoholic's binge on Third Avenue have done much with a drunken, disgraced British ex-consul staggering through the streets of a seedy Mexican town quoting Dante and Marlowe? When Malcolm Lowry died an alcoholic's death in a tiny village in Sussex, En-gland, in 1957, there was no edition of his book in print. As one who like the original reviewer became "this book's fool, mastered (possibly) by some trickery and not left alone," I have watched, even participated in, its takeover as an academic industry. It has not been as breathtaking as I would have assumed in 1947. My persistent, even if unmerited, proprietary rights have long since been taken over. What remains, incommunicable to my students or anyone else, is the likelihood that something that happened a half-century ago does not happen today: a life-changing book.

Pietà, Pelado, and "The Ratification of Death": The Ten-Year Evolvement of Malcolm Lowry's *Volcano*

Malcolm Lowry was a one-book writer. To say this is not to undersell his achievement, which was considerable, but to clear away some of the pettifoggery which in the thirty-five years since his death has delivered him over to the cultists or the exegetes. Neither path leads to an understanding of Lowry's extraordinary ten-year crucible which may have produced— Alfred Kazin expressed the opinion—the last masterpiece.[1] The cultists would have one believe that the life and works of writers like Lowry—the whole labyrinth of the addict—are evidence that only excess generates art. One of Lowry's misadventurous disciples, the late Conrad Knickerbocker, went so far as to declare that in his opinion the controlled artist provided no clues to the mysteries of the creative imagination; that only the demonic had interest for him.[2] Whatever academic claim to Lowry remains has been staked out by those whom Saul Bellow called the "deep readers of the world."[3] Their industry was climaxed by Perle Epstein's line-by-line gloss of *Under the Volcano* as a cabbalistic treasure-trove.[4]

Lowry was indeed an alcoholic and a symbolist. Those who knew him best describe a pathologically shy man in whom drink evoked a "Shakespearean jester" (Conrad Aiken's words) who manufactured a tragic myth while laughing at it all.[5] As to Lowry's fervor for symbols, one has to face up to the part of him that lived a life of its own: the part that was spiritual archivist, forever receiving and storing up correspondences out of thin air. His lifelong sense of being haunted, of being a human Leyden jar, of living perpetually in what he once termed in the punning manner he learned from Aiken, "introverted comas," produced all those Lowryan personae: guilt-ridden John Bunyans who live in hell but aspire to heaven; above all, the Consul (Geoffrey Firmin), the single creation for which Lowry will be remembered and perhaps literature's first character to reflect fully the noblesse oblige of the addict, the kind of pride that must be asserted to seek in drink a means of transcending the agony of consciousness.

But to understand how Lowry's novel evolved in a decade's constant and frustrating revisions from one addict's case history into what Philip Toynbee, coming on the book in 1962 after missing it for fifteen years, calls "one of the great English novels of this century,"[6] it is necessary to leave alchemy and addiction, the cabbala and black and white magicians, aside. It is necessary to forget Lowry's obsession that he was himself being written. For a decade during which the man knew all the miseries of Job, the artist prospered. Malcolm Lowry struggled with his book, but the struggle was as directive as a sculptor's and as strategic as a film-cutter's.

2

Even a cursory reading of an epic work, whether of a poem like *Paradise Lost* or of a prose work like *Ulysses*, is likely to make the reader think of the agonizing way huge masses of rock were hauled into place in the Age of the Pyramids. The architects of vast buildings and of epic literary works are alike in depending in considerable measure for their success on simple clarity in the initial massing and division of material. Arthur Barker is especially impressed, in the case of Milton and *Paradise Lost,* with the necessity of hewing out massive blocks of poetical material to gain sculptural control. The effect of balance, always characteristic of any work of art, frequently with Milton "arrives at a mathematical plainness almost suggestive of the counting of lines. We need not suppose that his muse worked quite so mechanically or laid so lowly a burden on herself; but Milton's mind operated at ease only when he perceived in or imposed on his material a precise mathematical division of some sort."[7] Professor Barker develops with complexity a theory about the direction of the "shifting" structural pattern in *Paradise Lost* as evidenced by Milton's redivision of the epic from ten to twelve books in 1674.

I should like in this essay to use Professor Barker's "block" concept as a point of departure. I propose to demonstrate that Malcolm Lowry also decided, as his view of his material deepened, upon a blocking-out technique, or something like it, as a way of discovering, exploring, developing his themes, of conveying their meaning, and, finally, of evaluating them. My aim is to show, largely by reference to Lowry's successive drafts and expositions, that he also decided upon certain blocks—certain alignments of theme and motif—to serve in a contrapuntal relationship. What Joseph Frank said of Joyce ("The reader is forced to read *Ulysses* in exactly the same manner as he reads poetry—continually fitting fragments together and keeping allusions in mind until, by reflexive reference, he can link them to their complement")[8] can be said of the author of *Under the Volcano.* Lowry speaks of his first and last chapters as the easterly and westerly towers of a "churrigueresque Mexican cathedral" for "the doleful bells of one tower echo the doleful bells of the other, just as the hopeless letters of Yvonne the Consul finally finds in the last chapter answer the hopeless letter of the Consul M. Laruelle reads precisely a year later in Chapter I."[9] This is the mosaic. A major theme, dramatized by one of Lowry's symbolic motifs, invariably recurs, usually several times, and is nearly always, as Lowry put it, "repeated with interest" in the final accounting. The toll on the reader who relies on a linear playing out of cause and effect is heavy. Yet Lowry's progress in composition is an evolvement from a profligacy to a clarity of counterpoint; his ability, after excruciating trial and error, is to make recurrences serve dually to crystallize theme while accelerating narrative.

Conrad Aiken spoke out after a long silence in an admirable effort to set the record straight; specifically, to prove that Lowry's Mexican phase—the demonic phase—was seminal in the evolvement of the book. He recalls during a memorable reunion in 1937 in Cuernavaca (Quauhnahuac of the novel) when, with Lowry virtually *in extremis,* his drinking uncontrolled, his marriage cracking, the younger man showed him "the whole of *Under the Volcano.* The first draft, but complete, and with a different ending: the horse theme had not then been developed. . . . In short, that book was going to be rewritten for the next nine years."[10] That is the point. Lowry lived his catalytic nightmares in Mexico, 1936–38, where he roughed out the essential Consular report on hell. But he managed, *soberly,* the *writing* of the great book between 1939 and 1945 in the "northern paradise," in Canada. It was only there that fictive "truth" evolved—it would never quite do so for Lowry again—and it is that progress, traced through the development of his "horse theme" and the evolving tableau of *pietà* and *pelado,* that I wish to chart.

3

One day about nine years ago, it was the end of 1936 . . . I took a bus to go to
Chapultepec. . . . There were several people with me, a person extremely dear to me
. . . Senora X my first wife . . . and two Americans, one of whom was dressed up in
cowboy costume. . . . We were going to a bullthrowing. . . . About halfway there we
stopped beside an Indian who seemed to be dying by the roadside. We all wanted to
help but were prevented from doing so . . . because we were told it was against the
law. All that happened was that in the end we left him where he was, and, meanwhile,
a drunk [a *pelado*] on the bus had stolen his money out of his hat, which was lying
beside him, on the road. He paid his fare with it, the stolen money, and we went to
the bullthrowing.[11]

I have let this quotation run because it describes the kind of experience a
controlled writer might have entered in his notebook to be fleshed out later.
Much of Lowry's later work reads like unfleshed-out notes, fragments fated
for the limbo of posthumousness. The above words appear two-thirds of the
way through *Dark As the Grave Wherein My Friend Is Laid*. They are spoken
by Sigbjrn Wilderness, an unpublished alcoholic novelist who has returned
to Mexico with his second wife in an attempt to exorcise the memory of
terrifying experiences a decade before. But to anyone familiar with *Under the
Volcano,* the quotation is a précis of chapter eight, an episode which successfully unifies the book's various levels. Wilderness goes on: "The whole
story [of *Under the Volcano*] grew out of that incident. I began it as a short
story. . . . There's far more to it of course than that, but out of this . . . came
the character of the Consul. . . ."

For a writer who wrote about nothing that had not happened to him, the
incident of the dying Indian had proved galvanic. It remained frozen in
Lowry's consciousness like a Hawthorne allegorical tableau. Here Lowry,
whose mysticism was inseparable from his messianicism, had found his *pietà*.
It became Aiken's "horse theme," a composite of the dying man, his tethered horse with the number seven branded on its rump,[12] his predator (the
pelado, the peeled one), and his witness the drunken Consul who, unable to
act, takes on the guilt for mankind's inaction against inhumanity). Although
Lowry had his most important blocks of correlatives, it was not until late in
the evolvement of the book that he was able to deploy these elements with
classic severity.

Lowry's composition of the short story[13] proved a kind of literary *felix
culpa*. It gave him an early opportunity to slide many pieces of his Mexican-
Gothic furniture into place. In formation were *Las Manos de Orlac* (the film

of Nazi origin about an artist with bloodied hands), the twin volcanoes Popocatepetl and Ixtaccihuatl (Lowry's emblem for true lovers), the Consul's overrun garden, which is his life, and the barranca, which will be his tomb. And, of course, the *pietà:*

> The Consul looked back again. No mistake. The man, receding quickly now, lay with his hat over his eyes, his arms stretched out toward a wayside cross. Now they were passing a riderless horse, munching the hedge. (Short story, 291)

Lowry incorporated the short story into the eighth chapter of the novel. He doubled its length, divided the viewpoint between the Consul and Hugh, but otherwise retained its exact configuration. In the short story, the Consul is named William Ames; Yvonne is his daughter; Hugh Fernhead is her fiancé. They continued in this relationship through the version Lowry completed in Mexico. With Lowry's overhaul of the manuscript in Canada, 1941–45, the Consul (William Ames has become Geoffrey Firmin) and Yvonne became husband and estranged wife, and Hugh became the Consul's half-brother and Yvonne's former lover. From the bland-leading-the-bland relationships of both the short story and the earliest version of the novel, there now emerged a sinister triangle through which Lowry could modulate the book's themes. These he was later to define as "the guilt of man . . . his remorse . . . his ceaseless struggling toward the light under the weight of the past."[14] Lowry's thrust toward dramatic viability led him to narrative viability as well. This double-barreled efficacy can be illustrated by a comparison of early, middle, and final versions.[15]

When he incorporated the short story into chapter eight, Lowry wisely allowed the Consul the narrative focus only until he has sighted the dying Indian from the moving bus. Once the bus is stopped and the unaided Indian robbed by the pelado, Lowry needed a clearer awareness than that of the mescal-fogged Consul. Thus he shifts the viewpoint to the sober, idealizing Hugh. The story and chapter eight both end with the arrival of the three protagonists at a saloon, ironically named the Todos-Contentos-y-Yo-Tambien. Knowing the *pelado,* "stepping high and with a fatuous smile of triumph on his face," has gone in, they linger outside. The door opens slowly; two old peons, in humble contrast to the *pelado,* struggle out.

> Bent double and groaning with the weight, an old, lame Indian was carrying out another Indian, yet older and more decrepit, on his back, by means of a strap clamped to his forehead. He carried the older man and his crutches—he carried both their burdens—
> They all stood in the dusk watching the Indian as he disappeared with the old man

around a bend in the road, shuffling through the grey white dust in his poor sandals. (Short story, 300)

Moving as it is, the description at this point distracts the reader's attention from the heart of the story. Lowry came to realize his error, but, never one to discard anything, he worked a transplant. He moved the two Indians one chapter further along—from the end of eight to the end of nine:

Bent double, groaning with the weight, an old lame Indian was carrying on his back, by means of a strap looped over his forehead, another poor Indian, yet older and more decrepit than himself. He carried the older man and his crutches, *trembling in every limb under this weight of the past,* he carried both their burdens. . . . (Published version, 310)[16]

Comparing the above from the book with the scene as originally written in the short story and then incorporated in chapter eight, the words I have italicized mark the only significant change: "*trembling in every limb under the weight of the past.*" In its new setting, the epiphany concludes the relatively light-hearted ninth chapter where Hugh participates, with a kind of serious absurdity, in a bull-throwing at Arena Tomalín, while Geoffrey and Yvonne, for one of the only times in the novel, speak together of reconciliation and rebirth. But the appearance of the aged peons brilliantly undercuts the redemptive mood as "the weight of the past," symbolically portrayed, returns the narrative to its course downhill.

"Downhill," in fact, is the first word of the eighth chapter. Lowry, of course, intends the word in its literal (descent of the bus) and in its metaphoric (the Consul's course toward the abyss) senses. Chapter eight became the tragedy's major peripety. Lowry's skill with "transplant" surgery is the key. Here, side by side, are the endings of eight as he blocked them in, respectively, in Mexico and for the final version nearly a decade later:

CHAPTER EIGHT ENDING

MEXICO, 1937

As the sudden piercing chords of a guitar were struck, Hugh, catching a glance from the Consul, thought he understood something of the *real tragedy of Mexico,* which was also the tragedy of the earthly paradise, of Adam and Eve, of Cain and Abel.

And for the first time in his life, Hugh hated Man, whose tragedy it was.

1947

They stared after them [the pelado and the bus driver] as the twin doors of the tavern swung to;—it had a pretty name, the Todos Contentos y Yo Tambien. The Consul said nobly:

"Everybody happy, including me."

And including those, Hugh thought, who effortlessly, beautifully, in the blue sky above them, *floated, the vultures—*

After a while they saw the driver and the peeled one swagger into a pulqueria, the latter stepping high, upon his face a fatuous smile of triumph.

The three stared after them and at the name of the saloon after the doors had swung shut: the *Todos-Contentos-y-Yo Tambien.*

At a distance the telegraph wires were singing like crickets: 'Everybody happy including me.' (Mexican version, 270)

Xopilotes,—who wait only for the ratification of death. (Published version, 253)

I have italicized a phrase whose early use (quotation left) indicates that Lowry was broadening his Mexican landscape to include analogues to contemporary political situations, not only of Mexico, as here, but of Spain and the entire West. The "loss of the Ebro" is a recurrent correlative for the Spanish Civil War which deeply influenced Hugh and was still being fought even as Lowry wrote. Near the end of the novel, in chapter ten, just before the Consul flees Yvonne and Hugh for the cantina refuge that will lead to his death, he engages in an invective-laden conversation with Hugh.[17] On the political level, the argument is about communism with the Consul lashing out at Hugh's "indoor Marxmanship" and at all those "people's revolutions" that were so much a part of the political climate of the thirties. The early drafts of chapter eight indicate that Lowry pushed his newly found political overtones hard. But what he finally seeks in his peripeteical chapter is much more: the failure in the principles of charity. He juxtaposes the default of humanity—no one comes to the assistance of the dying man— and the success of inhumanity—the *pelado* despoils the symbolic savior. Hugh, to whom the focus of narration is now fully given, makes a characteristically stylized gesture to help, but is warned off by the Consul and other onlookers. They remind him that he could be held responsible by Mexican law for aiding a wounded person. As for Yvonne, she cannot stand the sight of blood.

The published version eschews the singing telegraph wires and, as already noted, becomes a further tribute to Lowry's literary transplanting. He moves the memorable metaphor of vultures as ratifiers of death from their original place at the end of chapter one:

. . . the obvious vultures . . . hovered and tossed like burnt paper in their eternal ritual, fading as the screen grew bright, the lights flooded on, and the doors of the theatre were thrown open to the thunder—*xopilotes who wait only for the ratification of death.* (Mexican version, 42)

Since the first chapter is an epilogue in the place of a prologue—an elegy for the Consul precisely one year after his, and Yvonne's, death—the use of vultures as emblematic of the pall of death would appear to provide a perfect transition backward. It may even be that Lowry, who in the word's scientific sense was a *conductor,* a channel, for other men's works, had been influenced by "The Snows of Kilimanjaro," which appeared in 1936,[18] the year Lowry arrived in Mexico and began his book. Hemingway's use of the myth of the dying artist could not help but have had impact for the "dying" Lowry of the Mexican years. Harry, a dissolute writer, has long since died spiritually; now he is dying physically of gangrene. The setting is the plain before Mount Kilimanjaro in Africa. The "big birds" are Hemingway's major correlative for impending death.

The cot the man lay on was in the wide shade of a mimosa tree and as he looked out past the shade onto the glare of the plain there were three of the big birds squatted obscenely, while in the sky, a dozen more sailed, making quick-moving shadows as they passed.[19]

Lowry's shift of symbols reveals his deepening conception of the whole. He could not end his elegiac first chapter with a ratification of death but of *life.* The bright memory of the Consul must be preserved from mortal oblivion.

In a crucial letter, Lowry stressed that he came to conceive of his book as "essentially trochal, as a wheel, the image of which keeps recurring."[20] One could view the circular movement of *Volcano* —that is, the backward spin in time which occurs between chapters one and two—as a great circle voyage into time, the aim of which is to understand the tragedy of the previous Day of the Dead. To be truly trochal—that is, in the Proustian sense of eclipsing time and death—Lowry needed a more cogent conceit than vultures, what John Woodburn in an early review called "a magnificent sentence of elision": "Over the town, in the dark tempestuous night, backwards revolved the luminous wheel."[21]

The ferris wheel that bridges the time gap, an innovation relatively late in his revisions, relates to a major theme of the novel, what Lowry's friend, the novelist David Markson, calls the "timeless paradox" of death and rebirth in cyclical repetition.[22] This cycle moves only in relation to the fateful act of the Consul's fall which is linked to the peon's heartless death, hence to mankind's.

4

After having written the story about the Indian by the side of the road, and first got the inspiration to make the whole thing into a larger novel, I wrote the end of this book. . . . (*Dark as the Grave*, 151)

Lowry goes on in *Dark as the Grave* to recount his decision to have the Consul shot by a bunch of Mexican policemen in a cantina. He reports that the murder of the Consul, by turn tragic and absurd, with the victim unable to undo a simple protective ruse and prove he is not an *espider* (spy), was fleshed out from notes he made during a conversation with a group of fellow *borrachones* (drunks), they trying to speak English and he, Spanish. Elsewhere Lowry recalled a newspaper story that a man named Eriksen had been found dead in a barranca; that there was a barranca at the bottom of the Lowry garden in Cuernavaca; and that the Lowry telephone was on the "Eriksen" exchange.[23]

Here again loomed the Lowry demonology: his sense of being somehow—the word persists—a *conductor* for human agony. But the artistic fusing of all those currents, this was studied. And nothing illustrates Lowry's controlled operations better than the final metamorphosis of *pietà* and *pelado* from figures in an autobiographical fragment to principal icons in an infernal sojourn.

The horse theme—my *pietà* and *pelado*—actually dominates the pivotal first chapter, early version. It turns up eight times.[24] But since Lowry had not yet settled on the Consul and Yvonne as estranged husband and wife, it is not surprising that little is viable. However, Lowry's recovery from the failure of his original conception is worth examining as evidence of growth.

What makes the published *Volcano* so memorable is Lowry's ability to dissolve lucidly the boundary line between the objective and subjective worlds of his protagonists. The first chapter is related through the lens of a survivor, although a disenchanted one, of the tragic events of the recent past. The survivor is Jacques Laruelle, a French ex–film director, the only character whose world view is comparable in scope to the Consul's, a black melancholiac who is about to return to France. At this point, Lowry had not sketched in the abortive love affair between the Frenchman and Yvonne. Midway through the chapter, Laruelle enters a theater where *Las Manos de Orlac* is playing, sits down to watch it, and falls asleep, "drawing down with him the last image he had seen on the screen, that of Orlac's hands covered with blood and ceaselessly clutching them over the money, received for the murder he could not help committing." The dream becomes a complex and ambiguous state.

> Laruelle was sinking down, ever more rapidly downward until the sensation of sheer falling was paralyzing and then, when he felt that were it protracted a moment longer he must wake up and save himself, it was as if he entered, in some mysterious way, into the Consul's consciousness. . . . And waking from some strange sleep within sleep, Laruelle was instantly acquainted with all the events of that day of the dead long past which led up to this conscious moment. (Mexican version, 29)

The dream becomes the product of a nebulous state at first called "some strange sleep within sleep" but twenty words later referred to as "this conscious moment." One notes Lowry's inability, despite the high style, to convince the reader that there has been a breakthrough of the boundaries between dream and actuality. The language is self-consciously literary, but the feeling—the key idea, at this stage—that Jacques is inhabiting, inexplicably and simultaneously, *two* consciousnesses is missing entirely.

Jacques, however implausibly, is supposed to have *merged* with the Consul; become, in fact, one of the dead man's masks. He dreams of "plummeting" (a favorite Lowryan word) in pursuit of Yvonne and Hugh (the unabashed lovers of the first versions), "obsessed by the necessity of conveying some urgent message to these lovers" (Mexican version, 30). Although Lowry never gets around to revealing the nature of that message, much else is revealed: notably, his inability to make the parts equal the whole. When the dreamer dreams he hears the young lovers discussing the Indian, they say things that contradict the eighth chapter:

> "I wonder what's happened to that peon we had to leave beside the road," he added presently. "Gosh, that was an ugly business."
> "Oh, I expect somebody will have taken care of him." (Mexican version, 34)

Although never noted for his ability to write straight dialogue, surely such "gosh" and "oh" conversations would not have been written if Lowry had any idea of the cogency of their topic. Eventually, Laruelle fades out as Laruelle. Enter Laruelle inside the reincarnated Consul. Consularly, he recalls the bus ride and the *pelado:*

> [A]nd there, waving his arms, was a *pelado* . . . . He had got hold of a melon from somewhere and was approaching with a melancholy gait, swaying, walking straight, yet as if stepping over obstacles, as though the human frame were resentful of harbouring such a will as his and wanted to shake itself clear of it. . . . (Mexican version, 38)

The pelado boards the bus, stretches himself out on a seat, apparently asleep, but to the still-dreaming Laruelle, "aware of everything that went on." Several pages later, a horse and rider gallop in out of the black. Because Lowry retained a significant section in text and another in concept, it is necessary here to quote in detail:

> Once a horseman, crazy with tequila, drew up across the bus' path. The horse stood blinking in the headlights, its rider rolling over the horse, only holding himself on by the reins. The bus hooted nervously and the man rode off before them, almost falling over backwards but somehow saving himself by the pommel as he furiously beat the horse with his machete. Under the moon the sight was evidently frightening to Yvonne and she clutched Hugh, who was looking at her tenderly. Women drew their children into the side of the road as he galloped on, and men stood back against the hedges or into the ditches. . . . The sight of the man riding so wildly, whose eyes caught by the headlights were strange as *those soon to be familiar with death,* had been awe-inspiring, and perhaps there was fixed on her mind . . . some picture of *maniacal, uncontrolled, senseless force* . . . . (Mexican version, 40)

This discarded passage goes far toward clarifying Lowry's evolving conception. He retained, in essence, everything to the point where Yvonne's reaction is recorded. I have italicized two phrases from the discarded portion. The first is a foreshadowing that Yvonne is intended to survive, for she is one of "those soon to be familiar with death." More importantly, Yvonne's sense of the rearing horse as reflecting "maniacal, uncontrolled, senseless force" became Lowry's, added to the novel's injunction that man must exercise humanity and, above all, love, to control the life force.

But, even in this earliest stage, Lowry's sense of epiphanic *pietà* is sure. The chapter almost ends with Laruelle, waking at last, and realizing that he "was the only one who noticed that it was precisely here where the peon had lain bleeding, and seeing what he did see . . . he began finally to glide out of his sleep" (Mexican version, 41). Only the ratifying vultures remained to close out the epilogic prologue.

The horse theme is never wasted in the Published version. Horse and Indian, together or separately, make their appearance during those moments of that novel that are most "loaded."

As in the first drafts, a horse ridden by a drunken man thunders by Laruelle and interrupts his reverie. The horseman at that early point, wrote Lowry, "is by implication the first appearance of the Consul himself as a symbol of mankind."[25]

The next encounter, their first during the main action after chapter one, occurs in the fourth chapter as Hugh and Yvonne are crossing a river on their

morning ride. They see on the other side a pulqueria, talismanically named
La Sepultura (burial place), where

an Indian sat with his back against the wall, his broad hat half down over his face,
resting outside in the sunshine. His horse, or a horse, was tethered near him to a tree
and Hügh could see from midstream the number seven branded on its rump. (Published version, 109)

The Indian, having been viewed by Hugh and Yvonne, must now be seen
by the Consul. This confrontation occurs in Chapter seven, as the Consul
and Laruelle walk along the base of the Cortez Palace. They edge into the
palace wall to let a man on horseback pass,

a fine-featured Indian of the poorer class, dressed in soiled white loose clothes. The
man was singing gaily to himself. But he nodded to them courteously as if to thank
them. He seemed about to speak, reining in his little horse—on either side of which
chinked two saddlebags, and upon whose rump was branded the number seven—to a
slow walk beside them. . . . But the man, riding slightly in front, did not speak and at
the top he suddenly waved his hand and galloped away, singing. (Published version,
212–13)

Except for the needless proliferation in chapter one, all the appearances of
the horse and rider were in the manuscript from the start. All, that is, but
one. Since Yvonne must die, Lowry hit on the idea of capping her sense of
dread at the appearance of the rearing horse (chapter one, first draft) by
making the horse—this time riderless because the Indian lies dead at the
wayside—the instrument for her death in the penultimate (eleventh) chapter.
The tethered animal is released by the doomed Consul at his eleventh hour
in the befuddled yet benevolent belief he is doing a last penance to the
memory of the dead Indian whose horse his murderers (and they will be the
Consul's, too) have stolen.

Thus, symbolically and by cause and effect, Geoffrey and Yvonne are
united in death as they could not be in life. At the last, Yvonne envisions
their home in the "northern paradise" afire, dying like herself. But there is
one paragraph more. It is redemptive and suggestive as well of hope. The
dream of the burning house leaves her, and she "felt herself suddenly gathered upwards and borne towards the stars, through eddies of stars, scattering
aloft with ever widening circlings like rings on water, among which now
appeared, like a flock of diamond birds flying softly and steadily towards
Orion, the Pleiades. . . ." (Published version, 336). As for the Consul, at the
same moment (although a chapter later) that Yvonne finds salvation in death,
the dying Consul is borne ("born" is closer to the heart of the scene) to the

summit of the barranca and flung with a dead dog into its crater. But, like Yvonne's, the Consul's soul survives, ascending to the top of the volcano Popo which, like Hemingway's Kilimanjaro, had always beckoned.

5

The above attempt to carry through one major thematic complex is, at best, merely suggestive. What is true of the evolving nature of the horse theme could be applied to others from Lowry's cornucopia of symbols.

It should be added, finally, that my application of Professor Barker's blocking-out concept has its major relevance in terms of Lowry's arrangement of chapters. If leitmotifs flash like rockets to remind the reader of the footing of the terrain, the twelve chapters work like a vast check-and-balance network to condition expectation. The movement of the book is a concatenation of dark portents, occasionally penetrated by patches of light—an inevitability that in tragedy transcends any customary line of suspense. The Consul's fate, implicit from the first page, is affirmed in every scene, although the gloom is sporadically shaded by a series of set scenes of Pickwickian and punning humor.[26]

Dale Edmonds was the first to demonstrate that each of the four principals has at least one chapter in which the interplay of thought and action filters through an individual sensibility.[27] The Consul has five chapters (three, five, seven, ten, and twelve); Yvonne has three (two, nine, eleven); Hugh has three (four, six, eight); and Jacques has one (one). Lowry projects a related variation on the Miltonic efficacy of chapter arrangement which is tied to shifting character viewpoints. Where Milton's great poem gravitates between heaven and hell but has some of its most powerful scenes in the sublunary realm of the First Couple, *Under the Volcano* teeters between past and future, between despair and hope, and the Yvonne-Hugh shadings of the light play like a palimpsest over the Consul's night thoughts.

Lowry likened the architectonic progress of his novel, as earlier noted, to the construction of a cathedral whose east and west towers are the book's first and last chapters. "Doleful bells" in each tower toll their dialogue from the living to the dead and back again to the living. In the ten intervening chapters—a continuum between the towers—Lowry orchestrates contrapuntal theme music: the chords of the three principal players. Yvonne's chords, even at the moment of death, are translunary; Hugh's are redolent of the sea, to whose bosom he speaks of returning; the Consul's are more complex, for he is Promethean. What is perhaps his most moving soliloquy is pitched in the tones of the artist-addict. Shortly before he flees Yvonne for his Gethsemane, "oozing alcohol from every pore," the Consul wanders (and wonders) like a Jungian Prufrock:

> How indeed could he hope to find himself, to begin again when, somewhere, perhaps, in one of those lost or broken bottles, in one of those glasses, lay, forever, the solitary clue to his identity? How could he go back and look now, scrabble among the broken glass, under the eternal bars, under the oceans? (Published version, 293)

Malcolm Lowry plays the Yvonne-Hugh music as counterpoint to the Consul's solo. The chapters are carefully arranged for the always-sought contrapuntal effect. His aim is to make hope and despair interweave so as "to transcend even one's interest in the characters. Since these characters are in one way "Things," as that French philosopher of the absurd fellow has it . . . this hope should be, rather, a transcendent, a universal hope."[28]

What Lowry appears to be saying is that he envisioned his principals as interacting forces, out of whose triumphs and losses a human statement would evolve.

It is on the dark side of human nature that Malcolm Lowry looks. With texture reflecting maelstrom, Lowry has given us a book that is keyed to the contemporary rhythm. *Under the Volcano* is the story of a possessed man that could only have been written by a possessed man. Yet the always lucid evocation of the Consul's agony is the product of an artist in control of his labyrinth.

III.

The Ordeal of Margerie Lowry

As we know from her letters, Virginia Stephen left no doubt in the mind of Leonard Woolf, her caring suitor, that she felt no physical attraction for him ("When you kissed me . . . I [felt] no more than a rock"). However, as Virginia Woolf, she would leave a suicide note assuring him, her husband of thirty years, that "until this disease came on we were perfectly happy . . . all due to you. . . . from the first day till now." It was Leonard above all who helped Virginia stave off oblivion until, depressed by war and a sense of creative failure and fearful of a recurrence of her depression, she drowned herself. Modern literary history does not show a prevalence of husbands as caretakers for literary wives. More often, it is the other way around.

Five pages from the end of her harrowing memoir, Clarissa M. Lorenz, second of the three wives of Conrad Aiken, sadly declares: "Unfortunately, there's no training school for poets' wives. I learned too late that my real rivals were not women but the daemon."[1] At the end of her *Poets in Their Youth* (1983), Eileen Simpson, once the wife of John Berryman, writes almost triumphantly of Berryman's "subtle foe"—suicide—which had been waiting in the wings: "Many—I, too, at moments—blamed the suicide on John's having been a poet . . . [Then] I began to feel that I'd missed the obvious. It was the poetry that had kept him alive."[2]

In the case of Malcolm Lowry, a man who never wanted to be born and who lived every day in the grip of his daemon, no muse alone could have kept him alive to make his one great statement. Nurse and lover, helpmate and amanuensis, Margerie Bonner Lowry, by a fierce-if-often-misdirected loyalty, delayed the inevitable alcoholic's death. If her single-minded concern for his image (and hers) has not always served him—if her energy in attempting to see into print all that's fit to print down to the last poem scribbled on the back of an envelope often diminished him—it was she alone who paid the necessary price: drunkenness, in tandem with his.

In early March, 1969, Margerie wrote me that she would be in New York City at mid-month to see Peter Matson, her agent, about the upcoming publication of her late husband's last work, *October Ferry to Gabriola*. She planned to arrive on the weekend but could not see me until that Monday the seventeenth. She would be staying at the Hotel Elysée on East Fifty-fourth Street, just off Madison Avenue—"It's a quiet little pub. "Don't come too early! I have to work in the afternoon." I phoned my friend David Markson. The Marksons had hosted the Lowrys fifteen years earlier, in 1954, when Malcolm and Margerie left Canada and North America for the last time. Dave, the author of the then just-published *Going Down,* a fine novel about a hard-drinking writer in the Mexican interior, suggested I stop at a state store and buy a house-brand gin. There were no funds in our tight budget for air or even train and a hotel. I took the bus from Utica and reserved a room at the downtown Sloan House.

"Take it slow," Dave warned. "She can drink anybody under the table. But you'll need the fortification. You'll be sick of her in an hour."

None of the male Lowryans I had met could stand Margerie. Earle Birney, the dean of Canadian poets who had known the Lowrys early on throughout their Vancouver years, had once been a close friend. But Earle had come to a parting of the ways. Margerie had refused to authorize Birney's edition of Malcolm's poems—Earle wanted them to be selective; she wanted the whole unsorted crop. When I was able to bring Earle to Purdue and Utica College for readings, he pooh-poohed not only a complete-poems book but the idyll-by-the-bay featuring the fisherman's cottage that Margerie said they built. "Malc couldn't hammer a nail. It was his friends, I included, who built that shack." Expert swimmer that he was, Lowry did jump off the pier into the icy water every morning, Earle conceded, but did so mostly to sober up. But, from the start, I had bought even the publisher's blurbs. I believed "The Forest Path to the Spring," his lyrical novella about a jazz musician and his wife who brave the British Columbian wilds while he writes a symphony to

No happier-looking couple could be imagined than Malcolm and Margerie Lowry, shown in Dollarton, British Columbia, in 1946 just after his "contemporary classic" *Under the Volcano* had been accepted the same week on both sides of the Atlantic. "Downhill" was a metaphor both for the novel and the Lowrys' life for the next decade, culminating in his suicide at forty-seven. *Courtesy Malcolm Lowry Collection, University of British Columbia.*

the "northern paradise." There the lovers find daily renewal in walking to a spring for water. I could not accept that what the Lowrys had sought and found was a retreat whose principal advantage was its inaccessibility: Ten miles through dense forest from the nearest tavern. For me, Vancouver was Lowry's *Paradiso* and Mexico his *Inferno* ("pyre of Bierce and springboard of Hart Crane," as one of Lowry's poems has it) where he found peace to finish the book Alfred Kazin that very year of 1969 would call "the last instance of a masterpiece."

Besides, hadn't Margerie Lowry answered promptly and fully all my questions? Now I must digress for a moment.

The trick is to maintain throughout the long grind of writing a book the original passion. Two years earlier I had published a book on H. G. Wells, having begun the research while I was still on the *Utica Observer-Dispatch*. Nothing in journalistic immediacy prepared me for the five years it took. I didn't want to write another marathon book. Lowry was already a cult figure and *Under the Volcano* a subterranean work. Only then—twelve years after his death and twenty-two after original publication—was recognition being granted in his native England by such critics as Philip Toynbee and Anthony Burgess who, in company with all their peers, had missed it first time around. I submitted, on enthusiastic invitation, to Oxford University Press and editor Whitney Blake five chapters that expanded my doctoral dissertation at Purdue. I proposed not a biography, for that would call for various resources I deemed beyond me, but a study attempting to make sense of the near decade that Malcolm Lowry, in mostly bad spiritual weather, had required to finish the book.

In summer, 1966, I had spent six weeks at the Malcolm Lowry Special Collection, University of British Columbia, sifting through many hundreds of pages of tortured manuscript. I came to recognize the spidery hand of Lowry and the expertly unknowing one of Margerie. I saw how nightmarish Lowry's manner of composition, combining false starts exhaustively pursued and digressions and longueurs ruinously indulged, must have been for a writer whose hold on life was always tenuous. After keeping my five chapters for nearly a year, Oxford turned me down. At the bottom of the box— inadvertently there?—was the reader's negative report. It was in the form of a brief letter signed by Professor Douglas Day of the University of Virginia. Shortly after this turndown, Oxford announced that it had awarded a contract for a biography of Lowry. The beneficiary: Douglas Day. About the same time, Earle Birney wrote to tell me he had decided to relinquish his contract to do a book on Lowry. Would I care to take over his Twayne contract? I would and I did. But the memory of what I regarded as a near miss at Oxford haunted me. With Wells, author of one hundred titles, the Twayne format had provided a safety valve. I could be excused for relying on summary. But with Lowry, one major novel, one minor one, a posthumous story collection, two unfinished novels Margerie had ad-libbed into print, an edition of letters—that was all. This would be a far more demanding book.

(To recreate after twenty-five years my only encounter with the wife of the author of the book that changed my life, I hope to avoid hindsight. For hindsight is like a game you play with yourself to change—in your mind, anyway—the final score that circumstances totaled up for you. It's all about the futile business of if-I-knew-then-what-I-know-now. To avoid, so far as possible, the overlay of time—the relentless selectivity of memory as decoder—I have gone to my original notes. They were impressionistic, unstudied, but they best convey the way Margerie seemed, the way I was.)

Eyes virtually popping out of their sockets rimmed by hastily applied blue green eyeshadow. Hands often shaking out of control. Chain smoker, fingers endlessly shifting to and from the ashtray. Voice cold Bette Davis, rich, dispassionate, working at conviction. Black frock, white frills at collar and sleeves. Little-girl look in pathetic contradiction to the popping eyes and the nonstop smoking.

She asks me to place a pillow behind her back, wrenched earlier that week in the Washington, D.C., airport. I think again that this cannot be the woman of the only photo I have ever seen of them. He bare to the waist, shorts held up by a real belt, not the rope Earle Birney talks about, and no paunch. Right hand holding cloudy gin drink—Bols, their brand?—left hand lightly on Margie's shoulder. She with peasant blouse, flower print, bright colors no doubt, small breasts, her drink in one hand, cigarette in other. Just like now. But that was summer, 1947. The Volcano out from Reynal & Hitchock. Reviewer John Woodburn's words in *Saturday Review of Literature* (February 22, 1947, 9–10) still echoing in their heads: "I have never before used the word in a review . . . but I am of the opinion, carefully considered, that *Under the Volcano* is a work of genius."

After our third gin she talks of Malc's proneness to disasters. "I didn't dare leave him alone. Every time we were separated for more than a few hours there would be some terrible accident. Once when I had to go to Los Angeles from Canada because my mother was mortally ill, Malc fell off a pier onto cement. I found him out of his head, his back broken, in a Catholic hospital in Vancouver. It's all there in *The Ordeal of Sigbjørn Wilderness.* It's unpublishable, that book, but absolutely necessary to understanding the agony, moment to moment, of his life."[3]

I don't ask her just yet about the last night of Malcolm Lowry's life—June 26, 1957—when another enforced separation cost him his life. "Death by misadventure," the coroner called it. Malcolm popped twenty sodium amytals and died sometime during the night, choking to death on his own vomit ("better his own than somebody else's," a Cambridge friend had said at the time). Margerie, in fear of her life (she told the reporters), slept that night at Winnie Mason's next door. I hope we'll get to that.

For now, though, another quality—urgency—slips into her voice, but it is no less practiced: "Dick, will you do me the greatest favor?" She pauses, stretches fingers just short of the cigarettes. I assist once more—inexpertly again, for I have never smoked. "Dick dear, will you, in the event of my death, be Malc's literary executor? I am making out the will. Peter (Matson) thinks it's high time too."

"But what of Douglas Day?" I ask. (A ploy of mine to find out how the biography is going. Not well, I trust.)

She purses her lips. (A pout on the way?) "I haven't had even a card in eight months. And I write Douglas every week. Nothing for eight months. Peter finally took a plane to Charlottesville. Douglas says he'll have a manuscript in October. Dick, I don't think he will. I had such high hopes for Douglas. You cannot imagine how responsive he was when he came to see me in California. He had all the right answers. So bright. So kind. He was in the middle of an affair when we were supposed to be doing *Dark As the Grave.* Peter had to go down there and hold his hand while he wrote that introduction long after deadline."

"A brilliant essay," I offered.

(The pout in full bloom.) "But he called Malc 'silly.' *Silly!* Malc was a lot of things but he was never silly."

I tell her that I do not remember Day using that word. I tell her what I wrote in my 1968 review in *The Nation.* (I don't remind her that I had mailed it to her. I thought he pushed too hard the charge that Malcolm Lowry was not really a novelist. Yet anyone who has gone through the manuscripts at UBC, as Day says he did, and especially anyone who had to "finish" an unfinished novel, as Day had to do, could make a case for Lowry's missing circuits as a craftsman.) "If Malc wasn't a novelist, how could he have written the *Volcano?*" she sounds her one note. "Douglas Day has betrayed

Malc, just as Conrad Knickerbocker did." (*Conrad Knickerbocker, a suicide.* I think for a moment that she can only mean he betrayed Lowry by shooting himself three years ago while working on a biography of Malcolm Lowry— material now turned over to Day. Then I remember something she might regard as betrayal. *Paris Review* published an extraordinary essay left behind by Knickerbocker—extraordinary because of things Lowry's contemporary at Cambridge, critic John Davenport, revealed. Margerie can't have liked Davenport's first words to Knickerbocker—"You must remember that Malcolm was a masturbator.")[4] As I mull this, I only half hear her dressing down others—betrayers all. She lashes out at Conrad Aiken ("bitterly jealous, no-body reads him") and Birney ("I can't get a ten-page preface to the collected poems out of him. Why it would take him an afternoon!").

Having had nothing to eat since breakfast, I decline to pour a fifth gin. Dave Markson had been on the mark. Margerie is unfazed, unstoppable. It is past six; we have talked and boozed for two hours. I remember I had invited her to dinner. She knows of a French restaurant—Le Cygne—across the street. As soon as she excuses me so she can dress, I go down to the street to check the prices at Le Cygne. Everything is in French and no à la carte— prices an inflexible twenty dollars a person, not including drinks. I check my pockets. I have $22.07. I go back to the hotel and tell her my problem. "Oh, Dick, I wouldn't want to do that to you. I know another French restaurant— Le Bistro—that is inexpensive. It's in the neighborhood."

I excuse myself and go down again on the elevator to the lobby. I check the location of Le Bistro. We are on East Fifty-fourth, between Park and Mad-ison, and Le Bistro is on Fifty-first, near Third Avenue. I decide against hailing a cab, figuring her wrenched back doesn't preclude strolling. I phone Le Bistro. A girl with a French accent answers. Yes, one can do very nicely with fifteen dollars for two if one doesn't drink. I don't see why my bottle of gin can't suffice for a nightcap.

She is ready when I return. She asks me to pin her up in the back. I stifle a gasp. Her back is full of welts as if someone had whipped her. What I see looks *inflicted*, not caused by a wrench. I do not ask questions. She waits in the lobby for someone to open the door for her. An attendant obliges. On Fifty-fourth Street she grasps my arm almost voraciously. She tells me she weighs 105 pounds and is just an inch over five feet. I am under five foot six, not much shorter than the actual Malc (Hugh Firmin, the younger Lowry, is described early in *Under the Volcano* as rising to his "mental height" of six foot two). Lowry and Costa: pyknics both.

We talk as we stroll. She tells me Malcolm disliked New York. "He really was in Bellevue, you know. Really. I don't remember the year—can never remember years. That's why I always dated our pictures—four albums of them—from 1939, when I met him in California—in Hollywood—until the last ones in 1957, during our nostalgia tour of the Lake Country. Such happy days to be so near the end . . ." (But in the one with him sitting on a rock looking out to—what? The one that reminded me of a down-and-nearly-out Errol Flynn playing Mike Campbell in *The Sun Also Rises*. Lowry looked like that, burnt out. I always marvelled that however badly life was treating them, the Lowrys always had a camera at the ready.) She seems to think she ought to talk about this city—New York—and a desperate time before they met. "Malc had some very funny adventures here the year before he went to Mexico. He was drinking himself into Bellevue, trying to write stories for Whit Burnett and *Story*. He was surrounded by queer Bowery characters." She brings up *Lunar Caustic,* his unfinished Bellevue novel. Why had he given his alter ego of *Lunar Caustic* a name like Plantagenet? "That was Malc," she says. "Always using absurd names—Sigbjørn Wilderness, Kennish Drumgold Cosnahan, Roderick McGregor Fairhaven, you name it." A Cambridge Englishman in the Bowery! Why not a fantastic name to match the circumstances? For no reason I mention an old favorite of mine, *The Green Hat* by Michael Arlen. An Armenian in London in the twenties. Margerie ignores ignores my comparison. "Malc could never get *Lunar Caustic* right. It wouldn't jell. When Earle and I stitched it together for *Paris Review,* I think it jelled. The editors didn't change a word."

There is a short line at Le Bistro. A young hostess seats us at a tiny table against a wall. Margerie doesn't even glance at the menu. She orders a martini on the rocks. I have the distinct notion that she is going to make up in drinks any price differential between Le Cygne and Le Bistro. We have two each before ordering. She proclaims her love of French cuisine. I tell her I studied French in college but not French menus. She will order. "Like *escargots?*" "Never had them." "You must try them."

Le Bistro is not fancy, and our wait is short. The waiter brings the snails and a holder for the piping hot shell. Margerie, whose hands have never stopped quivering, cannot hold them. I use the tiny fork to pluck out the escargots. I feed her, literally. They are delicious. Our entrée is also some sort of shellfish whose name escapes—oyster-like, plentiful. The bill comes to just over nineteen dollars. I emerge from Le Bistro with seven cents. I ask her for money to tip the hatcheck girl. She hands me a quarter.

On the elevator at Hotel Elysée, I pet a grey schnauzer held on a leash by an older woman I somehow assume to be European. We could have dined in the hotel, or at Moriarty's next door. But Margerie had to have French. And I am flat. I had made a late date with an old friend who is an editor on the *New York Times*. Ray Warner is to give me a tour. Margerie will not hear of me leaving. She takes off her coat, reclines on the sofa "to rest my back." I arrange her pillow, light her cigarette, pour another gin. She calls room service for a bottle of tonic water. She signs for it.

For the first time we talk of my work. My five chapters have gone out again after the Oxford debacle. I had had a cold letter from John Erskine, Lowry's editor at Reynal & Hitchcock, now at Random House. The topic of editors brings her to a succession of stories of disasters—large and small—with her one serious novel, *Horse in the Sky,* the novel the late Maxwell Perkins accepted at Scribner's only to die before it received proper promotion. A crucial chapter from one of her two crime novels was once simply omitted. But I have read all about Margerie Bonner's novels in the *Selected Letters.*[5] Unlike Edmund Wilson, who never repeats a story, Margerie begins retelling stories from this afternoon. But I am pleasantly high. I ask if I can use the phone. I call Ray Warner. We arrange to meet at Moriarty's after his late shift on the *Times* national desk.

Margerie is not smoking when I return. She asks me to reach her a box on the nighttable. "Dick, you must look at these and tell me if you think we ought to publish some of them with the biography." The box contains a series of pencilled verse and drawings on cards and halfsheets. Malcolm's spidery hand is unmistakable, often as in the manuscripts: undecipherable. The accompanying sketches were either of a lion or of a gazelle. "Malc was '*El León*' and I was the hartebeest. He would write these notes to me nearly every day, collect them, and present them to me when I returned from Vancouver on the bus."

They are indeed charming. The poses of *El León* reflected that day's mood. Sometimes only the tail would show. That meant, she explains, that Malc was having a bad time. Often the lion was resting or prancing or assuming human postures. That meant Malc was having a good day. The writing or living or both had gone well. The verses were invariably prayers of thanks to the hartebeest for sticking by *El León* even *in extremis.*

"Malc begged me to leave him the last years in England. The doctors in the London rest hospital—he was there off and on from 'fifty-four until his death in 'fifty-seven—told me he had incurable cirrhosis. I always believed he would recover. We had our garden at Ripe, in Sussex. It was like the sea. And we made our last pilgrimage to the Lake Country. We were never happier. Everything was like one of his youthful voyages. And we believed his liver was well again."

This is the time. I reach into my breast pocket for a photostat of a letter she had written to Vancouver friends, the McConnells, Bill and Alice, from Taormina, Sicily, five months after Malcolm's death. "Can you take another heartbreak of a memory?" I ask, and it is not a disingenuous question. "I guess," she says. "I've had about all that life can dish out." The letter closed, ". . . My poor blessed Malcolm, his genius was a heavy burden to him and he fought it all the way . . ."

"And he did," she adds, her voice trailing off.

I decide to take the plunge. "He didn't die by misadventure, did he?" I hear myself ask. *"He committed suicide."*

"There is no question in my mind that Malc *intended* suicide." She stresses the verb. I had stopped noticing the bulging eyes. Now I am struck by them anew. We have been together almost nine hours. It is past time, and I am reeling. She shows no effects at all. I kiss her on the cheek and ask her if I might borrow a buck. She reaches for her pocketbook, finds her purse, and hands me a dollar. I phone Ray Warner at the Times to cancel our date. I make my way uneasily to the elevator. I am almost there when I hear her voice summoning me. "You pinned me up, now you'll have to unpin me." I have the absurd notion that I can go to bed with her. Male vanity—*my* vanity—is monstrous. I go back and kiss the reddened area of her back. I make no other move. It is all so grotesque. She hands me two letters to mail in the lobby. One is to a Raoul Ortiz y Ortiz in Washington. He is translating the *Volcano* for a Mexican publisher. I recall that she spoke of wrenching her back last week in Washington. Does she have lovers, *violent ones?* "Do you want those?" She points to a basket of fruit. I accept, eagerly.

I leave Margerie Lowry's small suite, 5A Hotel Elysée, and enter the elevator. Like the young Geoffrey Firmin who tried to look soberer the drunker he became, I attempt to navigate with dignity. The European woman with the schnauzer enters on the third floor. I stoop to pet the small dog. The animal, unaccustomed to drunks pretending to be sober, snaps at me and nips me on my right pinkie. "You have to let him come to you," the woman says, attending only to her dog as blood begins to flow from my finger. The elevator operator, a woman with a British accent, calls a bellhop. He ushers me to a men's room, tells me to bathe my finger in cold water. He returns with a bandaid. I don't feel a thing. I change the buck and phone Dave Markson, getting him out of bed.

"Dave, she admitted he committed suicide."

"Hell, Dick, nobody ever doubted it."

That afternoon she had phoned Elaine, he said, to insure her dinner for tomorrow night. "'Dave, you old duck,'" she had said in that phony accent everybody detests.

"Well, kid, you've met Margerie Lowry. Now you know." He rings off.

The finger begins to throb. I have visions of rabies, lockjaw. But I can still walk the twenty-five blocks to the Sloan House. The lobby is filled with men past forty wearing bellbottoms. *Why am I in New York?* I scrawl a note to Ray Warner and mail it. There is a white envelope under my door. It says I am to check at the desk. There has been an error. With ninety-seven cents I am not prepared for errors. But it is in my favor. There is a small refund.

I sleep only until 4:30—about four hours. I have sixty-cent eggs at Port of New York Authority terminal. I make the 6:00 A.M. to Utica. I buy a *New York Times*. My attention is called to a familiar name on the obituary page. Charlotte Haldane, once the wife of the great scientist J. B. S. Haldane, has died. But the name clicks in immediately to the curious circuitry of Malcolm Lowry. *I Bring Not Peace*, her 1932 novel about Cambridge, created a heroic undergraduate modelled in part, she acknowledged, on "a remarkable young man, the most romantic undergraduate of that period in Cambridge, Malcolm Lowry."

Margerie Bonner Lowry died in Los Angeles on September 28, 1988. She had been severely impaired, especially in her speech, since a massive stroke in 1979. A friend, Betty Moss, had cared for her during the last few years when she was rarely fully conscious. Ms. Moss took Margerie's body to England, to the village of Ripe, Sussex, for burial beside Malcolm in Ripe's single church cemetery. "We buried Margie as close to Malcolm as we could, but it had to be across the churchyard," Ms. Moss informed me in a letter.

Jo and I visited Malcolm Lowry's gravesite in early May, 1980, during my sabbatical. We sailed on the *QEII*, disembarked at Southampton, and traveled by British Rail throughout England. Only the extraordinary cooperation of A. Roger Gordon, the stationmaster at Berwick, made our pilgrimage possible. Neither he nor anyone else we talked to had ever heard of Malcolm Lowry, but the stationmaster got it into his head that we were on a mini–Alex Haleyan venture (the television series based on *Roots* was enormously popular in Britain at that time). We did nothing to disabuse him of that idea. We three divided our surveillance, and it was Gordon who located a small stone, almost hidden by unmown grass: *Malcolm Lowry 1909–1957.* That was all. Except for this, a detail I mention for the sake of other lovers of *Under the Volcano* who may be reading this: At the moment that Jo, Roger Gordon, and I entered the churchyard, a horse became clearly visible in the distant grazing ground beyond. The horse was moving fast, rearing, riderless.

IV.

Writing as Failed Therapy:
Tennessee Williams and James Baldwin

Just before Christmas break of 1987, the chance pairing of a week-long Tennessee Williams retrospective at Texas A&M—the plays and the man—and the death in France at sixty-three of James Baldwin raises anew the issue of whether putting one's private problems in one's writings actually helps keep the demons at bay. Writers like Williams and Baldwin give us all the proof we need that dealing in print with shattering personal problems in order to stave them off does not enable the writer to put them behind, but only, perhaps, to thrust them temporarily into some private drawer of the self.

"People think sexuality and death are the main themes of my plays," announces actor Ray Stricklyn, impersonating the author of *A Streetcar Named Desire,* in his powerful one-man show. "But they're not. Loneliness is. All of life is but an effort to escape loneliness. Promiscuity is really a distortion of love. I write in order to be loved."

"For me writing was an act of love," John W. Roberts quotes James Baldwin in *Dictionary of Literary Biography.* "It was an attempt—not to get the world's attention—it was an attempt to be loved. It seemed a way to save myself and to save my family. It came out of despair."[1]

I find no evidence that the quintessentially southern Williams and the Harlem-reared Baldwin ever crossed paths beyond the latter's brief stint, after the notoriety of his 1956 novel about homosexuality *(Giovanni's Room),* as an assistant to director Elia Kazan during rehearsals of Williams's *Sweet*

Bird of Youth. Where the two writers cross is in their conviction that suffering is the path to understanding and transcending the distances that separate us as human beings. Pain as prescriptive can generate a long writing career only if the artist keeps it concentric—that is, built around a controlled central force—rather than centrifugal—uncontrolled, destructively outward and downward from that center.

From opposite poles, Tennessee Williams and James Baldwin portrayed the misbegotten but lacked the larger vision that is only given to the truly great. The dramas of their literary careers lacked a final—and conclusive— act.

As long as Williams concentrated his compassion for the tortured and the broken in a gallery of unforgettable women from Laura *(Glass Menagerie)* and Blanche *(A Streetcar Named Desire)* to Catharine *(Suddenly Last Summer)* and Hannah *(Night of the Iguana)*, he could combine masterful language, realistic human confrontations, and empathetic response that were unsurpassed in the theater between the end of World War II and the early sixties. Later, after announcing himself as homosexual and a fervent practitioner of the art-grows-from-pain school, he insisted on parading across the stage the products of his sadomasochism. He termed the years after his last successful play, *Iguana* (1961), "my stoned age." He lost his longtime lover and friend to lung cancer in 1963, fell into two decades of depression that led to an even stronger drug and alcohol dependence than he had suffered during his earlier years, and became the flamboyantly desperate caricature of Dotson Rader's cruel memoir, published in 1985, two years after his subject's death. Donald Spoto's kinder and more accurate full biography, *The Kindness of Strangers,* describes Williams's last days in scenes that Ray Stricklyn brought to life at Rudder Theater:

He withdrew quietly to his bedroom with a bottle of wine. On his bedside was the traditional array of prescriptions—capsules, tablets, eyedrops and nosedrops . . . all the parapernalia . . . of hypochondria and chemical dependence. . . . [His last night] Tennessee Williams had ingested drugs—cocaine among them—with the wine [and] a barbiturate cap had somehow lodged in his throat; apparently he had used the cap like a spoon, to swallow two Seconal capsules. He had been, it seemed, unable or unwilling to summon help.
. . . One of his hands was resting gently, palm upward. At last there was stillness.[2]

The crises of identity that hounded James Baldwin never let up. Spared some of the violence of Harlem street life in the thirties by the demands of caring for eight younger siblings (the boy never knew his real father; his stepfather was an embittered New Orleans emigré preacher), Jimmy Baldwin read all the books in two Harlem libraries, came under the influence of poet Countee Cullen early, and observed racism and mistreatment, drugs, alcohol, and social-economic exploitation of his neighbors during the Depression.

Rare for a Negro in the New York of the 1930s, young Baldwin was accepted on the basis of academic brilliance at a nearly all-white high school. For the first time, he came into contact with classmates who were more academically sophisticated than he. Had he been white, he probably would have developed like his exact contemporary—and later antagonist—Norman Mailer. As it was he had to fight his stepfather's narrow sense that he was playing into the hands of the enemy.

He chronicled these conflicts of his youth in a series of essays which, taken together, I believe surpass in power and style those of any American writer since the Second World War. Edmund Wilson confessed that Baldwin was the only black writer he could enjoy with detachment because he could forget he was black. The finest of his essays, *Notes of a Native Son*, is the classic Oedipal theme translated to contemporary street life. Like a writer he much admired—James Joyce, who left his native country early but wrote only about that country—Baldwin became a voluntary exile in his early twenties. For the rest of his life, he returned to America only as a frequent commuter.

As with Williams, Baldwin's early fiction is considered his strongest. *Go Tell It on the Mountain* (1953) is a fictionalized version of *Notes of a Native Son*. In that first book, Baldwin acknowledged in 1985, he set the pattern of needing to deal in books with matters that most distressed him—the tyranny of, yet dependence on, his father, his fundamentalist early beliefs, his sexual ambivalence, the plight of blacks in America. "*Mountain* is the book I had to write if I was ever going to write anything else," he said.

No other work of his received so warm a reception. His later discussions of homosexuality in several novels and expressed preference for France "where at least I'm considered an American first and a black man second" (*1B*, 6) drew harsh criticism from within and without the civil rights movement. Like that of Williams, Baldwin's reputation slipped throughout the 1970s. "I'm very vulnerable to all of that," he said in an interview as the decade of his decline came to a close. He referred to the "dangerous, unending and unpredictable battle" of being a writer. His last published novel, *Just Above My Head* (1979), appeared to be a statement—rare for writers like himself and Tennessee Williams—that we not allow pain to destroy us.

V.

Cheerless Books That Cheer

At seventy, Edmund Wilson seemed out of sorts, unhappy with the year he was spending at the Center for Advanced Studies at Wesleyan University. Not even the effects of Johnny Walker at "happy hour" could lift his spirits. I told him that the book I always read when at lowest ebb was *Notes from Underground*. Contrary to the effect it is supposed to have, it always leaves me exhilarated. Five years later, after my arrival at Texas A&M, I would have been able to tell Edmund about the ROTC cadet who tried to beg off reading the book because it made him want to throw up. But Wilson demurred. Dostoevski was a terrible stylist, he said, and since he only read the Russians in the original, he would come out of the experience of reading *Notes from Underground* further depressed.

"I've been going back to Maurice Baring," he said. "In his novels, everyone is cultivated, well bred, cosmopolitan. I try to remember that society, even in America, used to be like that."

I never asked Edmund if he had read *Notes from Underground* in Russian *or* English. Even if he had not, I could never have succeeded in inducing him to do so. His reading was circumscribed in old age; he was *re*reading old favorites. But *Notes* still provides me the bracer most needed, perhaps, in old age. The Underground Man scowls at the world from the depths of his dark cellar. He is forty, a good age for scowling. I suspect that if he was told he had cancer he would have refused treatment just as the late Swiss jurist-teacher Peter Noll did in a powerful book, *In the Face of Death* (1989). Noll declined, at fifty-six, to submit to body-deadening surgery that might have extended his life but also forced him into a patient's role.

Now I can "play" the role of a healthy and normal person to the end. . . . People still take me for full; I sense a certain vague feeling of sympathy but not the embarrassing display of consideration accorded to patients, the endless conversations about the last operation, the further course of the disease, what the doctors said, when one has to return to the hospital.

From the opening lines, the Underground Man is like that: "I am a sick man. . . . I am a spiteful man. I am an unattractive man. I believe my liver is diseased. However, I know nothing at all about my disease. . . . [and] I don't consult a doctor." He keeps boasting that this attitude of his provides him with the "most advantageous advantage."

I have found only two other protagonists in modern fiction—that is, novels through the 1970s—who proclaim in the face of a seemingly paralyzing *acedia* their disposition to accommodate that state. One, of course, is Geoffrey Firmin, the Consul, of *Under the Volcano*. The other is Bob Slocum of Joseph Heller's *Something Happened* (1974). I have tried to link Slocum and Underground Man in the most challenging essay of my experience. "Notes from a Dark Heller" was originally published in *Texas Studies in Literature and Language* (Summer, 1981).

VI.

Notes from a Dark Heller: Bob Slocum and the Underground Man

Few works of contemporary fiction are so keyed to fear as Joseph Heller's second novel, *Something Happened* (1974). Within four paragraphs of the opening chapter ("I Get the Willies"), Bob Slocum, the book's saturnine narrator, has acknowledged closed doors as sure harbingers of disaster and recognized perspiration as a nightly visitant after "lies or booze or sex or just plain nerves and insomnia." Chapter two ("The Office in Which I Work") opens with the often quoted catalogue of the afraids:

[I]n the office in which I work there are five people of whom I am afraid. Each of these five people is afraid of four people (excluding overlaps), for a total of twenty, and each of those twenty people is afraid of six people, making a total of one hundred and twenty people who are feared by at least one person. Each of these one hundred and twenty people is *afraid* of the other one hundred and nineteen, and all of these one hundred and forty-five are *afraid* of the twelve men at the top.[1] (emphasis mine)

Long before he shifts his angst from office to home in order to build lengthy central chapters around the four members of his family, Slocum hints strongly that the real source of his fear lies neither at the office nor at home. He thinks of Andy Kagle, a crippled higher-up whom he will later shove aside, and finds in himself "a weird mixture of injured rage and cruel loathing that starts to rise within me and has to be suppressed" (*SH*, 44). A page later he admits to "something cankered and terrifying inside me that wishes to burst out and demolish him, lame and imperfect as he is." For all its apparent concern with the fragmented worlds of office and domestic politics,

Something Happened is really concerned principally with the forces in man which cause him to be terrified of himself.²

Slocum's terror is fed by his recourse to otherness, an involuntary slipping into someone else's personality ("There is this wretched habit I have of acquiring the characteristics of other people . . . even from people I don't like. . . . It's a weakness . . . a failure of character"—*SH*, 64). Even when he is apparently most fully his own person—even when, for example, he lashes out at his teenage daughter—he hears the invective with astonishment, as though

> [it] came from somebody else . . . directed harmfully at me as well as her, as though [it had its] source in some dark and frightening area of my soul with which I am not in communication. It is that same weird, perverse, glowering part of me that shelters my recurring impulse to kick Kagle's lame leg very hard, and to kick my daughter's leg under the table or strike her. . . . There are things going on inside me I cannot control and do not admire. (*SH*, 121)

Inwardly beached by the incalculable warp of time and change at some indefinite stage in his forties, Slocum collects the fragments of youthful personae—"hardy and impetuous patrol leader [seeking] merit badges," uniformed army recruit singing "those silly military songs exuberantly," insurance clerk riding daily "on a very stuffy subway car crowded with hostile, grimy adults who glared, snored, and sweated." He insists that that was somebody else's activity, generated outside himself, by "a second person who grew up alongside me . . . and filled in for me on occasions to experience things of which I did not wish to become a part" (*SH*, 123).

The later "things"—the seemingly upward spiral of jobs and downward arc of his domestic life, the dread monotony of his love affairs and fornications—do not formulate any self Slocum can recognize. *Something Happened* rivets attention anew on questions Thomas Mann posed at seventy in his single essay on perhaps the first novelist to raise disease to divinity.³ Mann excused his "cowardice" in avoiding Dostoevski on the basis that "the Daemonic is the poet's theme and not the writer's," but went on to imply a question: If life is not prudish, why might it not prefer fully confronted disease to unexamined health, the paradoxes of the irrational to the platitudes of the rational? Heller makes explicit the centrality of this question. In his search for a self that will speak up to hellish paradoxes in a voice he can recognize and accept, Slocum probes the same lower depths of Dostoevski's heroes, generally, and of the Underground Man⁴ in particular.

Slocum's reference to a kind of hierarchy of awareness is strongly suggestive of the Underground Man's hierarchy of confidences.

And there was a third person of whom I am aware only dimly and about whom I know almost nothing, only that he is there. And I am aware of still one more person whom I am not even aware of; and this one watches everything shrewdly, even me, from some secure hideout in my mind in which he remains invisible and anonymous, and makes stern, censorious judgments, about everything, even me. He hardly ever sleeps. (*SH*, 123)

Every man has reminiscences which he would not tell to everyone but only to his friends. He has other matters in his mind which he would not reveal even to his friends, but only to himself, and that in secret. But there are other things which a man is afraid to tell even to himself, and every decent man has a number of such things stored away in his mind. (*NU*, I, xi, 35)

It is the Underground Man's view that the more decent a person is, the greater the number of unmentionables that is stored away. Like Slocum, Dostoevski's hero, at forty, has "only lately determined to remember some of my early adventures" in an effort to understand why he has gone underground. Heller's hero, in the words of a recent popular song, wonders "if that's all there is." He remains *over*ground only to get the big promotion he both desires and detests. With him, as with the Underground Man, the only commitment is to secrecy. Both live in fear that someone might see them, meet them, recognize them.[5]

The broad purpose of this essay is to link those things-happening—more often, things-not-happening—in Bob Slocum's beleaguered consciousness with the workings of that favorite donnée of the great Russian: the nonstop inner warfare that animates life underground. More specifically, this essay will examine parallel and contrasting tonal and rhetorical devices they deploy in the interests of winning the war each wages for the survival of consciousness. It will conclude with a comparison and contrast of the price the two heroes pay for that inner survival.

However, before one can understand the efficacy of Slocum's long asides and the Underground Man's dialogic monologues, it is necessary to confront briefly the tonal oversimplifications to which, because of their chip-on-the-shoulder surfaces, the two personae are prone.

2

On most first readings of *Notes from Underground,* the difficulty with the eleven brief segments that make up the apparently confessional/masochistic first part is how to resolve their inertia-ridden, arrogance-fed, contradiction-oriented viewpoint. One tries to imagine what sort of audience would be "gentlemen" enough to put up with it. Wasiolek states the problem well: "The Underground man is vain, nasty, petty, tyrannical, vicious, cowardly, morbidly sensitive, and self-contradictory. He hates his fellow workers, never forgets an insult, tyrannizes over those who offer affection, and offers affection to those who tyrannize over him. He turns love into lust, friendship into tyranny, and principle into spite. He respects neither love, nor affection, nor friendship, nor principle, nor logic. He is a sick and spiteful man. And yet Dostoevski approves of him . . . makes him his hero."[6]

Where Bob Slocum continually wishes he could kick Kagle in his game leg or his daughter under the table, the Underground Man longs to give the Crystal Palace, the whole nineteenth century, a shattering cosmic kick. He begins, however, at the same fretful, almost hypochondriacal, level as Slocum, who at the end of the "office" chapter complains about bad feet and a deteriorating jawbone that will cost him his teeth. The Underground Man, later to apotheosize a toothache, glories in his bad liver, which he will happily leave untreated. Unlike Slocum, he was content to remain a low-ranked employee (civil servant) until he came into six thousand rubles, enabling him to retire and settle in his Underground corner. He further mirrors Slocum's fear of the demons within when he professes to see introspection as malady ("I am firmly convinced not only that a great deal of, but that any consciousness is a disease"—*NU,* I, ii, 6). However, later in the same paragraph, the Underground Man reveals that his is a selective resentment. The more he comes to know of what the world considers goodness, the more he opts for what the world takes to be dirt.

The more conscious I was . . . of all that "sublime and beautiful," the more deeply I sank into my mire . . . [until] the bitterness turned into a sort of shameful accursed sweetness and finally into real positive enjoyment! . . . Let me explain: the enjoyment here consisted precisely in the hyperconsciousness of one's own degradation . . .; that you could never become a different person; . . . [that] you probably would not want to change.

Throughout these early pages, the Underground Man wryly accepts his sentence, doomed as he is to envy insects, complain like a hunchback or dwarf, store up injustices in his mouse hole. He will moan as one with a toothache, but the moans, he warns implicitly, will be unceasing and soon prove to be not of physical but of cultural origin, those of "a man affected by progress and European civilization" (*NU,* I, iv, 13). The groans in Dostoevski's "existential overture"[7] have the same effect as the laughter in the allegorical tales of Hawthorne.[8] There is no mirth, only a kind of mordant heckle, in the latter; there is less pain than polemic in the former.

> Is it nasty for you to hear my foul moans? Well, let it be nasty. Here I will let you have an even nastier flourish in a minute. . . . It seems our development and our consciousness must go further to understand all the intricacies of this sensuality. You laugh? I am delighted. My jokes, gentlemen, are of course in bad taste, uneven, unsolved, lacking self-confidence. But of course that is because I do not respect myself. Can a man with consciousness respect himself at all? (*NU*, I, iv, 14)

The passage begins and ends in questionings. Dostoevski has seen beyond the Enlightenment and its emblematic Crystal Palace to what, resorting to effete French, he says has been overlooked by *l'homme de la nature et de la vérité.* He has seen that the sweep of *human nature*–extinguishing "laws of nature" has overrun, in William Barrett's words, "petty figures like that of the Underground Man who beneath their nondescript surface are monsters of frustration and resentment."[9] But the final question is the more important one. Constance Garnett's traditional translation is "Can a *man of perception* respect himself at all?"[10] For purposes of this paper, Matlaw's "*Can a man with consciousness* respect himself at all?*" is a crucial refinement (NU, I, iv, 14). The Underground Man, bearing replicas of Everyman's moral history, asks rhetorically if adversity, stress, chaos, and destruction can be other than concomitants of consciousness, an inner seismograph that is frequently incompatible with the calm of reason. Fuming at the toll exacted by exclusive reliance on the "laws of nature," the Underground Man concludes: "If desire should at any time come to terms with reason, we shall then, of course, reason and not desire" (*NU,* I, viii, 24).

More than three times as long as *Notes* and about sixteen times the length of the "Underground" section, *Something Happened* is also, on first reading, unrelieved in its tone of pressing desperation. Slocum's is, at best, "the fascination of the abominator . . . lost . . . with a profound emptiness. A sad, absurd, vicious, grasping, climbing, womanizing, cowardly, sadistic, groveling, loving, yearning, anxious, fearful victim . . . of being born human."[11] The book reflects the fashionable alienation that is endemic to much contemporary American fiction but carries it into a nether region of the mockingly demonic with what John Gardner, not without a grudging respect, calls "the Satanist's leer."[12]

That leer cannot, I believe, be attributed to the times, whether they are the 1970s or the 1960s or some indeterminate period between. If Slocum was in World War II—the book suggests he was—he must be well into his fifties.

Yet a passage near the end of the book—one that comes just ahead of the novel's crisis when some exact definition of age might be expected—is pitched to ten-year intervals looking ahead to fifty-five, presumably from the vantage of forty-five (*SH*, 523)

Heller implied in the *Playboy* interview that he was less interested in establishing precise "era" time than in "compress [ing it] into almost a solid substance."[13] It is outside the scope of this study to examine whether Heller may have ended in creating an encompassing frame for the times without providing a picture. For my purposes it is enough to say that, despite the novel's length, Heller's mindscape is not evocative enough of precise features of any time-terrain even to earn what one reviewer calls its "sociological scrim [from] . . . *The Organization Man*[14] or what another calls its incursion "into the liberated and vibrating 70's."[15]

True, Heller purports to see signs of entropy in aerosol whipped cream "that isn't whipped and isn't cream." He laments like an ecological Spengler in passages like this one:

From sea to shining sea the country is filling with slag, shale, and used-up automobile tires. The fruited plain is coated with insecticide and chemical fertilizers. Even pure horseshit is hard to come by these days. They add preservatives. . . . Towns die. Oil spills. Money talks. God listens. God is good, a real team player. "American the Beautiful" isn't. . . . (I hear America singing fuck off. . . .) (*SH*, 454)

Something Happens misses, I believe, the essence and feel of any era. Heller meets his commitment elsewhere. In its power to unfold, from the inside out, the anatomy of a fugitive psyche, he has created a schizoid sickness so controlled that Slocum can pause in his inventory of fears to hope "I never live to see the real me come out" (*SH*, 229).

It is tempting to try to apply the book's title to sequence or cycle, to assume that its words bear sociohistoric cause and effect. However, the sheer fecundity of Slocum's inner world is such that it forces the book's outer furnishings to take on distortion. One is ill-advised to infer themes from those few scenes that emerge as "rendered" from Slocum's underground.

Heller's best paradox has it that in Slocum's house "nothing is suppressed . . . everything is suppressed" (*SH*, 240). Suppression is always the effect of fear. Slocum's most fearsome fear—that of himself—leads to a book-long nihilistic solipsism whose only antidote is connection.[16] For 523 of the 530 pages of *Something Happened*, we are locked inside Slocum's desperately professed disconnection. Then, on page 524, in the novel's only "shown" scene, something *does* happen: connection. The "mercy-killing" of his nine-year-old son, an act of stunning horror, fuses dramatically what, until then, had been fused rhetorically: Slocum's outer and inner—the apparent versus actual—personae. It also produces the monochromatic tone of the final pages that defines the dreadful results of Slocum's interior *Bildungsroman*. I shall deal more fully with the implications of Heller's crisis scene later. I shall do so in terms of the equivalent "connecting" action of *Notes from the Underground*, the encounter between the Underground Man and Liza, the prostitute.

3

In the *Playboy* interview Heller declared that "I put everything I knew about the external world into *Catch-22* and everything I knew about the interior world into *Something Happened.*" "I have a universe in my head," Slocum thinks joylessly. A page later, he gives a characteristic twist to the cliché: "A man's head is his castle." Consciousness spares him nothing, but at least the silences are his own. The world is a place where he is sandwiched between people who will not speak. He confesses to missing his mother even though his only memory is of a human appendage he discarded, her resentments muted, though no less felt after a stroke. At times he even misses Derek, the forsaken—the idiot—son who could not speak from the beginning. Life outside consciousness is a series of tableaux in which the speaking members of the Slocum family fill the "cavernous voids" with strident sounds aimed at silencing. Not even in the unconscious can he be delivered:

In dreams I have trouble speaking. My tongue feels dead and dry and swollen enough to choke my mouth. Its coat is coarse. It will not move when I want it to, and I am in danger and feel terror because I cannot speak or scream. (*SH,* 332)

Aware of his own paralysis in the face of, even at the remotest prospect of, human distress, Slocum retreats inward, shuts out the disturbing external life by half-heartedly lusting for the latest girl in the office. But it is two other women—one living, one dead—who provide nourishment for "this crawling animal flourishing somewhere inside me" (*SH,* 102). One is his wife, whose dissolution he understands and contributes to and whose predictable infidelity he both encourages and fears; the other, Virginia Markowitz, the openly inviting "older" girl of twenty-one, the object of his erotic fantasies at seventeen, the suicide by gas whose death he learns about after his return from overseas a year and a half after it happened.

For the Underground Man, consciousness is a mediation between a zestful inability to make his behavior square with his emotional needs and what Edward Wasiolek calls "the circle of hurt-and-be-hurt . . . the basic psychological law of Dostoevski's world" (Wasiolek, 54). Dostoevski's hero, like Heller's, raises the perverse to a general principle of behavior, "the most advantageous advantage."

Man everywhere and always, whoever he may be, has preferred to act as he wished and not in the least as his reason and advantage dictated. Why, one may choose what is contrary to one's own interests, and sometimes one *positively ought* (that is my idea). One's own free unfettered choice, one's own fancy, however wild it may be, one's own fancy worked up at times to frenzy. (*NU*, I, vii, 23)

For both men external life is a lie. The Underground Man quotes Heine on the autobiographical fallacy but places his own testament outside the public world, "written for myself . . . a question of form, only an empty form" (*NU*, I, xi, 35). Slocum, for all his verbal thrashing inside himself, also appears to pay homage to empty forms:

I must remember not to smile too much. I must maintain a facade. I must remember to continue acting correctly subservient and clearly grateful to people in the company and at the university and country clubs I'm invited to who expected to find me feeling humble, eager, lucky, and afraid. (*SH*, 380)

Form is the men. The Underground Man's monologue contains an intersecting capability. His speech, from the start, accommodates to some other anticipated presence. The sheer number of times his responses are made in the expectation of either a question or a rebuttal is extraordinary.

Heller has been faulted by a number of critics on the one-dimensionality of his "form." Most recently, Susan Strehle Klemptner declared that "we are almost completely restricted to his version of reality" and concludes that Bob Slocum is an unreliable narrator and Heller a more subtle novelist for that fact.[17] In the interview cited earlier, Heller asserts that *Something Happened* is a "radical" work, but only in structure. He claims, without elaboration, to have fused first and third persons "in a way I've never seen before."[18] While respecting Klemptner's sense of Slocum's determinism—and, hence, unreliability—I would also suggest that Heller has gone to great lengths to deepen Slocum's self-consciousness. He has managed a fusion—his own word—of Slocum's perceptions at the *action* level and those of an even more candid—and reliable—persona who rethinks and *regrades* everything. Slocum seeks his own most advantageous advantage by what Klemptner, in another essay, refers to as his "parenthetical tic."[19] Perhaps a third of the novel is set between parentheses—a palimpsest (something like what Lillian Hellman means by *pentimento*)[20] on Slocum's less reliable sentiments.

These parenthetical overlays of Slocum's are the equivalent rhetorical devices to the Underground Man's anticipated refutations, those long asides invariably addressed to "gentlemen" who are never identified and, in fact, do not exist.

Both works, moreover, are in the tradition of the *monologue intérieur,* although neither Dostoevski, long before him, nor Heller, long after him, carries the form to the lengths Joyce did. Nevertheless, in both works readers are established, from the first lines, in the thought of the principal personage. The novels consist of an uninterrupted unleashing of that thought. Joyce, of course, goes to astounding lengths that need not be chronicled here to show how half-formed thoughts enter and leave consciousness with almost impossible rapidity. Dostoevski and Heller, although not so innovative, are also impatient with the usual means of narrative expression. Each in his own way is aware that the mind, a storehouse for injustices, keeps racing on.

In *Notes,* the Underground Man, in the guise of a cellar mouse, recognizes that even in the maelstrom nothing is lost:

For forty years together it will remember its injury down to the smallest, most shameful detail, and every time will add, of itself, details still more shameful, spitefully teasing and irritating itself with its own imagination. It will be ashamed of its own fancies, but yet it will recall everything, it will go over it again and again, it will invent lies against itself pretending that those things might have happened, and will forgive nothing. . . . On its deathbed it will recall it all over again, with interest accumulated over all the years. (*NU,* I, iii, 10–11)

Bob Slocum sees inner life as a series of nightmares whose course, like a runaway train, he tries to stop but cannot:

(. . . and I lie in darkness like a limbless baby while they run their ruthless course through me rampantly as though I were a helpless and disembodied mind, or this tiny, armless, legless baby still imprisoned motionlessly in a cradle or womb. I can't bear them. I forget them. They leave traces. I have them often. I have them whenever I want them.) (I know so many things I'm afraid to find out.) (*SH,* 154)

As important as the pathology of monomania is the thrust of both books to dialectic.[21] Dostoevski places his hero, spatially, in a dark cellar but, tonally, on a kind of podium with some of the resonances of an orator. This, as Matlaw points out, "gives the work the illusion of dialogue and makes it seem like a sustained polemic with an opponent, as if the narrator were anticipating objections."[22]

No doubt you think, gentlemen, that I want to amuse you. You are mistaken in that, too. I am not all such a merry person as you imagine, or as you may imagine; however, if irritated by all this babble (and I can feel you are irritated) you decide to ask me just who I am. . . . (*NU*, I, i, 5)

No question would find a readier respondent than someone who began by asserting that his greatest pleasure lay in talking about himself.

Bob Slocum builds his dialectic around the mystery of who he is. Heller equips him to deal with the only audience he needs—himself. His recognition of the "voice" dilemma—public versus private—also defines Heller's aesthetic problem.

(I wonder if the time will ever come when I will begin, without recognizing I am doing it, and without detecting the change, saying out loud the things I now say privately to myself or verbalize in contemplation and if I will therefore become psychotic or one of those men—more often than not they are women—who talk out loud to themselves on sidewalks and buses. If that happens, I will blend my inner world with my outer world. . . .) (*SH*, 227)

It is this paper's position that Heller attempts the blend through a powerful, if never precisely programmed, orchestration of outside and inside thoughts, the "overt" versus the "parenthetical" Slocum.

Now let us see in some detail how Dostoevski and Heller—literary ventriloquists both—"throw" their voices to accommodate, respectively, imagined interlocutor and parenthetical insider.

4

In *Problems of Dostoyevsky's Poetics*, Mikhail Bakhtin believes that "the emphasis of scholars and critics on the ideological problems of his work has overshadowed the deeper, more timeless structural aspects of his artistic vision."[23] Bakhtin praises Dostoevski as the practitioner of what English translator R. W. Rotsel renders as the "dialogical line" which leads to his creation of a "new variant of the novelistic genre—the polyphonic novel." Both terms, if I read Bakhtin correctly, stand as improvisations on, even refutations of, what we might appropriately refer to as "monological" or "monophonic"; that is, one-dimensional. To apply Bakhtin's notion to Dostoevski's *oeuvre* is beyond the scope of this paper. However, its application to *Notes from the Underground* provides a perspective that was more helpful to me than any other source in elucidating the voices of this book.

Bakhtin finds "extreme and acute interior dialogization" something that "amazes" the reader from the start. The confession, he declares, contains literally not a single monologically firm, undissociated word. "From the very first sentence the hero's speech begins to cringe and crack under the influence of the anticipated word of the other person, with which he, from the very first step, enters into a most intense polemic" (Bakhtin, 190). The Soviet critic goes through the Underground Man's opening tirades and dialogizes them; that is, he fills in the narrator's anticipations, giving them a kind of invisible "presence." This way we see that each "monologue" is intersected by expectation, a trimming of conversational sails. In short, the narrowness of monologue becomes the circularity of dialogue. To return for a moment to the aforementioned force that is capable of blunting nihilism—or monolog—a *connection* is made. The hero from the underground comes to understand the inevitability of this connection:

"This relationship to the other person's consciousness gives rise to a peculiar perpetuum mobile of his internal polemic with the other person and with the other person and with himself, an endless dialog in which one speech begets a second, the second, a third, and so ad infinitum" (Bakhtin, 193).

In the extended passage below, one which precedes the speaker's hierarchical view of reminiscence that I have stressed from the outset, Bakhtin's dialogization is especially well illustrated. One notes (1) the initial arrogance of his underground status, (2) a heated denial of that status, (3) a disavowal of all that he has written so far, and finally, (4) a selfdenunciation phrased in the inferred words of an invisible accuser:

(1) The long and the short of it is, gentlemen, that it is better to do nothing! Better conscious inertia! And so hurrah for underground! . . .
(2) . . . Bah! But after all, even now I am living! I am lying because I know as surely as two times two makes four, that it is not at all underground that is better, but something different, quite different, for which I long but which I cannot find! Damn underground!
(3) I will tell you another thing that would be better, and that is, if I myself believed even an iota of what I have just written. I swear to you, gentlemen, that I do not believe one thing, not even one word, of what I have just written. That is, I believe it, perhaps, but at the same time, I feel and suspect that I am lying myself blue in the face. . . .
(4) . . . "Isn't that shameful, isn't that humiliating?" you will say, perhaps, shaking your heads contemptuously. "You long for life and try to settle the problems of life by a logical tangle. And how tiresome, how insolent your outbursts are, and at the same time *how scared you are.*" (*NU,* I, xi, 33–34, emphasis added)

Bakhtin's sense of dialogization—his notion of the hero's dancing to the tune of another's words—links crucially with the "scared" Slocum and his awareness of an inside "filler-inner" for desperate occasions and a censor and judge who watches everything and never sleeps. Heller's version of dialogization is the monitorship of the overt Slocum by the parenthetical Slocum. The parenthetical Slocum, in a sense, reverses the action of id and ego.

I wonder what kind of person would come out if I ever did erase all my inhibitions at once, what kind of being is bottled up inside me now. Would I like him? I think not. There's more than one of me, probably. There's more than just an id. I know that I could live with my id if I ever looked upon it whole, sort of snuggle up and get cozy with it. . . . Deep down inside, I might really be great. Deep down inside, I think not. (*SH*, 229)

From Dostoevskian depths, something like id moderates something like ego in the interests of an insistent though, until almost the end, unknown self.

Toward the conclusion of his discussion of the dialogization of *Notes* ("The formal significance of . . . [the] dialogical oppositions in Dostoevsky's works is very great . . . [and] nowhere given in such abstractly clear-cut [or] . . . mathematical form"), Bakhtin raises an issue of style that is of extraordinary pertinence to serious readers of both books—a "deliberate uncomeliness" of presentation. This stylistic "inelegance," Bakhtin asserts, "is, however, subject to a particular artistic logic. . . . [The word of the Underground Man] is addressed to the other person and *to the speaker himself (in his interior dialog with him*self). . . . In relation to the other person it strives to be deliberately inelegant, to be in every respect obnoxious. . . . As a result . . . prosaism in the representation of his inner life attains extreme proportions" (Bakhtin, 193, italics added for emphasis). So extreme, in fact, has been the dialogic monolog that at its end the Underground Man, in words suggestive of Bob Slocum at his most desolate, sees in his lot a kind of memory of the species:

All the traits of an anti-hero are *expressly* gathered together here, and what matters most, it produces an unpleasant impression, for we are all divorced from life, we are all crippled . . . [and] we immediately feel a sort of loathing for actual "real life" and so cannot even stand to be reminded of it. (*NU*, II, x, 114)

Finally, anticipating to the end objections, the Underground Man appears to renounce the Conradian "one of us"[24] for the "most advantageous advantage" of life underground:

I have only, after all, in my life carried to an extreme what you have not dared to carry halfway, and what's more, you have taken your cowardice for good sense, and have found comfort in deceiving yourselves. So that perhaps, after all, there is more "life" in me than in you. (*NU*, II, x, 115)

Although entirely within himself, Bob Slocum's interior dialogue, at its most powerful, resonates outward, too, implicitly asking for acceptance of a hidden commonality"

I have noticed that people tend to grow up pretty much the way they began; and hidden somewhere inside every bluff or quiet man and woman I know, I think, is the fully formed, but uncompleted, little boy or girl that once was and will always remain as it always has been, suspended lonesomely inside its own past, waiting hopefully, vainly, to resume, longing insatiably for company, pining desolately for that time to come when it will be safe . . . to burst outside exuberantly, stretch its arms, fill its lungs with invigorating air, without fear at last. . . .
    . . . And hiding inside of me somewhere . . . is a timid little boy just like my son who wants to be his best friend and *wishes he could come outside and play.* (*SH*, 213)

In a curious way, coming out to play is a perfect metaphor for the parenthetical Slocum, even if the "play" is always, like Dostoevski's, a game of hurt and be hurt. This Slocum lives a life of his own. His presence, like the Underground Man's implied opponent, enables the novelist to open the insider's game to outside scrutiny.

A scene from a middle chapter ("My Little Boy Is Having Difficulties") reveals Heller's technique at its best. Against the boy's wishes, Slocum visits his son's school to look into his anxiety about gym class. He finds himself in the intimidating presence of an Atlas type named Forgione. Heller manages Slocum's ambivalence with great skill. The boy wonders "why he must . . . be better than all the other boys in pushball, kickball, throwball, shoveball, dodgeball, baseball, volleyball." The father also wonders, but parenthetically: "(It all does seem indeed like an awful lot of balls for a young man like him to have to carry around, doesn't it?)" When Forgione accuses the boy ("I don't like to say this, Mr. Slocum, but sometimes he acts like a baby"), Slocum would like to "kill" Forgione not only because he is sympathetic to his son's plight but because—and the words are in parentheses—"what [Forgione] says is true and I didn't want anyone to notice." His overt response—no parentheses—is different, bogus: "'He *is* only a kid, you know.' I fake an indulgent laugh." At the end of the conversation, Slocum fears that Forgione will tell the boy that his father has interceded. He pledges him to secrecy, begs him not to "take it out" on the boy:

"No, of course not," Forgione exclaimed[25] indignantly. "Why should I want to do that?" (Because you're human, I think.) "What kind of man do you think I am?"
    "Cro-Magnon," I reply crisply.
    (But that, of course, I say to myself. . . .) (*SH*, 224–27)

Some two pages, about one hundred lines, intervene between Forgione's question and Slocum's actual answer. We find him ruminating on what I have tried to identify as the aesthetic problem of *Something Happened*, the tension between inside and outside thoughts, the unlikelihood of any resolution. The problem, of course, was Dostoevski's too.

One is ill-advised to look for one-to-one correlations between overt and parenthetical voices as if the former were the lies of externality and the latter Slocum's invocation of that "part [or those parts] of me I can't find." Still, these unlocatable, though identifiable, parts always answer Slocum's inner roll call. The parenthetical sections invariably constitute response at the level of deepest resource. Parentheses always involve linking—an outsider's outside device to pair harsh experience with the mediating self. At the beginning the parentheses are most noticeable as a series of intrusive "ha-ha"s. At the end, as several commentators have observed,[26] the "ha-ha"s have become the repetitive "swish!" of his golf club, a kind of objective correlative for Slocum's promotion and subsequent participation in country club ritual.

A powerful scene between Slocum and son prefigures the book's dramatic ending and illustrates the narrator's awareness that the desired blend of outer and inner voices can never come off. Slocum has been battling his wife and daughter in his characteristically diffused way. Suddenly, amid it all, he reverts to "the deserted little boy I know who will never grow older and never change . . . bruised . . . lonely . . . thin . . . still alive, yet out of control" (*SH*, 145). As if on call, his son appears. He has been watching the domestic fireworks. Before he can restrain himself, Slocum stamps on his son's foot.

"Ow!" he wails.
"Oh!" I gasp.
He has been waiting there stealthily, taking everything in.
"It's okay!" he assures me breathlessly.
Clutching his foot, hopping lamely on the other, he shrinks away from me against the doorjamb, as though I had stepped on him on purpose, and intend to step on him again.
"Did I hurt you?" I demand.
"It's *okay*."
. . . (He is supplicating anxiously for me to believe he is okay, pleading with me to stop pulverizing him beneath the crushing weight of my overwhelming solicitude. "Leave me alone—please!" is what I realize he is actually screaming at me fiercely, and it slashes me to the heart to acknowledge that. I take a small step back.) "See?" he asks timorously, and demonstrates.
He puts his foot to the floor and tests it gingerly, proving to me he is able to stand without holding on. I see a minute bruise on the surface of his skin, a negligible,

white scrape left by the edge of my shoe, . . . (He is probably the only person in the world for whom I would do almost anything I could to shield from all torment and harm. . . . In my dreams sometimes he is in mortal danger, and I cannot . . . save him . . . He perishes, but the tragedy, in my dreams, is always mine. In real life, he is suffering already from secret tortures he is reluctant to divulge. . . .) He seems out of breath and waxen with fright as he stands below me now watching me stand there watching him (the delicate oval pods beneath his eyes are a pathological blue), and he is trembling in such violent consternation as he waits for me to do something that it seems he must certainly shake himself into broken little pieces if I don't reach out instantly to hold him together. (I don't reach out. I have that sinking, intuitive feeling again that if I do put my hand out towards him, he will think I am going to hit him and fall back from me in dread.) (*SH*, 145–46)

The intersection of outer/inner thoughts here has not only revealed Slocum's region of acutest vulnerability but has also prepared us for the fulfillment of his subliminal need "to be rid" of the person he loves most.

5

I am indebted to Professor Wasiolek for his profound analysis of the moral dialectic of *Notes from Underground* and his convincing demonstrations that the work, written when Dostoevski was forty-two years old, laid out themes that would be refined in dramatic form in the great novels that followed. Wasiolek's reading stresses the "dialectical nature" of Dostoevski's world in which the suffering of the Underground Man must be taken not as suffering but as willfulness and self-love. Following Bakhtin's lead, my emphasis on the Underground Man's unceasing polemic with a "felt" though invisible antagonist stands as an acknowledgement of his forensic tone.

There is no "reason" in Dostoevski's world, Wasiolek avers, only someone to reason. Ideas are always someone's and *"every act of reason . . . is a covert act of will"* (italics Wasiolek's, Wasiolek, 55). In the context of this essay, the important word is "covert." Deep in the underground of consciousness, this hero strives to seek confirmation of self in the syndrome of hurt and be hurt. So too, as we have seen, does Bob Slocum. Something happens to the Underground Man that enables a breakdown, however momentary, of the will to injure. It is his encounter, at the end of the novel, with Liza. To complete my argument for a fictional kinship, it now remains to determine whether anything happens to modify Slocum's "Satanist's leer" to allow him against his deepest fears, if only temporarily, to rise to the responsibility of being human.

6

First—and briefly—the resolution of *Notes:* The second part ("Apropos of the Wet Snow"), twice the length of the first, takes place sixteen years earlier. We are reintroduced at an earlier stage to the protagonist's resentments of the age in which "every decent man . . . must be a coward and a slave." Because the early words of part two are so similar to Slocum's catalog of the afraids, it is useful to quote from them:

Of course, I hated all my fellow-clerks, one and all, and I despised them all, yet at the same time I was, as it were, afraid of them. . . . It somehow happened quite suddenly then that I alternated between despising them and thinking them superior to myself. (*NU*, II, i, 38)

Throughout "Apropos of the Wet Snow," it is as if the twenty-four-year-old civil servant is determined to face in person *l'homme de la nature et de la vérité* and conduct in action what, in the monolog, he has conducted, at forty, in dialectic. His initial encounter is especially interesting because of an exact parallel in *Something Happened.* Having just observed a man being thrown out of the window of a tavern, the clerk envies the evicted one and enters the tavern to provoke a similar fate. The officer who had been the bouncer refuses to be provoked and merely moves him from one spot to another without seeming to notice him. Insults—even blows—would have been welcome, he thinks, "but I absolutely could not forgive his having moved me and so completely failing to notice me" (*NU,* II, i, 43). A fretful apostrophe on the wages of neglect follows from which only one conclusion emerges: the necessity to avenge.

Early in *Something Happened,* Slocum chafes over his neglect, generally, and over the matter of a three-minute speech he enthusiastically prepared for but is never permitted to read at the company convention in Puerto Rico:

It was downright humiliating to be the only one of Green's managers left out. The omission was conspicuous, the rebuff intentionally public, and for the following four days, while others had a great, robust time golfing and boozing it up, I was the object of expressions of pity and solemn, perfunctory commiseration from many people I hate and wanted to hit and scream at. It was jealousy and pure, petty spite that made Green decide abruptly to push me off the schedule . . . after I had worked so long and nervously (I even rehearsed at home just about every night.) (*SH,* 30)

Wasiolek is only one of many Russian scholars to show conclusively that the major scenes in part two—the one above, the humiliation of the clerk at the hands of Zverkov and his friends, even the brief love affair with Liza—are parodies of scenes in *What Is to Be Done?* (1863), a Chernyshevski novel Dostoevski despised. Such concerns lie outside my concerns here. It is enough to say, with Wasiolek, that these dramatizations of the dialectic of part one demonstrate that "between men . . . there can exist only an unremitting duel in which each strives to subject the other to his 'free' will. . . . The consequences of this dialectic of freedom are terrifying: every action of principle, every act of unselfishness, every good, beautiful, virtuous, reasonable act is only appearance . . . deceptions, for beneath them is . . . man's free will and his deadly duel with other 'free' wills" (Wasiolek, 44, 48).

Dostoevski foreshadows the Liza episode, which concludes *Notes*, much earlier. "I was already a tyrant at heart; I wanted to exercise unlimited power over him," the younger Underground Man admits while recounting a flawed friendship with a fellow student. "He was a simple and devoted soul; but when he submitted to me completely I began to hate him immediately and rejected him—as though all I needed him for was to win a victory over him, to subjugate him" (*NU,* II, iii, 60). This brief account of an unimportant relationship summarizes the evolvement of the vital adventure with Liza. Disheartened by the humiliation suffered at the hands of Zverkov, he finds in making love to a prostitute a perfect expression of his self-revulsion. Later, as they sit apart in the darkness, the sullen clerk determines to use her in other ways—first, by projecting silent hatred; then, by telling a coarse and fabricated story. But she hardly responds at all, neither involved nor intimidated. He invents an opposite strategy to unnerve her: a lecture on the joys of love and family life followed by an expression of sympathy for the lot of the prostitute. The result of his seeming compassion is to leave Liza distraught. Still later, his conscience bothers him ("the truth was already gleaming. The loathsome truth!"). That gleaming truth is this: that, although his compassion and hopes had converted her to a new life, he had been ridiculing her throughout. Like the forty-year-old Underground Man who would disavow his philosophy, the twenty-four-year-old has disbelieved his own counsel to Liza. A series of meetings between them merely extends the cycle of hurt and be hurt except for one astounding moment. Liza experiences an epiphany. In the painful ecstasy of an embrace, Dostoevskian *nadryv* (laceration) is transcended, love expressed.

What happened was this: Liza, wounded and crushed by me, understood a great deal more than I imagined. She understood from all this what a woman understands first of all, if she feels genuine love, that is, that I was myself unhappy. . . . Suddenly she leapt up from her chair . . . held out her hands, yearning toward me, though still timid and not daring to stir. At this point there was an upheaval in my heart too. Then she suddenly rushed to me, threw her arms round me and burst into tears. I, too, could not restrain myself, and sobbed as I never had before. (*NU,* II, ix, 109)

So lyrical is this scene by comparison with the rest of the novel that it is difficult to read it dialectically. None of my students can. Wasiolek views Liza's love as at once "liberation" from the trap of hurt and be hurt and a new motive for insult (Wasiolek, 52). It is as if the Underground Man, given an epiphanic taste of the power of human love, determines not to allow it to disarm the depravity with which he is more at home. So he accepts Liza's love only as a weapon for humiliating himself. He leaves her, convinced as he is that he has "saved" her. "Purification," he moans, "is the most stinging and painful consciousness." He is, of course, talking not only about Liza's consciousness but his own. "Which is better," he asks, "cheap happiness or exalted sufferings?"

7

In a book as long as *Something Happened,* Heller's skill in compressing the last two chapters into fewer than twenty pages may be overlooked. For that reason alone one wishes that Heller had disciplined himself in the first five hundred pages, had had some diffidence in liberating every "Slocumlocution" he could float upon the waters. Heller told the *Playboy* interviewer that he had allowed major editorial cuts. He might have considered even more of them, so as to concentrate and shape his effect more clearly.

Finally, what are we to make of the ending?

Very little, judging by some of the commentaries:

Calvin Bedient hardly deals with it at all, noting only that "in a muddled, undersized 'climax,' one of the children dies as a result of Slocum's panicky protectiveness."[27]

John Gardner accords the novel four pages in *On Moral Fiction* (1978),[28] but "despite Heller's novelistic power," he dismisses *Something Happened* as "finally not profound but only sad-sardonic and thus unsatisfying." Gardner commits a crashing error in his assessment of the climax, having the wrong son die: ". . . some such terrible miracle as happens in Heller's novel, releasing Bob Slocum from his own weakness and at least one of his painful psychological burdens, the existence of his loving, *pitiful idiot son* (emphasis added).[29] Derek, the idiot son, is not really portrayed, loving or otherwise, in the novel; after the normal son has died, Slocum makes it clear that Derek will not immediately be institutionalized.

Susan Strehle Kemptner's is by far the most searching analysis. She views Slocum's nine-year-old son as "the most compelling character in the novel . . . the unacknowledged hero." She argues persuasively that the son's words and acts "reveal an instinctual notion that people are free to choose." They provide an unused passport by which Slocum, whom she regards as predetermined to make poor choices, might have found agape. "Fulfilling his own prophecy," writes Kemptner, "Slocum succeeds in ridding himself of the poignant reminder of his freedom and responsibility."[30]

My own view of the significance of the son's death is just as bleak as Kemptner's but for different reasons. While I cannot elevate the boy to unacknowledged hero, I look on his death by strangulation as a terrifying fulfillment of a "prophecy" that was made more than three hundred pages earlier when his son asks Slocum, "'If you want to get rid of me, how will you do it?' 'With hugs and kisses,' I answer in exasperation" (SH, 217). The death at the distraught hands of his father, one which I regard as technically and fictionally accidental, fulfills, in fact, Slocum's dread prophecy about himself that he has enunciated throughout the novel. "Something did happen to me somewhere," he says at the beginning, "that robbed me of confidence and courage and left me with a fear of discovery and change and a positive dread of everything unknown that may occur" (SH, 6).

The book's first 523 pages thrust forward Slocum's deepest fears—of himself—and they are fatally confirmed by what happens when none of those surrogate voices from within can delay any longer the human challenge. The death scene, a marvel of concision, is brief enough to be quoted in entirety:

"Something happened!" a youth in his early teens calls excitedly to a friend and goes running ahead to look.

A crowd is collecting at the shopping center. A car has gone out of control and mounted the sidewalk. A plate glass window has been smashed. My boy is lying on the ground. (He has not been decapitated.) He is screaming in agony and horror, with legs and arms twisted brokenly and streams of blood spurting from holes in his face and head and pouring down over one hand from inside a sleeve. He spies me with a start and extends an arm. He is panic-stricken. So am I.

"Daddy!"

He is dying. A terror, a pallid, pathetic shock more dreadful than any I have been able to imagine, has leaped into his face. I can't stand it. He can't stand it. He hugs me. He looks beggingly at me for help. His screams are piercing. I can't bear to see him suffering such agony and fright. I have to do something. I hug his face deeper into the crock of my shoulder. I hug him tightly with both my arms. I squeeze.

"Death," says the doctor, "was due to asphyxiation." (*SH,* 524)

One notes a single parenthesis—"(He has not been decapitated.)"

It is not his son who has been "decapitated" but Slocum. It is he who in the five-page epilogue ("Nobody Knows What I've Done") shows himself to have lost his head and with it his mind: "[That] independent metropolis, teeming with flashes, shadows, and figures, with tiny playlets and dapper gnomes, day and night . . . only think[ing] of my boy or myself" (*SH,* 499).

Before the shopping center incident, the overt Slocum and the parenthetical Slocum coexisted. If this reading of *Something Happened* has merit, the first 523 pages of the novel evoke a Slocum who, victimized and cursed by being born human, *is* human. The Slocum of the epilogue—the postmortem father—has become "programmed" into a kind of eerie neutrality. The last two pages contain only three parentheses, and two of them are "(Swish!)." The third, appropriately, is "(I am fitting in)."

"Nobody knows what I've done" is the title—and those are the opening words—of the final chapter, a five-page epilogue which chronicles the overt Slocum. That persona has taken over for Kagle impressively, given his long-denied speech successfully, made domestic arrangements strategically. Slocum now "plays golf with a much better class of people. (Swish.)" The external Slocum has learned to "fit" in a limbo of executive inertia. "Everyone seems pleased with the way I have taken command" are the last words of the book. But *somebody* knows what he has done. That somebody, inaccessible now even to the parenthetical Slocum, is as dead as the unnamed little boy who was his son.

Afterword

"Our Last Man of Letters" and Other Legacies

(The publication in summer, 1993, of Edmund Wilson's *The Sixties: The Last Journal* may have concluded his long afterlife as a writer. His journals, published twenty-one years after his death, cover approximately the same decade of our neighborly acquaintance in upstate New York.)

Late on a Sunday evening in June, 1970, Edmund Wilson, who had recently passed his seventy-fifth birthday, drew his hand across the back of his bald and noble head in that way he had of signalling an announcement. He had been complaining all afternoon about his wife Elena who once again had refused to leave their main residence at Wellfleet to join him at his ancestral house in Talcottville, Lewis County, New York. Spending his summers in the old stone house was becoming increasingly difficult to endure. "One marries so as have someone to laugh with at night," he observed.

I have carried that remark in memory for twenty-three years as vintage Wilson, nonpareil. It came as a surprise, then, to encounter in *The Sixties* a version of his spoken words but attributed to Elena. In his entry of May 17, 1968—two years before our conversation—Wilson was warmly recalling a dinner set up for him at the Towpath, one of his favorite dining spots in those parts. The occasion, he wrote, had enabled him to know the maître d'. and his wife informally. They had recounted "hilarious" experiences as inn-keepers, moving Edmund Wilson to comment: "I remember Elena's saying that somebody had said that one of the great advantages of marriage was having someone to laugh with about things that you couldn't laugh about with anybody else."

Thus the man who had loved Edna St. Vincent Millay, married Mary McCarthy, and proposed to Anaïs Nin may have reconstructed from his fourth wife's allusion a truism for old age about his late discovery of conjugal joys with the right partner. In its formal setting as part of a journal entry, the words bore a localized significance. But in the context I remember, they revealed one of their aging speaker's profoundest needs in marriage.

"Elena always says she cannot stand the smell of cows." He repeated this line often for it always drew laughter up in the country. At other times he would present a darker picture: "Elena resents any reference I make to other women, especially attractive ones." Then he would add, his chuckle, assisted by tumblers of Johnny Walker Red, rising to a pitch of mock hysteria: "And all the young women I love *are* attractive—and married to other men!"

On another occasion, however, Edmund acknowledged with no apparent bitterness that "I have reached the time in life when Elena is the only woman I can sleep with." I never dared the intrusion a request for elaboration would have involved. I was not among his intimates. I simply took such a remark as at once an index of his gratitude to the family-oriented Elena for, as he once put it, "straightening out my life," and evidence that the once-chronic womanizer was, if not at last settling for less, at least settling for fewer. His final journal seems to indicate otherwise.

From the start of the 1960s, which were Edmund Wilson's late seventies, he agonized over the coronary artery disease from which he had suffered "for years" and for which "angina" was his only reference. The condition not only ruled out his only strenuous exercise ever—swimming—but slowed him down sexually. Once, when he was sixty-seven, he found that he was unable to perform satisfactorily all the libidinous acts with Elena that he exhaustingly described in *The Fifties,* his "recovery" years with the care-taking Elena after the mutually disastrous marriage to Mary McCarthy. "It [his heart] pinched me so hard I couldn't finish." Lying on the bed beside him, Elena said, "I've forgotten what it's all about." At such moments he could call back a pleasurable echo from the 1920s, Edna Millay saying, when he had made love to her for the first time in his life to anyone: "I know just how you feel: it was here, it was beautiful, and now it's gone!"

He never stopped trying to bring "it" back. In 1970, about two years before his heart finally gave out, he wrote of two trysts—one at the old house and the other at the Princeton Club—with women referred to only as

"Z" and "O". It was these late "conquests," occupying less than two pages of the 968 in *The Sixties* that *Gentlemen's Quarterly* (February, 1993) selected for prurient ballast in its six-page excerpt "Bunny in Winter." "Bunny," a nickname he regretfully told me originated at the Hill School and one he detested all his life, was a perfect choice for one of those slick magazines that pay high fees to lay low a polymath like Edmund Wilson whom Gore Vidal, who is rarely given to such praise, once called the owner of the era's finest critical mind.

"It's strange that now that I'm seventy-five and can only get an erection at half-mast, two such attractive women as she and Z should offer themselves to me. O. said, 'It's your brain,' but couldn't help giggling, as I did."

The dirty old man of these entries must be preempted by the desperate old man. Eva Thoby-Marcelin, the widow of exiled Haitian poet Philippe (Phito) Thoby-Marcelin—they were Edmund's favorite upstate couple—told me of having heard Katherine Anne Porter say this in conversation about the younger Wilson: With females, especially the sort who write poems, he was "like a fox in a wheat field with a flaming tail." During his seventies he attended as many porn movies as he could ("they're good for morale," he told me), but he thought the Ken Russell film of *Women in Love* was "rather silly. Two grown men fighting with their penises flopping about." He also attended *good* films. *The Yellow Submarine* was the cinematic milestone of his old age and *The Godfather* and *The French Connection,* sharers of most of the Academy Awards in 1973, his last. He found Doris Day "irresistibly attractive. So much the true female."

Edmund Wilson's attraction to women was a compound of certain contradictions. He was—first, last, always—a man of the book. All his wives had strong literary interests, and *The Sixties* is a who's who of literary ladies, usually written of with more affection than their male counterparts: (alphabetically) Léonie Adams, Marie-Claire Blais, Louise Bogan, Barbara Deming, Elaine May, Mary Meigs, Sonia Orwell, Dorothy Parker, Eleanor Perényi, Dawn Powell, Muriel Spark, Jean Stafford, Elinor Wylie. But he resolutely refused to learn to drive, a handicap which in old age he turned to sexual advantage. When Elena was not available, his chauffeurs were usually another kind of woman altogether: stable, motherly, all-purpose Valkyries who were always available to drive him around, type his manuscripts and letters, provide companionship and, finally, love.

Leon Edel, who scrupulously edited the four previous editions of Wilson's journals but turned over the editorship of the last volume to Lewis M.

Dabney so that he can complete the writing of his own memoirs, believes that Edmund's ideal of womankind was an amalgam of the mysterious, elusive, independent-hence-unattainable kind, of which Edna St. Vincent Millay was prototypical, and the "democratic earthly woman." Professor Edel believes that the story "The Princess with the Golden Hair," a self-contained segment of *Memoirs of Hecate County,* dramatizes the conflict between an idealized version of Wilson's mother, the self-confident and self-assured Helen Mather Kimball Wilson, and a dancehall girl who becomes the narrator's mistress.

In advancing age, the upstate Wilson was strongly drawn to stable and resourceful women. My belief is that the strong appeal of Edmund's one great love in old age in his region of last resort stems from this attraction. Of the late Mary Horbach Pcolar, he wrote in *Upstate,* the last of his books published during his lifetime:

> I never leave Talcottville nowadays [1965; he was seventy] without an uncomfortable feeling of never being able to do justice to my relation to Mary Pcolar. I am almost twice her age, and, as she says, she is to me like a favorite niece. Elena was later to reproach me for taking more interest in her than I do my own daughters. But the sole function I can have with young people seems to come down to instructing them, and neither Rosalind [daughter by Mary Blair, his first wife] nor Helen [daughter by Elena] has ever shown any signs of caring to be instructed by me. I can only in a small way teach Mary, and I cannot really educate her, as she ought to be and wants to be educated.

But they could be lovers, although not in the conventional way. He told me, when I was one of Mary's teachers at Utica College of Syracuse University, that "I'm putting her through college and I haven't even slept with her." His entries in *The Sixties* bear out a relationship that had affinities with *Pygmalion* and *Pamela.* Mary, a first-generation daughter of Hungarian farmers, had read neither, but she adored *My Fair Lady.* Although Elena referred to her as "the Madame Bovary of Talcottville," she was all things to a man who in the practical realm needed everything—a tireless driver, helper in his learning of Hungarian (language of the only country that had translated his plays), and helpmate in the quotidian, for which he had some interest but no experience.

When I returned upstate from Texas two years after the death of her "Mr. Wilson," I found Mary, to whom he refers in the final memoirs by her Hungarian name "Mariska," managing a book and record shop in Rome. She told me a story which I believe catches the spirit of the dying man. He was revising *The Dead Sea Scrolls* and had a sceptic's interest in the Mormon shrine at Palmyra. Could Joseph Smith actually have found on the side of a hill, right there in upstate New York, new Bible scriptures that an angel from heaven gave him? They had never ventured so far from Talcottville.

"It was growing late to be so far from home," Mary recalled. "There was a hotel at the place where we were dining. Mr. Wilson had consumed his usual large amount of Scotch, and I had not watched myself the way I had learned to; that is, keeping several highballs behind. 'Do you think you can drive, Mary?' he asked. I did a frivolous thing. It must have been the drinks. I reached into my pocketbook for the keys and dropped them in front of him. I laughed. 'Do you want to drive?' [It was unnecessary for her to remind me that Edmund did not drive.] 'We could stay here for the night.' Now it was Mr. Wilson's turn to laugh—mostly the Scotch, I thought. I would have done whatever he wished. 'No, Mary,' he said. 'Whatever should we do? You don't play cards, and I have no new tricks to show you.'"

Mary never completed her degree; family and the needs of her sponsor came first. When Edmund died at the old house at seventy-seven in June, 1972, she had a crackup. Somehow she survived the breakdown, a divorce, and the desperate—and disastrous—marriage that followed. Finally, however, she made a fine marriage with a widower who was also family-centered. Her happiness was brief. A decade after "Mr. Wilson" died, she perished with her husband in their trailer, victims of asphyxiation, en route south to visit her two daughters in Florida and Texas.

". . . and I have no new tricks to show you," he had told his Mariska in what may have been his insightful metaphor for the human condition—his condition—in advanced age. Card tricks and magic were his only hobby. He had done magic since boyhood and had known Houdini. For one such as he, who was Hemingway's first major reviewer and literary conscience to his own Princeton classmate Fitzgerald, the magic went out much more slowly than theirs. He had had the second act they and many others of his contemporaries had lacked. In old age, a lifetime's indulgences conspiring with angina, strokes, and the gout to bring him down, he may have wavered by trying to inject a sexual hint with women who cherished him as a kind of literary uncle. If he did not experience with Wordsworth "intimations of immortality" early on, he remembered during vacations from school at his mother's limestone house in rural upstate New York that he felt destined to be a poet or, "if not a poet, something of the kind."

His attitude was always let-*them*-qualify. At a White House dinner in 1962,

President Kennedy asked him his opinion of the Civil War and was told to read his introduction to *Patriotic Gore*. He met everyone of the new "cultural establishment" briefly lionized by JFK and Jackie (whom Wilson admired) but never took the "radical chic" of the 1960s seriously. He was at once impatient and sympathetic with writers of genius who had caved in at the end—Robert Lowell, Jean Stafford, Cyril Connolly. Only Moses Hadas, the Greek scholar, seemed "formidable." To the end, he who had done most to make the avant-garde modernists accessible to the general reader was inhospitable to a host speaker at a Wesleyan University think tank who lectured on something called "meta-criticism."

Edmund Wilson wore a McGovern button on his last journey to the old stone house three days before he died. When an admirer called him "the greatest living American," he told her that it was only the mediocrity of Nixon and the men around him that made it seem so. Throughout the memoirs woe leaks in. "I've seen the best and the worst that people can do, and I no longer have my old curiosity, sympathetic or antipathetic emotions," begins one of the journal's geriatric despairs. Then, almost immediately, will follow an ode to a rare orchid—a showy ladyslipper—or the joy in rediscovering George Eliot's *Middlemarch*. His journals jump over his shadow.

Finally, to one who recently passed the allotted three-score-ten, it came as a morale booster to see that in a survey at least one psychologist believes that in some cases "midlife crisis" should include seventy as prime time. I should like to imagine that I might still redress the pains of middle age. It is much harder to redress old biases. An admired economist, deceased, advised me late in his life that two factors take care of the anachronistic in our thinking and teaching: retirement and death. I find myself somewhere between the two.

Where I am depends on where I have been. I am much more likely to reread a favorite novel than begin a new one. Or to undertake one of the hundreds of books that I ought not to have missed first time around. "I am reading George Eliot in the evenings," Edmund Wilson told me when he was seventy. "I can imagine living life in the manner of a chronicle. In fact, I am, and I don't like it."

Some of the abiding gods of whom I have written are unlikely ever to be listed in any sacred canon. When I undertook this book it was deflating to realize that, except for Henry James, T. S. Eliot, and James Joyce, I had not looked to the literary Himalayas. In fact, James and Eliot only come into view because of their importance to Wells and Aiken. If there is any vitality in the preceding pages, that vitality rests with, even depends on, their limitations, my limitations. Can I do better than invoke in full at the end of this book Melville's tribute to Hawthorne?

> Give not over to future generations the glad duty of acknowledging him for what he is. Take that joy to yourself, in your own generation; and so shall he feel those grateful impulses in him that may possibly prompt him to the full flower of some still greater achievement in your eyes. And by confessing him, you thereby confess others; you brace the whole brotherhood. For genius, all over the world, stands hand in hand, and one shock of recognition runs the whole circle round.

By changing careers at forty—and I recommend it at any age for the unfulfilled—I returned to fiction and the novelists who were the gods of my late teens. By "confessing" the earliest of them, I grew to confess others. Some emerged for me in graduate school where I learned useful buzz words, most of which, I hope, I have learned to discard. The magic still glows, residue of precritical times, names and books and stories never to be lost in the conversion from plain reader to reluctant specialist and now reconversion back again.

Notes

PART ONE

II. Maugham's "Partial Self"

1. W. Somerset Maugham, *The Summing Up,* in *The Maugham Reader* (Garden City, N.Y.: Doubleday, 1950), 527. Quotations from *The Summing Up* are indicated as *SU,* with page numbers from this edition.

2. Edmund Wilson, "The Apotheosis of Somerset Maugham," in *Classics and Commercials: A Literary Chronicle of the Forties* (New York: Farrar, Straus, 1950), 324.

3. *Tellers of Tales* (Garden City, N.Y.: Doubleday, Doran, 1939). "The Death of Ivan Ilych" covers pp. 552–95; quotations are indicated as "Ilych" with page numbers from this edition.

4. W. Somerset Maugham, "Sanatorium," *Complete Short Stories of W. Somerset Maugham,* vol. 2 (Garden City, N.Y.: Doubleday, 1952), 515. Quotations from "Sanatorium" are from this edition and shown by "S" and page numbers.

5. Henri Troyat, *Leo Tolstoy,* tr. from the French by Nancy Amphoux (Garden City, N.Y: Doubleday, 1967), 461.

III. The Wages of Notoriety: An Update

1. Maugham, "El Greco," *The Maugham Reader,* 1208–1209.

2. "Selling Henry James," in Joseph Epstein, *Pertinent Players* (New York: Norton, 1993), 196.

3. "The Homosexual as Novelist: The Case of Somerset Maugham," *London Magazine* (August–September, 1992), 79. Quotations are indicated as "Harvey" with page numbers.

4. See Robert E. Scholes and Eric S. Rabkin, *Science Fiction: History, Science, Vision* (New York: Greenwood, 1968), 23.

5. Robert Calder, *Willie: The Life of W. Somerset Maugham* (London: Heinemann, 1989), xvii, hereafter cited as *Willie*.

6. Clive James, "What Happened to Auden, " *New Yorker,* Nov. 2, 1992, 84–85.

PART TWO

Prologue: In Deepest Regions

1. See *The Virginia Woolf Reader,* Mitchell A. Leaska, ed. (New York: Harcourt Brace Jovanovich, 1984), 192–212.

2. Michael Swan, "Henry James and H. G. Wells: A Study of Their Friendship Based on Their Unpublished Correspondence," *Cornhill* 997 (Autumn, 1953), 43.

3. See C. Hartley Grattan, "Good-Bye to H. G. Wells," *Outlook* 157 (Feb. 4, 1931), 178.

4. Leon Edel and Gordon N. Ray, eds., *Henry James and H. G. Wells* (Champaign, Ill.: University of Illinois Press, 1960), 98.

5. Jessie Chambers [pseud., T. E.], *D. H Lawrence: Personal Record* (New York: Knight, 1936), 54.

I. H. G. Wells and the Palimpsest of Time

I wrote this essay in 1986 for "H. G. Wells: Reality & Beyond," an exhibition and symposium at the University of Illinois at Champaign, whose library houses the world's major collection of Wellsiana.

1. Anthony West: *H. G. Wells: Aspects of a Life* (New York: Random House, 1984).

2. Anthony West, introduction, *Heritage* (New York: Pocket Books, 1984; originally published 1955), unpaged.

3. Henry James, "The New Novel," *Notes on Novelists, With Some Other Notes* (New York: Scribner's, 1914), 319.

4. James, "The New Novel," 320.

5. David C. Smith, *H. G. Wells, Desperately Mortal* (New Haven: Yale University Press, 1986), 113.

6. West, *H. G. Wells: Aspects of a Life,* 10–11.

7. H. G. Wells, *H. G. Wells in Love: Postscript to* Experiment in Autobiography, ed. G. P. Wells (Boston: Little, Brown, 1984), 82–83.

8. Norman and Jeanne MacKenzie, *H. G. Wells: A Biography* (New York: Simon & Schuster, 1973), 149.

9. H. G. Wells, *Experiment in Autobiography* (Boston: Little, Brown, 1962; originally published in 1934), 453–54.

10. Leon Edel, *Henry James: A Life* (New York: Harper & Row, 1985), 700.

11. H. G. Wells, *Boon,* in *The Works of H. G. Wells* (New York: Scribner's and London: Unwin), The Atlantic Edition, 1924–27, 28 vols.), vol. 13, 455. Works cited from this edition are hereafter indicated as Atlantic Edition.

12. Edel and Ray, *Henry James and H. G. Wells,* 265–68.

13. E. M. Forster, *Aspects of the Novel* (New York: Harcourt Brace Jovanovich, 1955; originally published in 1927), 162.

14. Richard Hauer Costa, *Edmund Wilson: Our Neighbor from Talcottville* (Syracuse, N.Y.: Syracuse University Press, 1980), 23.

15. G. K. Chesterton, excerpt from "Mr. Wells and the Giants," from *Heretics*

(1905), reprinted in Patrick Parrinder, ed., *H. G. Wells: The Critical Heritage* (London: Routledge & Kegan Paul, 1972), 103–109.

16. Anecdote related by Elizabeth Bowen in a lecture at the Art Alliance, Philadelphia, Nov. 10, 1958, and reported in Richard Hauer Costa, *H. G. Wells:* Revised Edition (Boston: Twayne, 1985), 128–29.

17. H. G. Wells, *Experiment in Autobiography*, 139.

18. Ibid., 37.

19. H. G. Wells, *Tono-Bungay* (Lincoln: University of Nebraska Press, 1978; first published in 1908), 44–45.

20. George Orwell, "The True Pattern of H. G. Wells," *Manchester Evening News*, Aug. 14, 1946, 10.

21. H. G. Wells, *Mr. Britling Sees It Through*, Atlantic Edition, vol. 22, 59–60.

22. Henry James, *The Art of the Novel: Critical Prefaces*, with an introduction by R. P. Blackmur (New York: Scribner's, 1962), 321.

23. Wells, *Mr. Britling*, 149–50.

24. MacKenzies, *H. G. Wells*, 57.

25. Wells, *Experiment in Autobiography*, 161.

26. MacKenzies, *H. G. Wells*, 55–56.

27. Thomas H. Huxley, *Evolution and Ethics and Other Essays* (New York: Doran, 1960), 16–17.

28. William Golding, "The Meaning of It All," *Books and Bookmen* 5 (Oct., 1959), 9–10.

29. Robert M. Philmus and David Y. Hughes, *H. G. Wells: Early Writings in Science and Science Fiction* (Berkeley: University of California Press, 1975), 60.

30. H. G. Wells, *The World of William Clissold* (New York: Macmillan), vol. 1, 112–13.

31. H. G. Wells, *The Research Magnificent*, Atlantic Edition, vol. 11, 48.

32. Costa, *Our Neighbor from Talcottville*, 43.

33. H. G. Wells, *A Modern Utopia*, Atlantic Edition, vol. 9, 13.

34. Edel and Ray, *Henry James and H. G. Wells*, 105.

35. MacKenzies, *H. G. Wells*, 430–31: "When H. G. saw that Orwell was repeating the claim that Wells believed that 'science can solve all the ills that man is heir to', he wrote Orwell an angry note insisting that 'I don't say that at all. Read my early works, you shit.'"

36. Gordon N. Ray, "H. G. Wells Tries to Be a Novelist," in *Edwardians and Late Victorians*, Richard Ellmann, ed. (New York: Columbia University Press, 1960), 158.

37. H. G. Wells, "My Auto-Obituary," in *H. G. Wells: Interviews and Recollections*, J. R. Hammond, ed. (London, 1980), 118.

38. Arnold Kettle, *Introduction to the English Novel* (London: Hutchinson, 1962), 82.

39. Walter Allen, *As I Walked Down Grub Street* (Chicago: University of Chicago Press, 1982), 14.

40. George Bolling is the hero of Orwell's *Coming Up for Air* (1939).

II. The Anxiety of Confluence

1. Unsigned article, *New York Times*, Aug. 6, 1972.

2. Postcard, Conrad Aiken to author, Sept. 29, 1972. It preceded Aiken's death—Aug. 17, 1973—by about ten months.

3. Postcard, Conrad Aiken to author, Apr. 7, 1967. He took issue with my attempt, textually, to fit him into a middle position between Joyce and Lowry. "Joyce doesn't really come into it at all," Aiken wrote. "I don't think you feel the immense difference between my work and Joyce's: our aims are widely divergent, the style in my case poetic, his much more prosy, and it was for these differences that Lowry came to me." In the face of Aiken's opposition, I published the long essay I had shown him during two interviews in Savannah, "*Ulysses,* Lowry's *Volcano,* and the *Voyage* Between: An Un-acknowledged Literary Kinship," *University of Toronto Quarterly* 36, no. 4 (July, 1967). I present a fuller account in the next essay, "Conrad Aiken and the 'Tom' Catastrophe."

4. H. G. Wells, *Experiment in Autobiography,* 423.

III. Conrad Aiken and the "Tom" Catastrophe

1. See James Merrill, "Prefaces: Five Poets on Poems by T. S. Eliot," *Yale Review* 78, no. 2 (Sept./Winter 1989): 209.

2. Stephen Spender, "Remembering Eliot," *Sewanee Review* 84, 1 (Jan.–Mar., 1966): 71.

3. *The Letters of T. S. Eliot,* vol. 1, 1898–1922, Valerie Eliot, ed. (Harcourt Brace Jovanovich, 1988), 391–92. Other quotations from Eliot's letters are from this edition, hereafter shown as *T. S. E. Letters.*

4. Peter Ackroyd, *T. S. Eliot: A Life* (New York: Simon & Schuster, 1984), 80.

5. T. S. Eliot, "Little Gidding," *Four Quartets, Complete Poems and Plays of T. S. Eliot 1909–1950* (New York: Harcourt Brace Jovanovich, 1962), 142.

6. See Joseph Killorin, ed., *Selected Letters of Conrad Aiken* (New Haven: Yale University Press, 1978), 323–25. Citations from this edition are noted as *C. A. Letters.*

7. My essay, an attempt to show how Lowry received a transfusion of Joyce and *Ulysses* through the veins of Aiken and *Blue Voyage,* was written originally for Maurice Beebe's graduate seminar on Joyce at Purdue, fall semester, 1965; expanded as "*Ulysses,* Lowry's *Volcano,* and the *Voyage* Between: Study of an Unacknowledged Literary Kinship"; and finally adapted for the opening chapter of my book on Lowry, the first critical study of his *oeuvre,* published and unpublished, *Malcolm Lowry* (New York: Twayne, 1972), 28–44.

8. Aiken, with his usual epistolary lightness of touch, responded promptly (letter to Edmund Wilson, Aug. 13, 1969): " . . . it scared the bjjesus out of me, flew right into my face where it fluttered affectionately, then went to heel. Lovely critter, which I will treasure" (*C. A. Letters,* 326).

9. Aiken's attitude to his "sometime protégé," as he frequently referred to Malcolm Lowry, was always conditionally admiring and insistently patronizing. The same could be said of his attitude to *Under the Volcano.* Although his first letter to Lowry after the publication of *Volcano* is ecstatic ("Your book is magnificent, magnificent, magnificent. . . ."—Aiken to Lowry from Rye, Sussex, and Jeake's House [near Lamb House, the English cottage Henry James occupied], in *C. A. Letters,* 277–79), Aiken never accommodated to the novel's critical acclaim. He consistently pooh-poohed Lowry as mythmaker. He only saw "old Malc" as a young man "drunk . . . with little variation in the density" in the two Cambridges; in Spain, where he introduced Lowry to Jan Gabrial, who would become the first Mrs. Lowry; and, finally, in Mexico, in summer of 1937, where he witnessed the confirmation of his worst fears for

his alcoholic pupil. Although Aiken became *in loco parentis* for Lowry, and for a time after Malcolm and Margerie married and settled in Canada doled out remittances from "the old man," he saw Lowry only once more. In 1954, Lowry's protégé David Markson (see *C.A. Letters, passim*) arranged a one-night reunion in Markson's Greenwich Village apartment.

There is no literal model for the Consul, a triumph of fictive metamorphosis, but the loving-unto-death rivalry Between Hambo and Demarest in *Ushant* (1952), Aiken's surreal autobiography, echoes the key relationship between half-brothers Goeffrey and Hugh in *Volcano.* The literary influence of the older poet on the younger, controversial from the start, is incalculable.

10. See "Europe's Day of the Dead," *Spectator,* Jan. 20, 1967, 74.

11. Edward Butscher, *Conrad Aiken: Poet of White Horse Vale* (Athens: University of Georgia Press, 1988), 335. Quotations from this biography are shown as *Butscher.*

12. Conrad Aiken, *Blue Voyage: The Collected Novels of Conrad Aiken* (New York: Holt, Rinehart and Winston, 1964), 24.

13. Frederick J. Hoffman, *Conrad Aiken* (New York: Twayne, 1960), 109.

14. Conrad Aiken, *Collected Poems, 1916–1970* (New York: Oxford University Press, 1970), 287–88.

15. Cynthia Ozick, "T. S. Eliot at 101," *New Yorker,* Nov. 20, 1989, 119.

V. The Sentence(ing) of Edmund Wilson

1. "An Interview with Edmund Wilson," *New Yorker,* June 2, 1962. This self-interview was reprinted, with a brief update, three years later in Edmund Wilson, *The Bit Between My Teeth: A Literary Chronicle of 1950–1965* (New York: Farrar Straus Giroux, 1965).

2. *Webster's Third International Dictionary* (1976).

3. Edmund Wilson, *Upstate: Records and Recollections of Northern New York* (New York: Farrar Straus Giroux, 1971), 4.

4. Edmund Wilson, "The Old Stone House," *The American Earthquake: A Documentary of the Twenties and Thirties* (New York: Doubleday, 1958), 496.

5. Wilson, *Upstate,* 205–207, 217–18, 286–88.

6. In *Upstate,* 216, 311, and Costa, *Our Neighbor from Talcottville,* 142.

7. See, among many essay collections, Alfred Kazin, *The Open Forum: Essays for Our Time* (New York: Harcourt, Brace & World, 1965), 160–73.

8. Joseph Epstein, "Edmund Wilson," an editorial letter, *London Times Literary Supplement,* Jan. 13, 1978.

9. Wilson, "The Old Stone House," in Kazin, *The Open Forum,* 173.

10. Wilson, *Upstate,* 244.

11. See, among many such interviews, Townsend Ludington, *John Dos Passos: A Twentieth Century Odyssey* (New York: E. P. Dutton, 1980), 372–73, and Virginia Spencer Carr, *Dos Passos: A Life* (New York: Doubleday, 1984), 374–75.

12. Edmund Wilson, introduction, *Letters on Literature and Politics,* Elena Wilson, ed. (New York: Farrar Straus Giroux, 1977), xxix.

13. George Orwell, "Inside the Whale," *A Collection of Essays by George Orwell* (New York: Harcourt Brace Jovanovich, 1953), 236–37.

14. George H. Douglas, *Edmund Wilson's America* (Lexington: University of Kentucky Press, 1983), 90.

15. Wilson, *Letters,* 265–66.

16. For Edmonds's and Birney's opinions, see Costa, *Neighbor from Talcottville,* 128, 138; for Trilling's and Steiner's, see Philip French, ed., *Three Honest Men: Edmund Wilson, F. R. Leavis, Lionel Trilling* (Manchester, England: Carcanet New Press, 1980), 40, 42.

17. Edmund Wilson, *To the Finland Station,* with a new introduction (New York: Farrar Straus Giroux, 1972), v–vi.

18. Wilson, *Finland Station,* v.

19. Edmund Wilson, *Patriotic Gore: Studies in the Literature of the American Civil War* (New York: Oxford University Press, 1962), xxxviii.

20. Edmund Wilson, *The Forties,* ed. Leon Edel (New York: Farrar Straus Giroux, 1983), xvi.

21. Wilson, *Upstate,* 116.

22. Costa, *Neighbor from Talcottville,* 26.

23. Joseph Epstein, "Living for Literature," *London Times Literary Supplement,* Nov. 25, 1977, 1372.

24. Carr, *Dos Passos,* 534.

25. Douglas, *Edmund Wilson's America,* 208.

26. The publisher is Jason Epstein. His comments on Wilson appear in French, ed., *Three Honest Men,* 41.

27. *Three Honest Men,* 43.

28. Wilson, *Upstate,* 340.

VII. The Triumph of Richard Ellmann

1. Richard Ellmann, *James Joyce* (New York: Oxford University Press 1982). Direct quotations and paraphrases of quotations will be drawn from this revised edition and indicated by *JJII* and page numbers. Professor Ellmann's biography of Joyce was originally published in 1959 by Oxford. Paperback editions were published by Oxford in 1965 and 1983.

2. Richard D. Altick, *Lives and Letters: A History of Literary Biography in England and America* (New York: Knopf), 381.

3. Richard Ellmann, *Literary Biography* (Oxford, England: Clarendon Press, 1971), 13.

VIII. Friendship, Francini, and the Triestine Joyce

In a much briefer version, I presented this material on Joyce and his Italian friend Francini at the Eleventh International James Joyce Symposium, San Giorgio Maggiore, Venice, during the week of Bloomsday, June 12–18, 1988.

I should like to express my debt to colleagues and others, without whom I would have been unable to proceed. My knowledge of Italian is rudimentary. I am grateful to Prof. Sonya Bašić of Zagreb University who, during her semester's exchange lectureship at Texas A&M (spring, 1988) graciously provided me with a line-by-line translation of Alessandro Francini Bruni's lecture, a small book, difficult to locate, and assisted me with Francini's later memoir. My thanks also go to unknown assistants at Yale's Beinecke Library Rare Book Room and the Texas A&M Evans Library Inter-Library Loan Office.

1. Fritz Senn, "Foreign Readings," *Work in Progress: Joyce Centenary Essays*, Richard F. Peterson & Others, eds. (Carbondale: Southern Illinois University Press, 1983), 82.

2. According to Richard Ellmann, Francini added his wife's surname Bruni "to distinguish himself from the multitude of other Francinis."

3. Silvio Benco, "James Joyce in Trieste," in Willard Potts, ed., *Portraits of the Artist in Exile: Recollections of James Joyce by Europeans* (Seattle: University of Washington Press, 1979), 52. Original American publication of Benco's memoir was in *Bookman* 72 (December, 1930).

4. Alessandro Francini Bruni, *Joyce intimo spogliato in piazza* (Trieste: La Editoriale Libraria, 1922). Although Prof. Sonya Bašić generously assisted me with an exhaustive translation of the two Francini memoirs on Joyce, I have also drawn on the authorized translation which appears in Potts's book (note 3), 7–38, titled "Joyce Stripped Naked in the Piazza." Potts credits a collaborative effort for this translation. The many references to this translated memoir are given as Francini I.

5. See note 4.

6. In his notes for chapter 13, page 766, Ellmann expresses his gratitude to Mrs. Vera Esposito Dockrell and to Professor Louis Rossi for help in the translation of Francini's "extraordinarily colloquial Tuscan." Ellmann does not attempt to do justice to Francini's lecture style.

7. See Potts's introductory matter to the Francini lecture, *Portraits of the Artist in Exile*, 5, in which Potts also quotes from *JJII*, 224.

8. *Letters of James Joyce*, Vol. III, edited by Richard Ellmann (New York, Viking, 1966), 58–59. Later quotations noted by *Letters III*.

9. For interesting accounts of the beleaguered Joyce's inferences of betrayal, see Herbert Gorman, *James Joyce* (New York: Farrar & Rinehart, 1939), and JJII, 467–68. References to the early biography are noted as *Gorman*.

10. Alessandro Francini Bruni, "Recollections of Joyce," in Potts, *Portraits of the Artist in Exile*, 44, hereafter cited as *Francini II*. This translation is by Lido Botti. The original memoir, "Ricordi su James Joyce," appeared in *Nuova Antologia* 82 (Sept., 1947): 71–79, a journal published in Florence.

11. *Francini II*, 77. Francini's reference to "four" women patrons of Joyce is puzzling. Certainly he had Sylvia Beach and Harriet Weaver in mind. Perhaps Edith Rockefeller McCormick, who became his sponsor for a year and a half when they crossed paths in Zurich during the Great War, was one of the "wealthy Americans" Francini was speaking of. She and Joyce were not close friends. Francini makes no mention of Ezra Pound, who was principally responsible for opening the doors of American and English publishers to Joyce. At any rate, Potts omits several pages from Francini's later memoir on the grounds that they contain a nearly verbatim repeat of passages from the earlier recollection, along with some critical commonplaces about *Ulysses* and *Finnegans Wake*. One misses, by these omissions, Francini's disbelief in the magnitude of his old friend's literary triumphs after the Trieste years.

PART THREE

I. Laughing with the Early Kingsley Amis
1. W. H. Auden, "One of the Family," *New Yorker,* Oct. 23, 1965, 228.
2. Kingsley Amis, *New Maps of Hell* (New York: Harcourt, Brace, 1960).
3. Kingsley Amis, "A New James Bond," in his *What Became of Jane Austen?* (New York: Harcourt Brace Jovanovich, 1971), 68–69.
4. See Dale Salwak, *Kingsley Amis: Modern Novelist* (Lanham, Md.: Barnes & Noble, 1992), 161.
5. Kingsley Amis, *Lucky Jim* (New York: Viking, 1958; originally published in England in 1953 and in America in 1954), 256. Quotations are from this edition and noted by *Lucky Jim.*
6. Kingsley Amis, *That Uncertain Feeling* (New York: Harcourt, Brace, 1956), 241. Quotations are from this edition and noted by *Uncertain.*
7. Kingsley Amis, *I Like It Here* (New York: Harcourt, Brace, 1958), 22. Quotations are from this edition and noted by *Like It.*

PART FOUR

II. *Pietà, Pelado,* and "The Ratification of Death"
This essay, "*Pietà, Pelado,* and 'The Ratification of Death': The Ten-Year Evolvement of Malcolm Lowry's *Volcano,*" was originally published in somewhat different form in *Journal of Modern Literature* 2, 1 (Sept., 1971).
1. "The Literary Sixties, When the World Was Too Much with Us," *New York Times Book Review,* Dec. 21, 1969, 1.
2. "Laying It on the Line," book review, *New York Times,* Apr. 2, 1966. Knickerbocker was a *Times* book critic who committed suicide in April, 1966, aged thirty-seven. He was working on a biography of Lowry.
3. "Deep Readers of the World, Beware!" *New York Times Book Review,* Feb. 15, 1959, 1.
4. Perle Epstein, *The Private Labyrinth of Malcolm Lowry: "Under the Volcano" and the Cabbala* (New York: Holt, Rinehart and Winston, 1969), makes an ingenious case for her belief that the Cabbala provided the "mythopoeic framework" for the novel. There are many reasons to believe she overstates her case. In terms of this essay, the principal one is that Lowry had barely heard of the Cabbala when he composed the essential drafts of *Volcano* in Mexico, drafts containing, although clearly undeveloped, most of the major talismans Ms. Epstein claims to be Cabbalistically oriented.
5. The best memoirs of Lowry, listed by the phase of his life with which they deal: the pre-Volcano Lowry—James Stern, "Malcolm Lowry: A First Impression," *Encounter* 29 (Sept., 1967): 58–68, and Clarissa Lorenz, "Call It Misadventure," *Atlantic Monthly,* June, 1970, 106–12. The Mexican years—Conrad Aiken, *Ushant: An Essay* (Boston: Little Brown, 1952), where Lowry is Hambo, a bibulous young writer. The post-Volcano Lowry—David Markson, "Malcolm Lowry: A Reminiscence," *The Nation,* Feb. 7, 1966, 164–67, and William McConnell, "Recollections of Malcolm Lowry," *Canadian Literature* No. 6 (Autumn, 1960), 24–31.
6. "Another Season in Hell," *London Observer Weekend Review,* April 29, 1962, 26.

7. Arthur Barker, "Structural Pattern in Paradise Lost," *Philological Quarterly*, 28 (1949), 19–20.

8. Joseph Frank, "Spatial Form in the Modern Novel," in John Aldridge, ed., *Critics and Essays on Modern Fiction 1920–1951*, (New York: Ronald Press, 1952) 44.

9. *Selected Letters of Malcolm Lowry*, ed. Harvey Breit and Margerie Bonner Lowry (Philadelphia: Lippincott, 1965), 85. All subsequent references to this forty-page letter to Jonathan Cape will be noted as Cape letter, with page number.

10. Conrad Aiken, letter to the editor, *Times Literary Supplement*, Feb. 16, 1967, 127.

11. Malcolm Lowry, *Dark As the Grave Wherein My Friend Is Laid* (New York: Meridian, 1968), 150.

12. Lowry's exhaustive explications include no clue to the importance of the number seven. An article by Victor Doyen, "Elements Toward a Spatial Reading of Malcolm Lowry's Under the Volcano," *English Studies* 50 (1969), 73, is instructive: "Finally we have the number seven, a symbol in itself. In the first chapter Laruelle's Day of the Dead ends shortly after seven o'clock. The action of the central story takes place between seven a.m. and seven p.m. In an allusion to the Indian belief it is revealed that a cock crowing seven times announced death . . . : at the end of the novel, when the clock strikes seven times, the cock appears also. . . . The number seven has the connotation of perfection. For both Yvonne and Geoffrey, it is the End of Time. In the context of the other biblical allusions the seventh stroke of the bell reminds us of the opening of the seventh seal."

13. The short story, perhaps embryonic of the novel that would emerge eventually, was not published in Lowry's lifetime. However, in a special issue devoted to Lowry, *Prairie Schooner* printed the story—vol. 37 (Winter, 1963–64): 284–300. Subsequent references are indicated as Short story.

14. Cape letter, 81.

15. The manner in which the novel finally meshed is the main concern of this essay. When, with my wife and eleven-year-old son, I spent two months in Vancouver at the University of British Columbia, summer of 1966, I was overwhelmed to find more than 1,100 pages of Lowry's working notes, which filled two large boxes in the Lowry Special Collection. They testify to the fact that Lowry compulsively reworked everything. If one included the short story, I found five drafts of *Under the Volcano* at UBC. The "first draft," for reasons less of accuracy than inferred sequence, is the typescript of the short story; the "second draft" consists of 364 pages; the "third draft" is a clear copy of the second, incorporating minor changes and bringing the page total to 404, but not yet changing the interrelationships of the three principals. This is the version rejected by New York's twelve most prestigious publishers in 1940–41. The "fourth draft" is of significance for the marginal and interlinear changes pencilled in.

It is impossible to fix exactly the dates of the revisions. For my purposes in this paper, I need only distinguish between three versions: the short story, the Mexican version, and the published version, and I shall so refer to them. Since the original publication of this essay, scholars more intense than I have determined that the short story could not be the first version of *Volcano* but is rather one of many equally tentative early efforts. I have retained the story in its position as, if not at, certainly near the beginning of the crystallizing process. Lowry's methods for revision can be seen by the successive stages these versions represent.

16. Malcolm Lowry, *Under the Volcano* (Philadelphia: Lippincott, 1965), 310. Subsequent references to the published version are to this edition.

17. For an account of the autobiographical overtones of this scene, see my "Lowry/Aiken Symbiosis," *The Nation*, June 26, 1967, 823–26.

18. "[T]he mails brought an advance copy of the August [1936] *Esquire*. It contained the final draft of Ernest's story about the writer dying of gangrene in Africa." Carlos Baker, *Ernest Hemingway: A Life Story* (New York: Scribner's, 1969), 289.

19. Ernest Hemingway, "The Snows of Kilimanjaro," *The Fifth Column and the First Forty-Nine Stories* (New York: Scribner's, 1938), 150.

20. Cape letter, 70–71.

21. "Dazzling Disintegration," *Saturday Review*, Feb. 22, 1947, 10.

22. David M. Markson, *Malcolm Lowry: A Study of Theme and Symbol in "Under the Volcano"* (M.A. thesis, Columbia University, 1952), 55. Novelist Markson vastly expanded this material twenty-five years later and published perhaps the best exegetical study of *Volcano* under the title *Malcolm Lowry's Volcano: Myth, Symbol, Meaning* (New York: Times Books, 1978).

23. "Malcolm Lowry," *Times Literary Supplement*, Jan. 26, 1967, 58.

24. Mexican version, 8, 9, 34, 37, 38, 40, 41, 42.

25. Cape letter, 69.

26. For a view of the novel as a major comic work, see Douglas Day, "Of Tragic Joy," *Prairie Schooner* 37 (Winter 1963–64): 354–62.

27. Dale H. Edmonds, *Malcolm Lowry: A Study of His Life and Work,* (Ph.D. diss., University of Texas, 1965), 190. Dale was also doing research on Lowry at UBC during summer of 1966. His essay, "Under the Volcano: A Reading of the 'Immediate Level'" *Tulane Studies in English* 14 (1968), is indispensable.

28. Cape letter, 80.

III. The Ordeal of Margerie Lowry

This memoir was originally published in *Cimarron Review* 106 (January, 1994): 97–107.

1. Clarissa M. Lorenz, *Lorelei Two: My Life with Conrad Aiken* (Athens: University of Georgia Press, 1983), 219.

2. Eileen Simpson, *Poets in Their Youth: A Memoir* (New York: Vintage, 1983), 253.

3. Prof. Patrick A. McCarthy, English, University of Miami, was completing an edition of *Ordeal* as my book went into production.

4. Conrad Knickerbocker, "Swinging the Paradise Street Blues: Malcolm Lowry in England," reprinted from *Paris Review* in *Best Magazine Articles: 1967* (New York: Crown, 1967), 135.

5. Malcolm Lowry, *Selected Letters of Malcolm Lowry*, ed. Harvey Breit and Margerie Lowry (Philadelphia: Lippincott, 1965). This volume, while woefully incomplete and misleading, does contain a bonus on pages 57–88. This is Lowry's extraordinary New Year's 1946 letter to publisher Jonathan Cape protesting the major excisions to *Under the Volcano* proposed anonymously by Cape's reader. The reader was identified

publicly some thirty years later as William Plomer, a fine poet and novelist in his own right. Plomer's report, which praised Lowry's surreal rendering of the Mexican mindscape but little else, merits respect for its early awareness of the recurrent theme of most of the adverse criticism of the *Volcano* for nearly a half-century: the excess of its virtues. Stephen Spender has gone on record as advising that Lowry's letter be made the standard preface for every new edition of the novel. Expected to help clarify some of the baffling aspects of Lowry's life left unsolved in Douglas Day's 1973 biography or presented one-sidedly in *Selected Letters* is Gordon Bowker's painstaking *Pursued by Furies: A Life of Malcolm Lowry,* which had not been published in America as my book went to press.

IV. Writing as Failed Therapy: Tennessee Williams and James Baldwin

1. John W. Roberts, master entry on James Baldwin in *Dictionary of Literary Biography* (Detroit: Gale Research, and Columbia, S.C.: Bruccoli Clark, 1984), 4. Quotations from this essay will be noted by *J.B.*

2. Donald Spoto, *The Kindness of Strangers: The Life of Tennessee Williams* (Boston: Little, Brown, 1985), 409.

VI. Notes from a Dark Heller

1. Joseph Heller, *Something Happened* (New York: Ballantine, 1975), 9. All quotations from *Something Happened,* hereafter cited as *SH,* are from this paperback edition.

2. Edmund Wilson, "A Treatise on Tales of Horror," in his *A Literary Chronicle, 1920–1950* (New York: Doubleday, 1952), 290.

3. Thomas Mann, "Dostoevsky—in Moderation," preface to *The Short Novels of Dostoevsky,* trans. Constance Garnett (New York: Dial, 1945), viii.

4. Fyodor Dostoevsky, *Notes from Underground* and *The Grand Inquisitor* selection, trans., and introd. by Ralph E. Matlaw (New York: Dutton, 1960). All quotations from *Notes from Underground,* hereafter cited as *NU,* are from this paperback edition.

5. David Magarshack, *Dostoevsky* (London: Secker & Warburg, 1962) explains that "the Russian title . . . *Zapiski iz Podpolya*—is variously translated as 'Notes from the Underground' or 'Notes from the Underworld,' but the Russian word *podpolya* simply means the dark cellar under a house used for preservation of food in summer. It was used by the revolutionaries for hiding illegal printing presses and literature. . . . Dostoevsky, however, does not use it in its political, but in its ordinary sense of a dark cellar—a place of retreat for the intellectual who denounces the *avant-garde* ideas of his time, who scoffs at 'the sublime and the beautiful' and whose attitudes towards men is one of embittered contempt" (p. 304 n.)

6. Edward Wasiolek, *Dostoevsky: The Major Fiction* (Cambridge: M.I.T. Press, 1964), 39.

7. Walter Kaufmann, *Existentialism from Dostoevsky to Sartre* (New York: Meridian Books, 1956), 14.

8. Robert Dusenbery, "Hawthorne's Merry Company: The Anatomy of Laughter in the Tales and Short Stories," *PMLA* 82 (1967), 285–98.

9. William Barrett, *Irrational Man: A Study in Existential Philosophy* (New York: Doubleday, 1958), 139.

10. Dostoevsky, *Short Novels*, 138.

11. William Kennedy, "Endlessly Honest Confession," *The New Republic*, 171 (Oct. 19, 1974), 17.

12. John Gardner, *On Moral Fiction* (New York: Basic Books, 1978), 90.

13. Sam Merrill, "*Playboy* Interview: Joseph Heller," *Playboy*, June, 1975, 75.

14. Calvin Bedient, "Demons Ordered from Sears," review of *Something Happened, The Nation*, Oct. 19, 1974, 378.

15. Edward Grossman, "Yassarian Lives," *Commentary*, Nov., 1974, 80.

16. George P. Elliott, "Never Nothing," *Harper's*, Sept., 1970, 83–93. Elliott's essay deserves a wide audience for its reasoned and invigorating cautions. He writes: "[Nihilism's] fulfillment would be to have all things cease to exist, the Void; failing that, its relief would be total lack of order in the motions of things, chaos. But no matter what Nihilism does, almost all things keep on moving describably almost all the time. It must substitute a relief which is occasional, fragile, and only sometimes permanent: disconnection" (83).

17. Susan Strehle Klemptner, "'A Permanent Game of Excuses': Determinism in Heller's *Something Happened*," *Modern Fiction Studies* 24 (1978–79):550–56.

18. Merrill, Heller interview, 75.

19. Susan Strehle Klemptner, "Slocum's Parenthetical Tic: Style as Metaphor in *Something Happened*," *Notes on Contemporary Literature*, 7 (Dec., 1977): 9–10.

20. See explanation at beginning of Lillian Hellman's memoir, *Pentimento: A Book of Portraits* (Boston: Little, Brown, 1973) especially her notation that *pentimento* is a painter's term that means the artist "'repented', changed his mind. Perhaps it would be as well to say that the old conception, replaced by a later choice, is a way of seeing and then seeing again" (3). The parenthetical "pentimenti" appear to work like this as Slocum incessantly "repents" for the thoughts that issue from the "surface" self and delivers countermanding thoughts within the parentheses from a "deeper" self.

21. The critical literature on *Notes from Underground* as dialectic is among the monuments of scholarship on nineteenth-century Russian cultural and literary studies. Among the works not mentioned in this essay but from which I benefited are the following: Joseph Frank, "Nihilism and *Notes from Underground*," *Sewanee Review* 69 (Winter, 1961): 1–33; Malcolm V. Jones, *Dostoyevsky: The Novel of Discord* (London: Paul Elek, 1976), 55–66; Avrahm Yarmolinsky, *Dostoyevsky: Works and Days* (New York: Funk & Wagnalls, 1971), 190–97.

22. *NU*, xvii.

23. Mikhail Bakhtin, *Problems of Dostoyevsky's Poetics*, trans., R. W. Rotsel (Ann Arbor: Arbis, 1973), 6.

24. Joseph Conrad, *Lord Jim* (Boston: Houghton Mifflin, Riverside edition, 1958), Ch. 5, 33.

25. A typographical error. The original hardback edition (Knopf, 1974) has Forgione speaking in present tense ("Forgione exclaims," etc., 246).

26. See especially Klemptner and Grossman.

27. Bedient, 378.

28. Gardner, 87–90. Gardner appears to rate Heller higher than Mailer and Von-

negut, but he lumps them together as "essentially transcribers of the moods of their time. They do not really think things out, though unlike post-modernists they to some extent claim to be truth-tellers" (90–91).

29. Gardner, 89.

30. Klemptner, "Determinism in Heller's *Something Happened*," 556.

Index